"A dynamic practical guide to enriching all of your relationships—Phyllis helps you to face your old self-defeating patterns and constructively re-create a new way of being."

—*Dr. Wayne Dyer, author of 9 books, including* **Your Erroneous Zones** *and* **Your Sacred Self**

"*Love Now, Here's How* is an excellent guide for those who need to heal old relationships or develop healthy new ones. It contains some very wise, practical advice presented in a style which is easy to read. I know from my experience as a physician and counselor to many that our life's memories are stored within our bodies. When they are not healed they take their toll, both emotionally and physically. The information contained here can help you to overcome the wounds of the past and create a healthier future."

—*Bernie Siegel, M.D, author of* **Love, Medicine & Miracles**

"Without love, we shrivel up and die. The most important thing is to free ourselves from the victim archetype and learn to love ourselves and others more fully and completely. This book will give you the techniques and knowledge you need to accomplish this, enabling you to deepen all your relationships—even with God. I can't think of anything more relevant and important in our world today."

—*Colin C. Tipping, award-winning author of "Radical Forgiveness, Making Room for the Miracle," Global 13 Publications, 1997*

"In this high-tech, ever-changing world, creating deep and meaningful relationships often seems hard to accomplish. *Love Now, Here's How* truly shares with us how to create the love that makes our life rich and meaningful. Packed with specific tools and techniques, this book leads us, in a clear, practical way, toward a life of joy, happiness and the fulfillment of our relationship dreams. This book is an absolute must-read."

—*Diane Alexander, President of The MindWorks, Inc., Columbus, Ohio*

"**Love Now, Here's How** is an outstanding book on relationships. Dr. Light does an exceptional job steering us through the "roadblocks" to healthy relationships—with ourselves and others. She guides us with clarity and humor. I recommend this book for anyone willing to embark on the adventure of self-discovery and relationship-building."

—*Christine A. Jones, M.S., Computer Education and Cognitive Systems*

"I shared the book with one of my clients who had been in total denial about her part in the relationship difficulties she was experiencing. It really helped her to see she was mentally creating the situation she was in. She realized it was her own fears of abandonment and of being loved that were causing the problem, and now she is quite willing to work on herself more deeply to resolve the issues. Also, both she and another client with whom I shared the book immediately wanted to know where they could get a copy."

—*S. J., Psychotherapist, San Diego, California*

"This book is terrific for getting to the core of relationship and personal problems, and I keep the book with me for reference. Reading from it, or showing my clients the section appropriate for them, quickly clarifies difficult and often confusing problems. Clients can easily relate to the 'Common Experiences,' and the 'Limiting Thought Patterns' are very helpful as well. At once, the client is validated, "Yes, you're not the only one," and given an immediate handle to gain power over his negative belief systems."

—*David Mumm, Educational Therapist & Clinical Doctoral Candidate, Columbus, Ohio*

"Your book really is a 'bible.' Love, to me, is the most important thing. And no other book has given me permission to pursue loving relationships with women and remain grounded spiritually. And this time, I am really ready to have faith in loving myself and asking for what I want. It is so scary for me but I want to be free of fear and free to be surrounded by love."

—*A. B., Physical Therapist, Dayton, Ohio*

"Phyllis Light is a wonderful healer. She has managed to place into her book her own healing energy. Students and teachers alike will benefit greatly from the healing energy (and the practical information) in this book and the impetus behind it."

—*Dorothy May, Ph.D., Clinical Psychologist*
Specialist in Codependency & Author

"This book showed me that there's a lot I can do to help myself, particularly when I'm feeling overwhelmed and hopeless about being able to change my circumstances. I learned that there is something I can do, when I used to think that there was nothing I could do."

—*S. L., Business Technology Instructor, Syracuse, New York*

"**Love Now, Here's How** has helped me to identify all the patterns that have kept me from experiencing a truly great relationship in my life. I am now able to start healing myself by using all the wonderful affirmations and techniques provided in the book. I'm extremely grateful to learn that there is, indeed, something I can do on my own to improve the quality of my relationships."

—*A. K., Administrative Assistant, Dallas, Texas*

"**Love Now, Here's How** gives readers an opportunity to understand how we can perceive life's trials and tribulations as wondrous opportunities to see inside ourselves. This enables us to grow beyond our current limitations and do what we could not do before. Empowered with insight, we can change the direction, form and function of our lives, making it possible to live life at a higher level of enjoyment and fulfillment than ever before."

—*Mary O., MBA, Marketing & E-Commerce, Chicago, Illinois*

"**Love Now, Here's How** is a remarkable tool for clearing and healing our subconscious minds, and equally important, our hearts. This book is not just an intellectual construct, but a viable tool for healing and recovery at very deep levels, on an ongoing basis! I found this book deeply insightful and very applicable in everyday life."

—*Bryan B., Holistic Health Practitioner, San Diego, California*

Love Now

HERE'S HOW

_26_ ROADBLOCKS
TO HEALTHY RELATIONSHIPS
AND HOW TO CLEAR THEM

Phyllis B. Light, Ph.D.

Light Unlimited
Austin, Texas

*I*n this potent and informative guide, you will learn to:

- Trust the love that flows within you and express it more freely and spontaneously to those around you.

- Penetrate the subconscious mind to discover the real causes of your relationship difficulties.

- Use intuitive skills to determine which particular subconscious patterns are yours.

- Apply a new technology to your affirmations that can help you heal your patterns at their roots.

- Heal your relationship with your parents in a deeper way than ever before, creating greater love and harmony in your current relationships.

Phyllis Light, Ph.D. and Telepathic Healer, takes you on an empowering journey through the inner workings of your subconscious mind—the storehouse of negative programming that often undermines happiness and success in relationships.

By shining the light of Truth onto your negative subconscious patterns, a deep level of clearing and healing can take place, which will ultimately enrich and enhance all of your relationships throughout your life.

This journey, when undertaken with commitment and dedication, will result in a heart that is freer to love and to enjoy life.

Acknowledgements

I want to thank all of you who were kind enough to share your relationship stories with me. I truly acknowledge you for feeling safe in discussing the personal details of your lives and for trusting me to impart that sacred information in a way that supports healing and transformation for others. For each one of you, may your journey through life be blessed with true love, peace, and happiness!

Dear Friends,

When I went to shop publishers for my first book, **Prince Charming Lives!*** (***Princess Charming Does Too**), the metaphysical ones told me, "it's too mainstream," while the mainstream publishers told me, "it's too metaphysical." In truth, I am a bridge between the two worlds, and what I have to offer is highly relevant to both.

The information in **Love Now, Here's How** is extremely useful in helping people resolve their relationship issues, and I ask you to approach it with an open mind. I am an avid "seeker of truth." My studies and explorations have indeed taken me beyond the physical world as we know it. Yet, the information I have to share here is quite practical and has helped a number of people not yet aware of or interested in the metaphysical.

I have had several therapists share this book with their clients, who then made major breakthroughs in their lives. Where they had once felt stuck, unhappy, and victimized by their partners, these individuals began to understand their own role in creating their problematic circumstances. This, then, empowered them to feel confident and capable of transforming their relationships.

I share this with you—metaphysical and mainstream alike—so that you can use the information in this book to your best advantage. It can truly help you to create positive, even miraculous changes in your life, particularly in your experience of relationships. If, however, my early explanation of the "nature of reality" uncomfortably stretches your boundaries, move past that into the actual subconscious patterns that I describe and how to transform them.

Use the parts of the book that work for you. Everyone can get value from working with this information. Trust that there is something for you here, whatever your philosophical orientation.

Phyllis

Contents

Introduction

*"All men should strive to learn before they die,
what they are running from, and to, and why."*
— *James Thurber*

Today, we all face the challenge of creating and sustaining healthy, loving relationships based on intimacy, safety, and trust. To keep our hearts open and able to share love with those around us remains the greatest challenge of all. Many of us were raised in "dysfunctional" families, cared for by people unable to meet our emotional needs for love and nurturing. We sought desperately to be loved and accepted, but received much criticism and disapproval instead.

As a result of our upbringing, we often felt misunderstood, unimportant. We learned that our loved ones couldn't be trusted, that it wasn't safe to communicate our true feelings. Eventually we learned that it was easier to shut our feelings off—even from ourselves! We have become stuck, at some level, in our early learned attitudes about what it means to love and to be loved, and have re-created old hurts, pains, and resentments in our present relationships. Many of us are aware of being co-dependent, needy for others' approval, addicted to any form of love we can get—no matter how destructive to our self-worth.

The time has come to awaken to the possibilities that await us as we heal our wounds from the past. There exists now, within human consciousness, the possibility to experience joy, ecstasy, and intimate union with another. Fulfillment, self-actualization, and spiritual development can be realized within the context of relationships. We can now realize our relationship dreams and satisfy the deepest longings of our hearts.

Love Now, Here's How can help make this true in your life. You will learn how to work on yourself, from within, in order to make positive and lasting changes in your external world, particularly in the crucial area of relationships. Working with this book will enhance your ability to love and accept yourself and to create relationships that support your needs for love, intimacy, creativity, and self-expression.

Because of the many years (and perhaps lifetimes!) of negative programming that we've received, most of us have forgotten how good, kind, and loving we truly are at our essence. When you think that you are bad, unkind, or wrong in some way, it is difficult to extend true love toward another person. If you don't feel love within yourself, just for being who you are, it is extremely difficult, if not impossible, to truly love another person for being who he or she is.

Love always starts within the self—for the self, and then extends from one individual to another. If you don't feel love for yourself, you will continually struggle to get that love from someone else, and such a relationship can only be characterized by conflict and strife. You can't get from another person that which you are not giving yourself. If you are harsh or ungenerous with yourself, you will, for the most part, encounter harsh and ungenerous people throughout your life. If you are miserly with yourself, you will tend to attract people with similar attitudes and beliefs.

So, in order to effectively open your heart to love and heal your relationships with others, you must begin with yourself. You must clear the negative subconscious patterns that cause you to feel less than whole, complete, and secure within yourself. Otherwise, any time you deal with a relationship partner and you experience insecurity, fear, or neediness within yourself, you will have difficulty feeling as if your partner is truly there for you, loving you the way you want.

Any negative feelings you have probably stem from deep subconscious beliefs, such as: "I need my partner in order to feel love," "I can't make it on my own," or, "No one loves me or wants me the way I am."

And the problem is that when you believe such negative ideas, you can only experience them as true. They color your thinking and make it difficult for you to perceive life differently. If you believe, for example, that no one really loves you the way you are, then you may ask your partner again and again to reassure you that he (or she) truly loves you. But, at the same time, it will probably be hard for you to believe that the person does.

If you believe that no one loves you, then, ultimately, that is what you will experience. And nothing anyone says or does will make you change your mind. That is why, in order to open your heart and genuinely share love with others, you must heal yourself of your negative beliefs.

In actuality, your thoughts, attitudes, and beliefs—both conscious and subconscious—always determine the quality and content of your life. Your conscious mind occupies about five to ten percent of your total mental processes at any given moment. Your subconscious mind makes up the remainder—about ninety to ninety-five percent.

What this means is that even if you make a decision to think positive thoughts all day long, you still have a huge mass of subconscious material continually attracting circumstances to you, many of which are unpleasant and undesirable. And since, by nature, the subconscious is out of your awareness, it remains, for the most part, a mystery, affecting you in insidious ways, without your knowledge or consent. Negative programming that could have come from infancy or childhood is still affecting you today; yet, it remains undetectable in the murky depths of the subconscious mind.

Love Now, Here's How was written to help you effectively deal with this mass of negative subconscious programming. It will guide you through the subterranean maze of your mind and help you to see exactly what has been affecting you, and consequently your relationships, for so long. It will also give you the necessary tools to help you release the hold this negative programming has had on you.

Having worked with thousands of people over the past thirty years, I have been able to isolate twenty-six problematic relationship patterns and the subconscious programming that causes them. These are the roadblocks we all face as we travel the path toward true love, seeking happy, fulfilling, lasting relationships.

Many of these may sound familiar to you. Many are fairly universal (unfortunately!). These subconscious patterns cause co-dependent feelings and behaviors, create unhappiness in our lives, and hamper successful relationships. Essentially, these patterns shut out hearts in fear and prevent us from feeling genuine love for ourselves and others.

Although there are many negative subconscious patterns that exist within the human psyche (e.g., fear for survival, fear of not having enough, etc.), I have chosen to focus on those negative patterns which directly and specifically hamper successful, loving relationships between human beings—those which will surely prevent you from experiencing unconditional love and support from another.

These patterns are described in detail in this book, which can be used as a reference guide. You can read it all at once, if you choose, or you can refer to portions of it that seem to apply directly to your life experiences. As you work with these subconscious patterns and release your negativity regarding relationships, you will begin to heal in wondrous ways.

You will feel a renewed sense of power and joy within you, along with a growing excitement at the new possibilities relationships have in store for you. You will see old patterns of relating to others crumble. New opportunities for sharing love and enjoying others' company will appear in your life. Your intention to heal yourself, coupled with your commitment to working with this guide, will produce the loving relationships that you have always dreamed possible!

1

What Is Love, Anyway?

"The way is not in the sky.
The way is in the heart."
Gautama Buddha

Love is simple. It is the natural expression of our essential nature as spiritual beings. Love is the energy that spontaneously flows from one heart to another, when we are being who we are, at our deepest core. This fundamental energy underlies all of life. Love occurs naturally and effortlessly, in the absence of fear and other negative emotions.

So, why does love seem so difficult? How is it that our hearts get broken so easily by being in love? Where do we go wrong? How can we reclaim the loving essence that is our natural birthright?

THE SIMPLICITY OF LOVE & THE COMPLEXITY OF RELATIONSHIPS

Love has become a complex issue because we, as human beings, have become so complex. We have lost touch with who we really are and have been programmed, over eons, to be other than our true spiritual selves. As a result, most of our behavior arises from the multitude of beliefs and attitudes that we have learned about love and relationships, not from what we feel and experience to be the truth in our hearts.

Most of us, unfortunately, are not at all in touch with what our hearts experience. And even when we are, there is usually a stern voice within letting us know that we are wrong for what we feel. We have learned from our parents, as they have from their parents, that trusting what we feel in our hearts is not acceptable behavior. We have learned a myriad of rules as to how to behave, how to respond to others, and even how to

1

love. These rules are based on logic, social mores, and expectations that others have of us, rather than what we feel to be right for ourselves, deep within our hearts.

How many times did our parents give us a choice about what we wanted to do? Weren't we often made to do what they wanted us to do, based on what would make them feel or look good? We were never trained to look within our hearts and tell the truth. The truth was always far too threatening to those around us. It might have forced them to look within and question their behavior and motives. No, looking within was not part of the training we received in how to deal with life. (This is not about blaming our parents, by the way, for they, too, had their own programming, which unconsciously influenced their attitudes and behaviors toward us.)

So, we accepted that in order to make it in the world, we had to follow the path of those around us—which was to learn the appropriate rules and behaviors—and then carry them out to the best of our ability. In fact, carry them out as if our survival depended upon it. That's how deeply ingrained our programming is. We believe that we must continue to follow all that we've been taught, or, in some part of our subconscious, we fear that we are not safe.

The mind thrives on the familiar. When you follow the path of the familiar, you get a sense of comfort and safety. "It's worked for me before; it'll work for me again," you tell yourself, in the deep recesses of your subconscious. "I made it before, doing it this way; so, in all likelihood, I'll make it again. I just need to make sure that I don't change my way of doing things."

So you see, change is very threatening at a deep level. Change brings up the feeling that you won't make it. You are leaving the familiar behind. "I'll be a stranger to myself if I have to change too much," is how the subconscious thinking goes here. "I won't know who I am anymore." It may feel so uncomfortable that, in the deepest parts of yourself, you may feel as if you're facing a sort of "death."

However, such change is death only to the shadows that you carry, buried deep within the subconscious, the negative beliefs and programs that keep your true light from shining forth. So, in truth, it is safe to change. It is safe to choose the unfamiliar, which, in this case, is trusting your heart and letting love flow between your heart and another's.

In order to experience the simplicity of love and return to the purity and innocence of your essential nature, you must bring the shadows forth and shine the light of truth upon them. You can no longer follow the rules that you once learned, obeying the programming that continually leads to feeling separate and alone. You must be willing to re-think how life can be for you and eradicate the negative programming buried deep within your subconscious mind, which is keeping you from trusting the wisdom of your heart.

THE MECHANICS OF LOVE

Here is how love happens, from an energetic standpoint. Energy, the life-sustaining energy of "Love," is always you flowing into you, through the chakra system, from the plane or dimension where God[1] resides. Each chakra is an energy vortex, often described as a "wheel," that spins and brings through energy for your use.[2] In other words, a basic outpouring of life-sustaining energy, "Love," from God, is constantly being made available to you, flowing into you through the energy center at the top of the head, the "spiritual chakra."

This energy continuously spirals around to the right, moving rapidly down through your body and back up again, where it then "fountains out" the top of your head and surrounds you completely. So, technically, it is a natural part of the human experience to literally be filled with and surrounded by a "cocoon" of God's love. However, because of your negative subconscious programming, this natural flow of energy often gets

---

1. Creative Intelligence," "Infinite Life Force," or whatever name you choose to call that Higher Creative Power.
2. There are seven main "chakras," or energy centers, throughout the body, each representing a different energetic aspect of life. The first chakra, located near the tailbone, deals with survival energy; the second chakra, just above that, deals with sexuality and creativity. The third chakra, near the solar plexus, deals with the ability to be in control of and manage your life. The fourth chakra, near the center of the chest, deals with love. The fifth, at the throat, deals with self-expression. The sixth, the "third eye," deals with the ability to discern and understand in a deeper way, and the seventh, "the crown," at the top of the head, deals with spiritual energy.

disrupted and you are not able to experience the Love that is your birth-right.

When the energy is flowing properly through you, it passes through all the different chakras, or energy centers, which allow you to experience the different qualities of your nature that each chakra represents. Problems arise when your negative subconscious programming gets activated, because this often causes the energy centers to dysfunction and the "wheels" to stop spinning properly.

At times, your negative programming can even shut down a chakra completely. When any of these energy centers are shut down, they no longer allow you to use or experience the energy or quality that is normally available to you, and therefore, you are unable to experience harmony and balance in that aspect of life.

Here is an illustration of how you experience life with a properly-functioning chakra system. When the energy moves unimpeded through your first chakra, which deals with survival issues, you feel as if you can easily make it in life, that you have the all the energy and resources you need. You feel confident in your ability to "make it" and survive with ease.

Likewise, when your second chakra is working properly, you feel empowered, strong, creative, and in tune with your sexual energy and needs. Your drive and motivation are high, and your basic life force is strong. You are able to move forward, with purpose, to accomplish your goals.

Your third or solar plexus chakra spinning normally allows you to feel in control and quite capable of managing the circumstances in your life. You are easily able to stay on top of things and create a sense of order in all that you do. Likewise, when the fifth or throat chakra is working properly (we'll go back and focus on the fourth chakra shortly), you are able to express your will and enthusiasm and be in tune with what you want. You feel confident to ask for what you want and communicate your needs and desires clearly to others.

The sixth or "third eye" chakra spinning properly enables you to discern more clearly, make decisions that are best for you, and use your intuitive faculties in order to know what's right for you in any moment.

When the seventh chakra functions normally, you feel a connection to God, to Spirit, to the unseen nature of life and the realm of spirituality. You feel as if God is there for you, and you have an inherent trust in the process of life from a spiritual point of view.

So, you see, each chakra allows you to experience different aspects of your nature. And the degree to which the chakra is working properly and the "wheel" is spinning smoothly, is the degree to which you experience ease and comfort in that area and are able to express the particular qualities of that chakra.

Now, let's go back and examine the fourth chakra, the heart center. When this energy center is working properly, when it is open and spinning correctly, you feel love. Love is your birthright. It is natural and appropriate for you to feel love all the time—for yourself and for the other people in your life.

Again, the life force that activates and flows through all the chakras is an outpouring of Love from God. Love is the basic impulse of Life. And, the way you are allowed to experience this heavenly outpouring of love is by means of your heart chakra, through which energy pours constantly, allowing you to feel love on an ongoing basis. Having your heart chakra open and functioning normally is the key to being able to experience the energy moving through you as love.

So, if the energy of love is always available to you and is a natural part of your birthright, it should be easy to feel love all the time, for yourself and for others, right? Absolutely.

However, it's not quite that easy. Many lifetimes[3] of negative experiences and programming about love and the consequences of love have served to shut down your heart chakra and keep you from being able to experience the energy of love. In other words, as long as your negative subconscious programming prevents the heart chakra from functioning properly, then the energy that continuously passes through it cannot be experienced as the feeling of love. You are literally keeping yourself from

---

3. If you don't believe in past lifetimes, please bear with me. Many years ago, I was quite skeptical of this as well, but as my intuitive gifts developed, I actually began to get glimpses of my own and others' past lives. Nothing like personal experiences to make you a believer!

feeling love because of your old negative thoughts, attitudes, and beliefs about love.

Here's the good news: since your past negative programming about love has shut down the heart chakra and prevented you from experiencing love, clearing that programming will normalize the functioning of the heart chakra and allow you to reconnect with your loving essence.

Here we've been torturing ourselves for eons in the name of love. We have struggled to be loved, killed for love, died for love, and suffered from the heartbreak of love lost. People have massacred each other for centuries in the name of God (which surely had something to do with Love), and the truth is this: the love we have been seeking has been inside each one of us all along! It has simply been our negative programming that has kept us from feeling it.

The search for love, which has driven us to try and possess the woman (or man) we desired, to conquer our enemy, or to destroy those who have eyed our beloved too fondly, has been an outward quest, from which we have always come up empty-handed and unfulfilled. We have been looking outside of ourselves for love, trying to manipulate people and circumstances, in order to obtain that which can only be found within!

This book will help you to open your heart and discover that glorious fountain of love that flows endlessly inside of you. And this will be accomplished by your willingness to acknowledge and let go of those deep shadowy fears and beliefs lurking in your psyche from the ancient (and sometimes more recent) past that are keeping your heart shut and making it difficult, if not impossible, for you to feel true love.

All you need is a willingness to tell the truth about your negative patterns, transform your attitudes about life that do not support genuine joy and happiness, and work on "re-wiring" your subconscious programming. That being so, you are about to embark upon an exciting and inspiring inner journey, with wondrous rewards along the way.

HOW YOU COMMUNICATE WITH YOUR ENERGY

Each time you communicate with someone, what happens specifically is this: you (unconsciously) extend your energy outward through one particular chakra, which indicates what you are feeling and which of your subconscious programs are operating at that time. For example, as you communicate to another person, if you extend your energy outward through your first chakra, whatever you say is coming from a primal desire for survival. Perhaps it is an emergency. You are probably operating from a deep fear underlying your communication. People will intuitively sense your fear and distress and respond accordingly.

Maybe they will feel compelled to rescue you from your plight. Maybe they will feel burdened because you apparently need something from them so badly. They might even feel bored being around you because you are so stuck in a survival mode, whereas they just want to have fun and enjoy themselves. Wherever you're coming from energetically, whatever message you radiate from deep within yourself, albeit unconscious, people will respond to you accordingly.

Genuine love can only be expressed and felt between two people when each person spontaneously extends energy outward through their heart chakra. If you're stuck in a survival mode and fearful about your circumstances, as in the example above, it will be very difficult to give and receive love from your heart. When your energy is focused in your first chakra and your communication emanates from there, you are unable to feel the love that naturally radiates from your heart center, the fourth chakra.

> The way you select a chakra from which to communicate happens unconsciously and automatically. It is controlled, for the most part, by your subconscious attitudes and beliefs.

Sometimes, when people (unconsciously) choose to communicate from the second chakra, their communication will have sexual overtones to it. Often, advertisers will hire people whose communications—including speech, thoughts, and body language—emanate from this chakra. In this way, they use sexual energy to lure the public into buying their product.

In personal relationships, if you believe, as some people do, that the only way to get a person to do what you want is by flirting with them or making them think you're interested in them sexually, then you will automatically communicate from your second chakra in your attempts to convince someone to do something for you. Or, perhaps you don't feel that someone could love you for who you are, in which case you may feel compelled (unconsciously, of course) to lure them in sexually to ensure their interest in you. Here, you would also communicate from your second (sexual) chakra and thus prevent genuine love from flowing between your hearts. The person may indeed become interested in you sexually, but this in no way guarantees that you will truly feel loved by him (or her).

A person who radiates energy from the second chakra in a manipulative way is commonly known as a "charmer." He (or she) uses their sexual energy to make another person feel loved. Again, this isn't the genuine love that comes from the heart. This is merely the energy designed to hook you into believing that someone cares about you.

If you feel unloved or unwanted and someone radiates energy from their second chakra, indicating an interest in you, you will probably light up with excitement. "Oh, he (or she) really likes me. Gee, maybe I'm not so bad after all. It feels so good to be wanted. At last, someone loves me!" This person has hooked you into feeling loved, even though the love is actually sexual energy directed toward you, ultimately designed to manipulate your attitude and behavior. Neither the intent nor the love is sincere.

People mistake sexual energy for love all the time.

"If you want to have sex with me, you must be interested in me and perhaps even love me," is how the thinking goes here. However, such is usually not the case. Many men, unfortunately, have been programmed to disconnect from their hearts, since it has been traditionally unacceptable, by our culture, for a man to be in touch with his emotions and express his feelings.

Since men have been trained to be strong and not to feel, it is challenging for many men to love from their hearts, the only place where true love can be felt and shared with another. Instead, society and tradition dictate that the only way for men to feel the loving connection they are seeking is through sex, although this doesn't really satisfy the true longings of the heart.

Thus, many men have become captivated by their desire for sex, and as a result, they can lure women into a sexual encounter with the false promise of love. Although these men are unconsciously seeking love, they are simply unable, because of eons of negative programming, to love women in the way they want to be loved, that is, from the heart.

Women, on the other hand, are generally more in touch with their feelings and the loving energy flowing through their hearts. After all, they are the traditional nurturers and caregivers and are programmed to be in touch with their feminine, loving nature. When a woman meets a man who seems interested in her, she is eager to have love in the equation and can often fool herself into perceiving an exchange of heartfelt love, when in fact there is none. Thus, women may be easily duped into thinking they are loved when their partner is only looking for sexual fulfillment or release.

When you're in an intimate loving relationship with another person, warm flowing sexual energy is a natural expression of a loving heart. Making love and sharing yourselves physically is a beautiful extension of the closeness and love that you feel for each other in your hearts. Energy emanating from your second chakra in this way is normal, natural, in balance, and adds a thrilling, passionate element to intimate relationships. It is only when your energy becomes "stuck" in this chakra and you are unable to access love from the fourth chakra that difficulties occur.

> It is simple and natural to connect with others from your heart (chakra).
> It is only your negative programming that prevents you from doing so.

Because of your past relationship experiences, you may feel that in loving someone, you are vulnerable and will get hurt. This will (unconsciously) cause you to communicate from any chakra but the heart—in order to avoid feeling love. In other words, your subconscious beliefs will determine how you express yourself and whether or not you feel safe in letting love flow from your heart to another's.

So, why is love often hard and complex? Because we have so many twisted beliefs about what to do and how to behave in order to make people love us! Since we were not trained that we are lovable and okay for being who we are and that the love we seek is already inside us, we have developed complex, deeply-layered, multi-dimensional belief systems about how to get that love. This has separated us further from our innocent, loving essence, causing us to manipulate and play games in a desperate attempt to get someone to love us.

To have healthy, loving relationships, we need to learn a whole new way of being, which starts with loving and accepting ourselves. The better we feel about ourselves, the safer we feel with love—since that is who we truly are, at our essence. As we feel safer with love, we can begin to drop the façades and games we have learned to play as ways to survive and cope in the world. Then, we can communicate from our hearts and begin to give and receive love—as we were meant to do by nature. We can reclaim the simplicity and purity that love truly is.

2

Love and Truth Grow Hand In Hand

Since love is the fundamental energy that underlies all of life, love, in its essential nature, is real and true. One way you can be more in touch with love is by being real and true with yourself and others. Living life in a truthful manner absolutely supports you in feeling more love. When you are not being real and true with others, it is harder to look them in the eye. You don't want them to know the truth about you and how you are feeling. The more you avoid the truth, the more you deny yourself the possibility of sharing love and good feelings with others.

As you clear the negative programming that causes you to fear living in truth, it will become easier for you to let people know who you really are and experience loving interactions with them. As you grow more comfortable being true with others, your heart will simultaneously soften and become safer in sharing your true loving self with them. The truth will set you free and allow you to become more in touch with your deep loving essence. Love and truth do indeed grow hand in hand.

So, let's examine the bigger picture here and the possibility of opening yourself to an even higher level of truth about the reality and nature of life. As you deepen your awareness of the truth and meaning of life, you also open your heart in ways that have heretofore been impossible for you. As you open your mind to a deeper understanding of what life is all about, you open your heart as well.

MY PERSONAL QUEST FOR TRUTH

I used to joke and say that my first word out of the womb was "why." I was always asking that question! Nothing made sense to me; I wanted an explanation for everything that happened in life. What was I doing here? Why was I female? Why was I so different from everyone else? Why didn't anyone understand me? Why didn't others feel the same way I did? Why did everyone else seem so happy in life?

I probably drove my parents crazy with my constant questioning. My good friend Donny, however, seemed to be able to handle it. I remember how my confused state would always show itself in my language, and I'd end every statement I made with a perplexed "I dunno..." Donny used to end all of his statements with a confident "Lemme tell ya..." I *loved* talking to him. At least someone seemed to know something!

My perpetual questioning led to nothing but frustration. No answers ever really satisfied me. I remained unhappy deep within myself, and feeling love was not even an option. My heart remained shut to love— for myself and for everyone else in my life as well. It wasn't until my senior year of college that a breakthrough finally came. The light of Truth, at last, was able to part the gloomy clouds of discontentment that had surrounded me for so long.

At school, I met a woman selling health foods from a "restaurant on wheels"—her truck! Interested to hear her story, we chatted a bit, when suddenly she began telling me how she had recently started meditating and no longer felt unhappy.

"No longer unhappy?" My ears perked up. That was nothing short of incredulous to me! I couldn't even remember what it felt like to be happy. Making careful note of the name and address of the meditation center, excitement filled me. I knew that I had nothing to lose—and *everything* to gain! I followed through and learned how to meditate.

Admittedly, I was quite skeptical. Fortunately for me, however, they said that no belief in the program was necessary in order to see results. As it happened, my experience was indeed profound. The high level of stress and negativity, with which I had been struggling for so many years, began to diminish, leaving behind an underlying peaceful awareness that the Universe somehow made sense after all. *Something* in my life started to ease my struggle and satisfy my questioning mind! My heart started to open to love.

My search for "Truth" continued. And, as a result, numerous seminars, training programs, and techniques appeared in my life, all supplying key portions of the information I sought. For many years, I diligently practiced all that I had learned, until one day, the most miraculous thing occurred. I began to know things—about myself and others—without knowing *how* I knew them. It was as if some great storehouse of knowledge suddenly opened its doors to me and began flooding me with answers to all the questions I had ever asked—and *more*! How thrilling!

"Ask and ye shall receive" became my newfound motto and modus operandus—on a 24-hour basis! I awoke asking questions—and getting answers. I lay in bed at night asking questions—and getting answers. I kept a pad and pen with me wherever I went to be sure and document the answers I received. I was in heaven. *Anything* I wanted to know—and all I had to do was ask!   I even figured out how all of this was possible.

THE TRUE NATURE OF REALITY

I discovered that two basic "arenas of play" are available to us humans: 1) the third dimension, and 2) the fourth dimension. The third dimension refers to that which exists in the physical universe—the material world, the realm of *physicality*. The fourth dimension refers to the realm of consciousness, inner wakefulness, or aliveness—the *spiritual* realm, deep within, which underlies our ideas, feelings, and moments of inspiration. All aspects of third-dimensional reality are tangible, concrete, and able to be perceived by the five senses. All aspects of the fourth dimension are intangible and *lack* physical form. They can be perceived only by our "sixth sense," our intuition.

Both dimensions are very significant, and in order to live a full life, we need to live fully—one hundred percent—in both. Many people, however, have learned to give very little credence to the fourth dimension because of its "invisible" or intangible quality. Since they are unable to perceive it through "normal" methods of perception, it doesn't make sense, it can't be real, and consequently, for them, it doesn't even exist.

Thus, some people appear to live one hundred percent in the third dimension. That is, they're fully here and present in the physical world but remain unconsciously shut down to the fourth dimension, unable to perceive, appreciate, or comprehend anything that exists outside the realm of the five senses. This keeps people stuck and limited, unable to take advantage of the magnificent opportunities available to human beings when they become aware of a higher understanding of how life truly works.

When you think that the physical world is the only reality that exists, you may tend to take things very seriously and identify completely with the world around you. The physical universe is all that gives your life meaning—since that's all there is, according to your belief system—and your attachments to the people and things in your life may become extreme. After all, if you were to lose your job, husband, girlfriend, car, dog, etc., you might actually believe that you have nothing left, no future, no possibilities, no hope. When any aspect of the world that you know seems to end, it truly feels like the end of your world, with no good coming from such unfortunate changes.

On the other hand, when you understand and experience fourth-dimensional reality, you have the sense of an underlying order, flow, and meaning to life, and you feel more comfortable with the experience of love. You are also better able to deal with the changes that inevitably happen in the third-dimensional world. The fourth dimension adds a more eternal, unchanging quality to an ever-changing and temporal third dimension.

> "Do not close your eyes to acts or events that are not always measurable. They happen by means of an inner energy available to all of us."
>
> Bernie S. Siegel, M.D.

THE REALM OF ALL POTENTIAL, ALL KNOWLEDGE

Not only is the fourth dimension very real, but an openness to *that* reality further opens the grand gateway to "The Realm of All Potential or All Knowledge." The bridge or link from the fourth dimension to this infinite realm is commonly called our "Higher Self." Through this lofty aspect of our being, we are able to travel, in an instant, to unseen realms, in order to perceive truth at a higher and deeper level.

This "Realm of All Knowledge" equates to the concept of "Universal Consciousness," or "One Mind" that is often discussed in different religions. This is the energetic realm from which our intuitions and inspirations spring. It is from here that we get our brainstorms, our flashes of genius, our visions for the future. The energy transmitted from this realm provides us with the courage to move forward with our hopes and dreams, even when no one else understands or supports us. It fills our hearts with joy, providing the inner knowing and deep certainty that we are following the right path, even when those around us scoff and disapprove.

This means, in practical terms, that there is a great "bank of information," or body of knowledge—of the past, present, and future—available to everyone. It is part of the glory of being human. It is a gift accessible to us all, as we grow and develop our full potential. It is only *consciously* available, however, to those who have done the inner work necessary, as described in this book, to establish a clear link to this realm. And, once that link is established, *anything* (when appropriate) can be known.

SKEPTICISM, YOUR DOWNFALL

You have certainly heard: "By your faith, ye are healed." Equally accurate is: By your skepticism, ye are kept from seeing the Truth. When you ignore the reality of the fourth dimension, you miss a valuable opportunity to grow and develop yourself. You shut down your heart to a deeper fountain of love from within. You ignore many ideas and inspirations that enter the fourth dimensional realm of consciousness from the "Realm of All Knowledge."

These are the intuitive hunches that many of us have learned to discount or ignore. Most of us, when we were young, never received support or understanding from those around us for following such inner promptings or intuitions. Now, as adults, we continue the same pattern of discounting information when it comes from within, because it simply "does not make sense." Not based on logic or reason, it doesn't fit into our "normal" ways of doing things, so we dismiss it and choose familiar though often unfulfilling activities or behaviors. We feel safe following the dictates of society, believing that if we act in the same way others do, we will fit in and be accepted.

Often our link to these unseen realms gets broken, or unrecognizable, because we have ignored it for so long. We have lost our ability to trust ourselves at the deepest level of our being. We trust the world of appearances more than we trust what we feel within ourselves. We have been programmed to be skeptical, just in case someone is trying to con us. Alas, it is this skepticism that keeps us skimming the surface of life, making it impossible to dive deeper within our own being and make contact with who we really are.

> *"Knowledge alone effects emancipation.*
> *As fire is indispensable to cooking,*
> *So knowledge is essential to deliverance."*
> Shankara, one of the most renowned
> spiritual leaders in India

DROPPING ANCHOR INTO THE FOURTH DIMENSION

We are incredibly powerful beings who have lost touch with our ability to create life according to the true desires of our hearts. We have forgotten that we are multi-dimensional beings who exist in vitally important unseen realms, along with that of the physical. The problem is this: once we think that we are merely third-dimensional beings, existing solely in the physical universe, we are unable to make real and lasting changes in our lives. We are stymied because we do not understand the necessity of going *within* to make those changes.

In truth, the fourth dimension, the dimension of consciousness, underlies and permeates the entire physical universe in which we live. The third-dimensional world, the world we see, was actually *created* by the realm of consciousness. From a purely energetic realm, i.e., the fourth dimension, the physical universe sprang. First there was the thought, and then that thought manifested into form. Consciousness underlies all elements of the physical world.

By ignoring or denying the existence of the fourth dimension, you are disconnecting from your source of power and creativity. Creativity happens in the fourth dimension, and then physical action or manifestation takes place in the third dimension. This is how athletes can win games or competitions by first visualizing or creating their goals on the inner planes of consciousness, which then "drop into" the physical and appear as concrete, "real" results. It all starts in the realm of *consciousness*.

Everything that exists in the physical world was first an idea in the mind of someone. Buildings, roads, houses, clothing, movies—everything existed as a seed thought in someone's mind before it found expression in the physical world. Every physical object is a direct reflection of the consciousness that created it. To truly change the outer, we must first change the inner!

When a problem arises in the physical world, most of us try and manipulate the circumstances. We change jobs, partners, cities, cars—whatever we think will make us happier. And yet, our experience of life generally stays the same. We can't seem to leave our problems behind. Vacations may help temporarily, but then it's back to life as we know it.

In order to make real and lasting changes to the physical world in which we live, we must step inwards and examine the consciousness which holds our physical universe in place and structures life as we know it. The bottom-line: our thoughts create our reality. What we believe to be true within our minds and hearts, deep within our psyches, is what we experience in our world. There's no getting around it.

To truly change anything in your life, you must "drop anchor" into the fourth dimension and be willing to make changes *inside* yourself. You must begin to trust your "inner" life and give it as much credence and validity as your "outer" life. When you sit down and close your eyes, does the world stop, making you feel bored? Or do you feel excited, alive, and inspired by a world of unlimited imagination and creativity?

Much happens in the mind that we ignore or discount. When something isn't going well for us in life, we commonly blame our boss, spouse, children, lover, mother, job, city, country, etc. We rarely look within, acknowledging that something inside of us—within our minds, our psyches, our consciousness—is actually creating our experience of life. What takes place in our consciousness, in the realm of thoughts, attitudes, beliefs, and ideas, directly gives rise to everything that happens in our lives. Consciously, it is important to watch what we think and say. All thoughts and words have an impact on us and create particular circumstances in life. We must also learn to tap into our subconscious mind, for it, too, is creating our experience of life!

> *"Within a couple of decades, it will be widely accepted that inner conscious awareness is a cause of reality in the Universe and our daily lives."*
>
> Dr. Willis Harmon,
> former Stanford University Senior research scientist

3

The Secret To Changing Your Life

When life isn't giving you what you want and love seems absent, when you're not able to hear that deep inner voice that inspires and guides you toward your highest good, you'll find the culprit in the unseen realm of the *subconscious* mind. The subconscious mind is a vast storehouse of programming, both positive and negative, that makes things happen (or not happen!) for you. All that you have learned while growing up is stored there—the good, the bad, and the ugly.

When I say "all that you have learned," I am referring not only to what your parents or teachers taught you *consciously,* (e.g.,"Don't play in the street—it isn't safe," or, "Get good grades in order to get into a good college,") but to *ALL* the messages that you have ever received, both conscious *and* subconscious.

A client of mine once said that every time he came in from playing ball when he was a child, his parents would yell at him for wasting time and not doing his homework. They didn't come right out and say, "Don't have fun; it's not okay to have fun," but *that* was the hidden message beneath their scolding words, and *that* was the message his subconscious mind received and stored. (That man, by the way, has never since allowed himself to have fun; the thought of taking time for fun makes him feel guilty!)

All the decisions that you made about life while growing up, all the thoughts and feelings that you've ever had about yourself and others over the years—billions of bits of information—*all* experiences are stored in the subconscious!

So, who wants to deal with all that anyway? Why bother digging up what lies in the subconscious? If it is *sub*-conscious, that is, "below" or "out of" my awareness, wouldn't I be better off just ignoring it? In other words, isn't ignorance really bliss?

The answer is no! Ignorance can actually be quite painful and lead to feelings of being hurt, controlled, abused, or victimized in some way. When you are not aware of what is in your subconscious mind, you will often believe that other people are hurting, abusing, or controlling you for no apparent reason—except that they're just "bad guys." You are also ignorant of the fact that *you* are responsible for how the people around you act toward you.

This last statement might outrage some. "How could *I* be responsible for what *they* are doing to me?"—a common response from those in ignorance of the true nature of life. The explanation is simple: *Your thoughts create your reality!*

What you think, both consciously and subconsciously, structures your experience of life. Your thoughts come from the attitudes and beliefs about life which you have formulated in the process of living. They act like filters through which you view your world. You cannot see anything that does not fit into your belief system of how life is!

For example, suppose you were raised to be distrustful of strangers. As a result, every time a stranger enters your midst, you "instinctively" bristle, suspicious of his motives, certain that he is untrustworthy until somehow he proves otherwise. Whether he is or not doesn't matter. Your "programming" says that he's not to be trusted; so *that* will be your experience. In fact, with this type of programming, you will *often* attract a stranger who does indeed prove to be untrustworthy, thus validating your belief system about "strangers." This is how your thoughts structure your reality.

> You always attract people and circumstances that validate your thoughts and beliefs about life. Whatever you *think* is true, you experience as *being* true.

Now, here is how the subconscious mind comes into play: Let's say you meet someone and feel very attracted to him or her. *Consciously,* you may feel positive about the encounter. You may even date the person a few times, thinking surely this one will work out. Then, suddenly the person stops calling; your messages aren't returned. Or perhaps you're even bluntly told that he or she has met someone else. You can't imagine how this could have happened. Things seemed so good!

"Is it that he or she is a bad person? Did I judge the person incorrectly? Is it that I should date someone a bit older and more stable who might be more willing to commit to a relationship?" These are the kinds of questions that people often ask themselves. However, they are questions founded in logic, regarding *external* aspects of the third-dimensional world. Rarely do people look *inside* and ask, "What subconscious thoughts do *I* have that attracted this situation? What beliefs stored in *my* subconscious are causing me to experience *this* in my life?"

By asking yourself these last two questions, you would discover negative subconscious beliefs such as, "Love doesn't last for me," "The people I love leave me," or "Love never works out for me." These are the negative beliefs that you must change in order to open your heart to love and experience something different in your relationships!

Your thoughts always create your reality! When your reality isn't giving you what you *consciously* think you want, then be willing to dive into the *subconscious* mind and make some changes. In doing this, you will begin to experience your power to change your life in significant ways.

Again, "Is ignorance *really* bliss?" In ignorance, you don't care what's happening in your subconscious mind. You do whatever you do in life and hope to hell it works out. If it doesn't, you'll no doubt find someone whose fault it is and blame him or her for your lack of success. Then, you may or may not try again. (Some people actually get "stuck in blame" their whole lives and *never* try again!)

Once you wake up to the fact that no one "out there" is doing it to you, you open up to the possibility of true relief, for you may, at last, be able to let go of the anger, hurt, and resentment you've been carrying for so long. When you finally realize that your negative thoughts are the only ones "doing you in," you can start to rejoice—all negative thoughts can be changed!

As you change your negative thoughts and clear the subconscious "debris" that has blocked you for so long, you will begin to reconnect with the enlightened, powerful, loving Being that you are at your essence. Your skepticism and negativity will diminish, and you will feel more in control of your life than ever before. Your natural ability to outpour loving energy from your heart will be rekindled. Feelings of greater happiness and inner peace will begin to well from within.

This clearing work will help you re-establish your link to your Higher Self, so that you can begin to view life from a different, more lofty perspective. You will start to sense your connection with a power and energy greater than yourself to help you direct and organize the events of your life. You will move from the role of victim to the role of creator in your life.

As time goes on, you will experience a growing sense of being in the right place at the right time, guided by an inner knowing as to where you need to be and what you need to be doing. Life will start to make sense in a new and deeper way. Work diligently to clear the negativity from your subconscious mind, for this is a task well worth undertaking!

BEWARE OF THE "INSTANT GRATIFICATION SYNDROME"

Although you may want the love and other rewards promised, the thought of reprogramming the subconscious mind and clearing out all of your negative attitudes and emotions may cause you to feel overwhelmed. "There's so much to do," you may groan. "I'll *never* get it all done!" Then, you give up in dismay. However, the only reason you might feel overwhelmed is because you are secretly pressuring yourself to get the job done now, all at once! You are not allowing yourself the luxury of taking whatever time is necessary to complete the process to your satisfaction.

Unfortunately, in today's world, we've been programmed to require *instant* gratification. We've learned to ignore, dislike, or lose interest in anything that *takes time* to achieve. Our attention span has become absurdly minuscule. In short, we have lost touch with the natural flow of life.

In nature, everything takes time. You may be able to go to your pantry and open a can of peaches and enjoy the taste of a peach immediately, but in truth, it took time to grow that peach. That's how life is. It takes time to grow and evolve. Our speeded up, "microwaved" version of life doesn't help us to develop the motivation or habits that we need to properly nurture and foster the growth of our true inner selves. This is a process that takes time.

As you work on reprogramming yourself, changes *will* occur, but rarely are these instant. You cannot go from "black to white" overnight. Remember, it is not fair to judge your progress by how quickly your outer circumstances change. Be willing to witness "shades of gray" when they appear before you.

If you are looking for the dramatic overnight change and do not see it, you will get frustrated and abandon your quest for inner fulfillment, thus giving in to the "Instant Gratification Syndrome." In doing so, you are stepping off the path to true love and fulfillment, and taking a detour that could lead you far from your heart's desired destination.

A RAY OF HOPE

Aware for many years of how much subconscious negativity I was carrying, I searched for a quicker, more effective way to heal myself. (Yes, I, too, was a member of the "instant gratification" generation!)

Upon discovering the "science of affirmations," I was thrilled. I now had a tool at my disposal to "re-wire" my negative subconscious programming and open my heart to love. However, as time passed, I became aware of how limited our current technology is for working with affirmations.

For many years, I had had great success using all the techniques I had learned for "making affirmations stick." Yet, I'd been aware, for quite some time, that the subconscious mind is a multi-layered affair, and the techniques I was using were only "scratching the surface" of the subconscious! Thinking a new thought once, twice, or even a dozen times, would do little to change the very deep layers of programming ingrained within us from many years (and I believe *lifetimes*) of experience. I began to search, and pray, for a way to clear my subconscious mind more effectively—and more quickly!

If you have read my first book, **Prince Charming Lives!* (*Princess Charming Does Too),** you'll recall my accounts of my "invisible helpers."[1] They came to my aid once again and delivered an extraordinarily valuable piece of information, helping me to advance my own level of clarity as well as my ability to help my clients. They informed me that there are thirty-three levels to the subconscious mind, that is, thirty-three different levels at which programming is stored that can hamper our clarity and effectiveness in life and our ability to experience genuine love. This is why certain problematic situations recur, even when we thought we had "cleared" the source of the difficulty or "worked through" our particular issues. We have simply allowed ourselves to go *deeper* within our own being, and as a result encountered a deeper place inside where negative programming is stored.

Needless to say, receiving this information opened new vistas for me, and my work deepened dramatically. At the same time, I also received an *advanced technology!* This new technology would help a person clear negative programming all the way to the depths of the subconscious mind; i.e., thirty-three levels deep! I was informed that current usage of affirmations today generally clears subconscious negativity only three to four levels deep at best! My prayers had been answered: I received a more rapid and effective technique for clearing the subconscious mind!

---

1. Phyllis Light, Ph.D., **Prince Charming Lives!** (Austin, TX: Light Unlimited, 1994), Chapter 10.

4

Understanding The Process

Although you are about to learn an "advanced technology" for working with affirmations in order to release negative subconscious programming, this still doesn't mean that you can think a new affirmation once or twice and then the work is done. This new technology is not the equivalent of a "mental microwave" or an "instant cure." However, it *can* take you where you want to go. It can help you clear out those deeper layers of stress and negative programming that very few have been able to access until now. This is the exciting part—that an effective tool has arrived to help you get the job done.

To further illustrate: suppose you bought a piece of property covered with trees and wanted to build a house. To do so, you must first clear the land and cut down many of the trees. If you had only a pocket knife to do the job, you would never accomplish your goal. If, on the other hand, you had a chain saw at your disposal, you could get the job done. Using the chain saw would still require time and effort, but eventually you would see the results that you wanted!

This new technology will help you get the job done. You simply need to be patient and give yourself whatever time you need, as you work toward your goals. Remember, don't shortchange yourself by looking for instant gratification. The process of healing yourself by "rewiring" your subconscious mind necessarily takes time, effort, and commitment. The new affirmations technology you are about to learn is incredibly powerful, and you will definitely see results over time, as you continue to work with it.

AFFIRMATIONS: A NEW APPROACH!

To effectively use this new, advanced affirmations technology, you must first understand a bit more about the subtle aspects of human nature.

THE HUMAN BEING AS AN ENERGETIC SYSTEM

In **Prince Charming Lives!** *(*Princess Charming Does Too)*, when the "compatibilities" between two people were discussed, the "subtle bodies" that exist within the human structure were also explained.[1] These are the aspects of a person's nature that are not *visible* in the third-dimensional world, but which are a very real and essential part of our fourth-dimensional human "package." The six subtle energies that surround a person are the etheric (the energetic "blueprint" of the physical body), emotional, mental, will, higher mental,[2] and spiritual "bodies," the spiritual occupying the outermost layer, away from the physical. Each subtle body allows us to experience different aspects of life—our thoughts, our feelings, our ability to be in touch with our will or desire to do things, and the deeper energies coming from the spiritual realm. As mentioned before, the physical realm is created first in the subtle realms.

Energy actually forms in the subtlest of all bodies, the spiritual, and "descends" into matter. That is, energy first becomes a faint hint or whisper from our highest spiritual self and inspires us to move in a certain direction. Thoughts and feelings of what to say or do accompany such inspiration, and we feel compelled to take action. All of this energy

---

1. Ibid., Chapter 10.
2. There are actually six subtle bodies. I mentioned only five of them in **Prince Charming Lives!** because, for all intents and purposes, the higher mental body and the spiritual body serve similar functions and are not easily distinguishable when it comes to determining compatibilities between two people.

then affects the subtle physical body (the etheric) which finally manifests as something occurring within our actual physical body.[3]

This is why it is possible to heal our bodies—as well as our circumstances in life—by focusing on our thoughts and attitudes. Again, we are going inward to the dimension of consciousness in order to re-structure our physical reality.

THE "ADVANCED SUBCONSCIOUS CLEARING" TECHNIQUE ("A.S.C.")

This new technique will allow you to "plant" your affirmations into a deeper part of your being, in order to effect a more profound change in the circumstances of your life. Using this technique will help you to clear deep layers of negative subconscious programming that have plagued you in insidious ways for longer than you could possibly know. The "A.S.C." Technique will give you access to "old baggage" so deeply ingrained in your subconscious mind, that it has previously been impossible for you to reach, and therefore to clear or release. When you "A.S.C." you shall indeed receive!

When working with affirmations, most of us have learned to read them or think them, in order to help change our negative programming. While there is definitely a benefit to using affirmations in this way, the "A.S.C." Technique allows you to impact your subconscious in a far

---

3. I heard two fascinating accounts that validate this concept of reality occurring first on the subtle levels and then manifesting into the physical. First, I heard a story about Edgar Cayce (often called "the Sleeping Prophet" because he received visionary information while in the sleep state) who was standing waiting for an elevator. The door opened and he looked at the people and was able to see clairvoyantly that no one had a subtle energy field around them. He had a split second to make a decision and backed away, choosing not to get on the elevator. The doors closed, and as the elevator went down, the cable broke and all the people fell to their death (at least the death of the physical bodies).
The second account: a scientist had been working in a lab for a number of weeks with Kirlian photography, which takes an actual photograph of the energy field surrounding a person or other living organism. He had been measuring his own energy field, along with that of the leaves of plants, on a daily basis. One afternoon, he measured his own field and he couldn't get a picture. Nothing would register on the machine. So, he assumed that the machine was malfunctioning and decided to go home for the day. Ten minutes after leaving the office, he had a car accident and died. No one had realized the significance of his not being able to detect an energy field around him until after the fact.

deeper way. Rather than just thinking the affirmations mentally, you will actually be working with them at the spiritual level first.

To do this technique, focus on the area around the center of your chest, at the same level as your physical heart, but in the middle of your chest rather than off to the left. This is where the heart chakra is located, the energy center that can feed tremendous love and joy to your entire being.[4]

Then, move your awareness to approximately five inches outside the physical body, staying in the area at the center of your chest. It is from this point, which is located in the "spiritual body," that you will do the technique. Once you have read these instructions, your intention to do this correctly is good enough. You don't need to worry if you're in the exact right place or pull out a ruler every time you practice it.

Pick the affirmation you want to work with (for example, *I'm good enough the way I am; It's safe to let love in;* and so on). Work with one affirmation at a time. Then, with your eyes closed, focus on the area described above (five inches outside the body at the "heart center") and say your affirmation to yourself mentally, from there, repeating it seven times. Once you do this, the magic begins!

You may feel an energetic shift in your physical body (or subtle bodies) immediately. On the other hand, you may feel a gradual change begin to occur in those areas. What will actually happen is this: you will receive a clearing of whatever negative programming you are ready to release at that time, and this clearing will continue for a half hour.

You don't need to repeat that exact affirmation more than seven times during that particular half hour to receive the maximum clearing. You may, of course, want to perform the technique again, in the next half hour, or in every half hour, if you wish. Working with the same affirmation over a period of time is an excellent idea to ensure that the deeper layers of negative programming it addresses get cleared.

As you repeat the affirmations to yourself, you may choose to say them slowly and deliberately, with feeling. This way, you can emphasize

---

4. Unfortunately, however, because of our negative subconscious programming, this energy center, for many people, is inactive and not functioning as it should. All the work that you do to clear your negative programming about love will help to revitalize and restore the heart chakra to normal functioning.

the meaning that they have for you by paying attention to the words and focusing on the positive message you are giving yourself. Or, you can say them rapidly, one after the other, without concentration or focus, simply repeating the words in succession, until you've said them seven times. Either method will work. The clearing will begin, once the affirmation has been repeated seven times.

Of course, saying the affirmations slowly and with feeling will make the process more conscious, reminding you of the reality that you intend to create for yourself. This is good. However, if, for example, you're getting ready to start a meeting with your boss and you feel anxious, it is much more practical to be able to say the affirmations (such as *"I now receive support from the authority figures in my life,"* or whatever you choose to work on) as quickly as possible, to elicit the clearing right away and enable you to return to the business at hand with minimum distraction. Both ways of activating the technique will ultimately produce the same results—negative programming deeply stored in the subconscious will be cleared during the following half hour.

Another way to use the technique is this: Take three different affirmations you want to integrate. Repeat the technique for each affirmation, one after another (i.e., repeat the first affirmation seven times, then the second one, then the third). Wait a half hour while the clearing and healing take place, and then you can work with all three affirmations again, in a similar fashion, to evoke additional clearing. There is no limit to how many rounds you can do, working in this way. However, a limit of three different affirmations at a time, per half hour, is advisable in order to avoid overloading the system, which can happen when you try to work with too many affirmations at once. You may be eager to clear *all* of your past negative programming *immediately*, but, realistically, the mind and body can only dump so much at one time.

Remember, this technique is designed to help you clear thirty-three levels deep, so it's not a good idea to try and do too much at once. The technique will lose its effectiveness if you do. Asking for too much to be cleared at once will definitely overload your system and bog down the process.

It's okay to take time to heal and clear yourself. Enlightenment doesn't happen overnight! It is a long-term process, but one well worth the effort. Take heart, the results of your work won't take that long to show. Just be easy on yourself, trust the process, and watch what happens with innocent eyes.

Let go of your expectations—which put pressure on you—and stick with your intention, which is to heal and develop yourself as deeply as possible, in order to reconnect with your true Loving essence. This process *will* work for you. Give yourself all the time and space you need to achieve the results you desire. This new technology will take you where you want to go. Stick with it!

You can use the "Advanced Subconscious Clearing" Technique whenever you're feeling down or are aware of certain negative thoughts floating through your mind. Stop and figure out what you're telling yourself and create an affirmation or two (or three) to specifically counteract your thought(s). For example, let's say your partner doesn't do something that he or she promised to do, and you feel extremely upset about it. Notice your deepest negative thoughts about the situation.

How are you reacting to your partner's behavior? Which of your beliefs are being validated by your partner breaking his or her promise to you? Do you feel that you must not be important because of what your partner did? Perhaps you are having feelings of being betrayed, coupled with the belief, "I knew I couldn't trust men (or women)." Maybe you've been programmed to believe: "I can't be happy being with a man (or woman)," and that's the piece of programming triggered by your partner's behavior.

There is no "right" answer here. You will react to what your partner did, based on *your* programming. Your job is to figure out what that is.[5] Figure out which negative thought or thoughts are making you feel the way you do, and then create the *opposite* thought(s), e.g., *"I am important to the man (or woman) I'm with."* Or, *"I now experience how trustworthy men (or women) truly are."*

---

5. There is a specific technique, "The Discovery Process," in **Prince Charming Lives!** (Chapter 9) that can assist you with this. It is not *necessary* for your success here, but it may prove to be helpful.

Then, practice the technique, repeating each positive thought or thoughts seven times, one at a time, from approximately five inches outside the heart center. Do this every half hour until you feel a significant shift. You will definitely notice a change in how you feel!

Remember, the negative programming is layered in so deeply that you might have to do the technique dozens, even hundreds of times, before you notice the specific results you seek in your life. Understand that this is due to the inherent massive nature of the subconscious mind, not a lack of effectiveness on the part of the tool.

Let's say your goal is "Z" and you're starting at "A." "Z," for example, may represent attracting the relationship of your dreams or perhaps experiencing your current partner truly loving you. It is important to look for progress on your way to "Z," even before your ultimate goal is realized.

You may start attracting people who are kinder and more loving than previous partners, even though they may not yet be your ideal partner. You may find yourself less anxious or needy about finding your ideal mate—which is always helpful to the manifestation process. (Any time you are holding on tightly to a goal, your underlying fear always pushes it further away.) Remember to look for "shades of gray," in order to see the progress you've made.

Sometimes early progress can be felt by a greater inherent understanding of fourth-dimensional reality. That is, the changes you are making will not be visible right away in the third-dimensional world. Yet, you may begin to *feel* differently about things, about your life. You may begin to feel a stronger connection to your intuitive self, even though your ideal relationship partner hasn't yet arrived. All such changes are significant, and you want to watch for progress on all levels.

Enjoy the process of growth and development that results from using the new affirmations technology, and avoid thinking that you can't be happy until you achieve "Z." If you think you can't be happy *until* you reach "Z," then you may lose motivation on the path and quit. In other words, since it's going to take time to get from "A" to "Z," you must have the faith to keep practicing the technique until you get there.

Ideally, you should notice shades of improvement along the way to give you the encouragement you need to stay with the process, but if you're really looking for "Z" and only "Z," you must simply persevere in order to achieve your goal. Sometimes, if you have been solidly grounded in third-dimensional reality, but unfamiliar with the realm of consciousness (i.e., the fourth dimension), you may not be used to perceiving subtle changes—the kind that occur as you use the new affirmations technique. In this case, it is only faith and perseverance that will support you in continuing the journey.

THE ROLE OF FAITH

Faith is a very powerful ally that allows you to keep moving forward on this path of healing and transforming yourself, even while your old programming is still operative and manifesting in your life. Faith gives you the inspiration you need to continue clearing your subconscious negativity, even when the going gets rough (as it will, at times, since you can't clear *all* of your negative programming at once). Without faith, you may give up too quickly, and giving up will NEVER get you where you want to be.

In having faith, you are trusting what you cannot yet see. You are making changes in the unseen fourth dimensional realm of consciousness, in order to see results in your third dimensional world of relationships. This process of changing your inner self in order to see changes in your outer circumstances absolutely works. But, you must have faith in the process, since it does take some time.

Sometimes your outer world seems so terribly real that it looks as if nothing can change it, and you're stuck with it forever. This isn't necessarily true, but without faith in the process, your circumstances may discourage you from continuing your inner work. Faith will carry you forward and give you the courage to persevere, until you finally experience the results you want.

ENJOY YOURSELF ALONG THE WAY

It is best, of course, if you can enjoy the process along the way. Keep a journal, and note any time you experience that a person or circumstance in your life is reflecting more of your goals than previously. Give yourself credit for the progress you've made to date, rather than bemoaning the fact that you haven't yet reached your final destination. Acknowledge yourself for how far you've come. Focus on what you *have* achieved, rather than on how far you have to go.

You can actually choose whether you want to enjoy the ride or wait until you reach your destination to experience the happiness you seek. The problem with the latter is that reaching your destination actually represents a singular moment in time, and once you reach it, life continues.

Life is constant movement. Once one goal is accomplished, another springs into your mind to replace it. The natural movement toward greater understanding and growth is imminent. No singular goal, once accomplished, can give you lasting peace and satisfaction. A case in point is how we've all been programmed about marriage.

Most of us have been raised by an old myth: find your dream mate, get married, and you'll live happily ever after. This implies that marriage is the main goal, and once you achieve that, you can coast in bliss forever. Has anyone found that to be true? Definitely not! Do any of us still harbor hopes, deep down, that this will happen? You'd better believe it!

Your journey through life continues, even after marriage! Dealing with the manifestation of your thoughts—both conscious and subconscious—and learning to master this process represents an ongoing path toward true fulfillment and self-actualization.

Life is full of opportunities to learn and to grow. You can count on that! Relationships, as well, are full of opportunities to learn and to grow—there's simply no getting around it. So, are you willing to enjoy the ride, or do you want to wait until you've arrived? I recommend enjoying the ride and taking advantage of whatever learning opportunity presents itself in the moment.

In other words, use the tools that are at your disposal for clearing and healing yourself, and be willing to experience as much love and joy as possible on your journey through life. But, don't beat yourself up or criticize yourself for not yet being where you want to be. It's okay. The process of waking up to the joyful Being that you are, deep within your heart and soul, takes time. You *will* get there. Just be gentle with yourself along the way and give yourself all the time you need.

When we do the necessary inner work to free ourselves from our past fears, hurts, and sorrows, we will experience a positive and wondrous shift in our experience of relationships. As each of us finds greater love and self-acceptance within our own being, the world will become a better place to live for all of us.

5

The Practical Application

Now let's examine, in greater depth, the twenty-six roadblocks to healthy relationships—the subconscious patterns that shut our hearts in fear and hamper our ability to feel and express genuine love. Each pattern is listed separately and discussed in detail. The information about the pattern is divided into the following four sections:

1) **"Common Experiences in Relationships,"** which gives you an idea of the kinds of experiences you will attract if you have that particular pattern.

2) **Explanation of the Pattern**, which includes insights as to how the pattern originated and what you can do about it.

3) **Real life Stories** of people who have that particular pattern, which illustrate how the pattern can affect someone's life and relationships.

4) **"Common Limiting Thought Patterns"** and **"New Thought Patterns to Integrate,"** which contain the negative beliefs you might have and the corresponding positive beliefs you will need to incorporate into your thinking in order to heal the pattern.

As you look over the material in this section, notice if anything "jumps out at you," or sounds familiar. For example, if your eye is drawn to a particular passage and you feel to read it over several times, *pay attention!* Your intuition may be telling you which subconscious pattern you need to work on.

If you read something that seems to relate to your partner (or to the people you attract), but not to you, *don't be fooled!* There is a common phenomenon called "projection," in which you tend to project *your* subconscious patterns onto your partner (and onto other people in general). What *looks* like your partner's issues (and not yours), you are well-advised to examine more carefully in yourself!

It is never an accident whom you attract to you or what you perceive in the people around you. You will always attract people who have subconscious patterns that match your own. All partners you attract need to learn lessons similar to yours. (Yes, indeed, there is an underlying wisdom to the game plan of life!) So, take responsibility for what you see in your partner, or in those around you.

For example, under "Common Experiences in Relationships" you may read, "partners who leave you after a short time." Instead, you might experience the "flip side" of that pattern and find the opposite to be true: that you leave your partners after a short time. Either way, the pattern is still yours! In other words, whether you or your partner seem to experience the pattern, you need to own it yourself, since all of this is a part of *your* reality.

Whichever pattern you choose to work on first is fine. Each pattern is an "entry point" into the whole fabric of your being, as it expresses in relationships. Therefore, any healing that occurs in one area will have a positive effect on all areas. For example, if you change your negative thought patterns related to "Fear of Rejection," you will surely feel more comfortable in the area of sexuality as well. Every change that you make will be valuable for you in all aspects of relationships.

TO BEGIN THE HEALING PROCESS:[1]

1) **Determine which particular pattern** you want to change. (You may want to select the pattern based on the "Common Experiences" listed in the Index.)

---

1. You can apply this process to all relationships with all people. It's not just for romantic relationships, but for friendships, business associations, and family relationships as well. Simply substitute the names of specific people or groups where necessary; e.g., for "men/women," you could substitute "businessmen," "children," "teachers," "Mom," "Dad," "Bill," "Jane," or even "people" in general.

2) Turn to the section on that pattern, then **find the negative beliefs that you think you might have** (under "Common Limiting Thought Patterns") or that seem to relate to your situation. If you're not sure which ones to choose, it's fine to work with them all.

3) **Tell yourself that you are ready and willing to change your thoughts** in order to experience life in a new way. (This can take place silently in your mind, aloud to yourself, or by writing your intention down on paper.)

As you examine the limiting thought patterns, some of them may still *seem* true for you (e.g., "Men cheat on me," or "The people I love hurt me"). However, you can forgive yourself for *believing* them and experiencing them as true for you—*until now!* Know that you are ready, at this time, to create something different in your life. You are ready to create a reality in which relationships work for you!

4) **Select and work with the new, desirable beliefs** that you want to experience in your life (under "New Thought Pattern to Integrate"). Feel free to modify the beliefs in whatever way you choose, in order to feel maximally comfortable working with them. Continue this work until you are able to fully integrate the new thought pattern.[2]

To fully integrate a new thought pattern means to work with it until it becomes an integral part of your essential nature; i.e., until it is automatically and spontaneously a part of your thinking and being. This new thought pattern has to sink in deep enough to begin creating emotions and behaviors that will produce the satisfaction and fulfillment you seek. Using the new affirmations technology will greatly facilitate this process.

"Thought patterns" refer to deep beliefs stored in the subconscious mind. You are often, for the most part, unaware of even having them. The mind holds these beliefs as general operating principles (e.g., "Men

---

2. All of the new thought patterns are written to accommodate both sexes (e.g. "men/women love me and want to be with me."). Simply choose which gender is appropriate for you. To make the affirmations flow more smoothly as you read them, you may want to scratch out or blacken whichever gender is inappropriate for your circumstances.

leave me"), which you then express in your life in specific situations (e.g., your father leaving the family when you were young, or your high school boyfriend leaving you when his family had to move out of town, etc.).

These deep operating beliefs guide and shape how you think and feel, and ultimately what and whom you attract to you. They form the underlying sub-structure of your awareness, which then gives rise to conscious thought. For example, you may not be aware that you have a deep thought pattern, "Men leave me." You are aware, however, that whenever a man leaves you, you experience *conscious* anguish, often accompanied by blame, "I *hate* when this happens to me. That son-of-a-gun turned out to be just as untrustworthy as all the rest of them!"

You don't normally examine the deeper operating belief in your subconscious mind! However, changing this deep belief is the only way to give you true relief from the negative pattern. Integrating the new thought pattern means changing the deep operating beliefs in the subconscious mind so that your entire way of thinking, feeling, and being is transformed, and you begin to attract different experiences in relationships.

As you work with the new thought patterns, it's okay if you feel dubious or skeptical. That's natural. But do your best not to let disbelief or skepticism prevent you from at least participating in the process. Then, be willing to give it some time to work for you.

Do your best to be open-minded. Work with the new thought pattern for a while before you pass judgment. You deserve to have what you want in your life, and only by persisting with this process will you experience the changes you seek. "Re-programming" the subconscious mind takes time, but the effort will always be rewarded! As you change and upgrade your subconscious thoughts, you will experience improvements in the quality of your life and in your ability to feel and express love.

Never be afraid to learn what is in your subconscious! Any "skeleton" there is just a negative thought that you chose to believe at some point. Unfortunately, because you believed it, it became true in your reality. Now, you are ready to make some new decisions about life and create more positive relationship experiences.

By the way, none of your thoughts are "bad." They are just mistaken beliefs about the true nature of life, and all can be changed. So, take on this task of reprogramming lightheartedly. Don't judge yourself or take yourself too seriously as you discover which negative thought patterns have been controlling your life. It's time to lighten up! Acknowledge yourself for your willingness to move forward and clear up the negativity from your past.

You're ready for a new beginning. It's time to adopt new attitudes and beliefs about the possibilities life holds for you. You are about to create a new life for yourself in which relationships work for you and enjoyment is the norm.

IDENTIFYING YOUR PATTERNS

As you read through the twenty-six patterns, you may naturally sense that some pertain to you directly. (Most people have nine to twelve patterns.) When you are not certain which patterns are stored in your subconscious mind, simply familiarize yourself with them all. That is, read through all twenty-six patterns until you feel that you have a good grasp on how they operate in a person's life.

Then, as you go through life, stay aware and notice any feelings or behaviors that characterize a particular pattern, and continue to watch how you or your relationships may be affected. In other words, by staying conscious of the process of relating with others, one or more of the patterns may suddenly emerge, within your awareness, as a key piece to understanding your subconscious make-up. When this happens, you will know, at last, which subconscious culprit had been adversely affecting you or your relationships in some way. Once you become aware of your patterns, then you can work on integrating the new, positive beliefs, in order to heal your subconscious negativity and transform your experience of relating to others.

By working on yourself in this way, you are allowing life to help you prioritize the patterns which require your attention. In other words, rather than trying to heal all your negative patterns at once, simply work on them as the need expresses itself through your life's circumstances. The most important part of this process is to observe how you are as you experience and participate in relationships, and then to do the healing work necessary to "re-wire" your subconscious mind. Life will always let you know which aspects of yourself need healing. Your job is to be diligent and catch the "red flags" as they present themselves to you.

MORE HELP IDENTIFYING YOUR PATTERNS

In addition to the "third-dimensional approach" of attempting to use logic to match your life experiences to the information presented within each pattern, here is a special technique which employs your intuitive faculties, for determining which specific patterns are stored in your subconscious mind.

1) **Select a pattern** you think you may have.
2) **Read the entire section** on that pattern (if you haven't already done so).
3) **Turn to the first page** of that section and **look at the pattern heading** ("Fear of Boredom," "Fear of Commitment," and so on) for a few seconds, **allowing yourself to relax**.
4) Then, **close your eyes, take a slow breath, and let it out**.
5) **Ask this question** in your mind:
   "Is this one of my subconscious patterns?"

If the answer is "yes," a flash of light will immediately appear in your mind's eye. If the answer is "no," the flash will *not* appear. The answer will come to you within three seconds. If nothing happens within three seconds, assume the answer is "no."

Do this exercise sitting quietly, i.e., where you are not disturbed by external stimuli. Be innocent and trusting. Don't *try* to see the light or *make* it happen. It will either happen spontaneously or not. Your job is simply to relax and allow the answer to come to you.

Note that an *inner* flash is not the equivalent of a *physical* flash of light, as in a camera flashing. It will be more subtle; yet, you *will* be able to determine its presence. Some will see the flash. Others will feel as if something flashed in their mind's eye. They will simply sense that a flash just occurred. Trust whatever you get.

You may even need to practice the technique several times in order to distinguish between *your* version of "yes" and "no." Since this is an intuitive experience, your unconscious may "speak" to you in a unique way, giving you particular images whose meaning you will have to interpret.

For example, one woman who tried it a number of times discovered that if the subconscious pattern was significant for her, she would experience a bright flash in her mind's eye. If the pattern was relevant for her, but its effects weren't so all-pervasive in her life, she saw "teeny little sparks." In this case, her intuition also revealed how much the pattern was actually influencing her.

Another person experienced the technique with an unusual twist, but his answers, once he determined their meaning, were equally valid. When he asked about a pattern that he knew had a dominant influence on him, he would experience a heavy dark wave coming over him, in his mind's eye. When the pattern had a less dominant influence on him, he would instead see small waves, like "little dark dots." When the pattern was irrelevant to him, he experienced nothing, no change on his "inner screen."

So, you see, there is no right or wrong experience of this. The important part is to trust your ability to do it, and then to trust the response you get. If you do not see images when your eyes are closed, do not fret. The technique will still work for you. Everyone has a way of accessing knowledge and understanding from within. Do the technique and simply trust the manner in which the answer comes most naturally and spontaneously to you.

Remember, you may not *see* a light, you may *feel* it. Or, you may simply know that something just happened, during the few seconds when the flash is supposed to occur. If you don't see *or* feel it, you may simply be aware that, indeed, something just happened. This is fine. Again, trust your ability to know. What you're really looking for is the difference between *something* happening and *nothing* happening. And, there will be a difference, no matter how it comes to you.

In any event, a "yes" will be a distinctly different experience from a "no." If you absolutely *can't* detect a difference, take a few days and work on integrating the following beliefs, using the "A.S.C." technique:

"I can follow instructions the way they are given."

"I am capable of understanding what I read."

"I am aware of the meaning of printed words I am told to read."

Then, practice the "flash of light" technique again. Once you have successfully integrated the above affirmations, this technique will work for you! Simply continue to work with the above three beliefs until you experience success with the technique.

ANOTHER USE OF THIS TECHNIQUE

You may also use this "inner flash" technique to help you select which affirmations best suit your needs, in the section called, "New Thought Pattern to Integrate." Whereas it can't hurt you to work with all of the positive beliefs, you may want to use this intuitive technique to select the particular ones that would best serve your own transformational process.

You will first need to determine which of the negative thought patterns you have, that are stored in your subconscious mind. So, look at the list of "Common Limiting Thought Patterns," and point to the first one. Then, close your eyes, take a slow breath, and let it out. Ask this question in your mind: "Is this one of my negative thought patterns?"

If the answer is "yes," a flash of light will immediately appear in your mind's eye. If the answer is "no," the flash will not appear. As before, the answer will come to you within three seconds. If nothing happens within three seconds, assume the answer is "no."

If you are unsure, you may want to work with the corresponding positive thought pattern anyway. Again, it won't hurt you to work with them all, if you so choose. It is actually quite probable that you have something akin to all of the negative thought patterns lurking in your subconscious somewhere, and any work you do with the positive ones will have a beneficial effect on your life and relationships!

FEAR OF REJECTION

"God has given you one face and you make yourselves another."

Shakespeare, Hamlet

COMMON EXPERIENCES IN RELATIONSHIPS

- Creating relationships with unavailable men/women (e.g., those who are married or live far away)

- Pushing your partner away or feeling pushed away by your partner

- Feeling afraid that your partner doesn't love you

- Feeling afraid that your partner will find fault with you (or finding fault with your partner, to reject him/her before he/she can reject you)/being critical or judgmental

- Feeling unloved, unwanted, undeserving, unattractive, or inadequate In relationships

- Having affairs or attracting partners who have affairs

- Avoiding relationships or not finding someone you want to be with

- Feeling as if you aren't okay in others' eyes, and therefore, not allowing them to be nice, kind, or loving to you

- Feeling as if you can't have love here, and therefore, resisting getting to know people who are kind and loving to you

- Being constantly "on the go" or committed to activities outside the relationship and never spending quality time with your partner (or having a partner like this)

- Having "one-sided" relationships or "unrequited love"—where you give far more than you receive

- Avoiding someone who is interested in you (you reject him/her before he/she can reject you) or vice-versa (when you are interested in someone, he/she avoids you)

- Sacrificing your needs and wants to make your partner happy (then surely he/she won't reject you)
- Holding back your true feelings and thoughts, or being an "actor" in the relationship, so that your true self is never known and thus can't be rejected
- Attracting bragging or egotistical partners (who have to prove how good they are since they don't really believe it themselves) or being this way yourself
- Avoiding intimacy in relationships
- Being unable to be intimate with your partner (or vice versa)
- Creating superficial relationships

When you have this pattern, **Fear of Rejection**, you are often afraid of being discovered for who you really are, because you think that you are bad or unworthy. At some point in your life, based on the way people treated you, you got the distinct feeling that something was wrong with you, and you began to believe that you're not okay the way you are. Because of this, you may now feel compelled to act as if you are superior to others, or put up a falsely impressive façade, so that they won't find out who you really are.

When this pattern, **Fear of Rejection**, is operating, difficulties with intimacy will occur. Your fear is that your partner will reject you, once he (or she) gets to know the real you. As a result, you won't let the person get too close! To be intimate with someone requires revealing yourself at the deepest levels of your being, without hiding or holding back what's really happening inside you. However, with this pattern, you do not feel safe letting others know who you really are, because of your negative beliefs about yourself. Because you believe that you're a bad person and not okay the way you are, you avoid getting close to others to prevent them from discovering what you believe to be true about yourself.

The problem with this pattern is that as long as you fear being rejected, that is precisely what you will experience as you relate with others. Either they will overtly reject you in some way, or you will avoid the risk of asking for what you want, in order to avoid being rejected. Either way, you will probably find yourself feeling unloved, unwanted, and left out. Because of the deep sense of unworthiness or undeservingness that accompanies this pattern, it is often difficult to believe that others could love you, even when they do. More often than not, you try to push their love away, because you believe, deep down, that you couldn't possibly be worthy of it.

BEN'S FEAR OF REJECTION

Ben was a soft, gentle-spirited man. As a child, he was sensitive and bright, finding pleasure in art, nature, and the more refined things of life. His father, on the other hand, was a hard-core, yet well-respected scientist, and was quick to let Ben know that he was not okay. Ben experienced endless, heart-breaking rejection from his father throughout his entire life. His father wanted Ben to be different and never hesitated to express his opinion. Ben's two older brothers grew up and received Ph.D's from Harvard in math and economics. Ben, being an artist by nature, had no place in such a family—or so thought his father.

His father would enter his room, at times, in a fit of rage and throw Ben's prized stamp collection all over the room. He would yell at him and tell him that the decisions he had made were stupid and wrong. He would tell him that he just couldn't be an artist, but if he did, he would simply have to become an architect—at least that would be respectable art.

Ben never really dated much because, when he did, all the girls that he dated tended to reject him. He did finally get married though, but during the seventh year they were together, Ben discovered that his wife had been having numerous affairs on the side, and the marriage soon ended in divorce.

He had only one or two girlfriends in the twelve years that followed, and then he met Bonnie and married her. Interestingly enough, that marriage hit the rocks around the seventh year as well. But this time, Ben did the rejecting. Ben had been very mean to their oldest child. In fact, the girl stuttered until she was five, unable to complete a sentence because she was so afraid of Ben's anger. Ben was treating her the same way his father had treated him.

Ben continually hassled both Bonnie and their oldest daughter. He would tell Bonnie that she wasn't a good parent and that she should be nicer to their children. He gambled away much of the family's income and complained that Bonnie was spending too much. His abusiveness and accusations were unbearable, but Bonnie just put up with it all. Finally. Ben threatened to leave, and Bonnie let him, unable to justify staying in such an abusive situation any longer. Apparently, Ben was prepared to be rejected in the seventh year of his marriage—just as it happened before—but this time he (unconsciously) decided to do the rejecting before it could be done to him.

FAYE'S FEAR Of REJECTION

Faye was a real loner. She stayed at home a great deal. She waited for her friends to call her, and didn't make much effort to go anywhere if they didn't. She kept to herself most of the time, reading and listening to music.

Faye, now forty.two years old, had experienced nothing but heartbreak and unhappy endings in all of her relationships. (Faye also had **Pattern 10—Being Victimized by Love**.) Somehow she seemed to attract men who were happy to take from her, but not give to her in return. Faye always bent over backwards to please the men she was interested in, but somehow, they never seemed to reciprocate the effort or caring. Faye did everything that she could to "get men to like her," but her efforts never seemed to pay off.

Some of her relationship partners would criticize her to her face and tell her what was wrong with her. This upset Faye terribly and made her feel worthless and unloved. On a number of occasions, Faye would get involved with a man who would then become interested in another woman shortly after meeting Faye. This frustrated Faye greatly, who began to think that there must be something wrong with her.

Faye wondered if she wasn't somehow pushing men away from her, but she couldn't figure out how or why. Unhappily, Faye decided that she must be "jinxed" as far as love is concerned, because no matter how hard she tried, she couldn't get relationships to work out for her.

Faye's mother was extremely domineering and critical and had always found fault with Faye while she was growing up. Faye felt that she was never acceptable the way she was, since her mother always found something wrong with her at every turn. As a result of the constant criticism from her mother, Faye was convinced that she was not good enough, that no one could possibly like her the way she was. The low self-esteem that resulted from her upbringing caused Faye to fear being rejected by those she loved. Then, her fear unconsciously drew such circumstances to her—again and again.

HEALING YOUR "FEAR OF REJECTION" PATTERN

You need to learn that your negative thoughts about yourself are not the ultimate Truth about who you are. They are simply beliefs that you've formulated while growing up, all based on what you were told about yourself or how you were treated by the people you loved. *No one* is bad or unworthy at his (or her) essence. We are all essentially lovable, capable, powerful beings who have, for the most part, lost touch with our essential nature. That you are bad or unworthy is not the truth about who you are. However, because you *believed* this, it became true for you.

As you change your beliefs about who you are, you will start to love and appreciate yourself more, realizing that others feel the same way about you as well. You will recognize your own value and feel at ease being yourself around others. Because of this, you will no longer need to keep people at a distance. As your inherent sense of self-love and self-worth increases, you will feel more comfortable knowing yourself in greater depth. At last, you will be free to experience greater depth and intimacy in all your relationships!

Common Limiting Thought Pattern	New Thought Pattern to Integrate
Men/women don't like me for who I am.	Men/women like me for who I am. It's safe to be myself around men/women and trust that they like me.
I'm unacceptable the way I am. I have to be different to be okay. Something is wrong with me.	I am okay the way I am. I now find myself acceptable to men/women the way I am. Men/women enjoy and appreciate me the way I am.
Men/women reject me.	Men/women accept and love me for who I am.
I'm a bad person. I don't want men/women to know how bad I really am.	I am a good person. I forgive myself for thinking I am bad. I am innocent for being who I am. It's safe to let men/women get close and know me for who I am.
I am a bother to men/women. Men/women don't want to be with me.	Men/women enjoy and appreciate my company.
I push men/women away. I am too powerful/too intense for men/women.	Men/women accept and enjoy my presence. Men/women like how I am. Men/women appreciate and accept the powerful and intense aspects of my nature.
I destroy love.	Love thrives in my presence. I express and create love wherever I go.

Common Limiting Thought Pattern	New Thought Pattern to Integrate
I'm not good enough. I'm not as good as I could be.	I am good enough the way I am. I am good enough to have the love I want in a relationship.
I displease men/women. Men/women disapprove of me.	I am naturally pleasing to men/women. Men/women approve of me and accept me for who I am.
I am unattractive to men/women. My body is ugly.	I now appreciate my appearance and find myself naturally attractive to men/women. I now accept and love my body. I now attract men/women in my life who are loving and accepting of my body.
I'm afraid that men/women think I'm not good enough.	I trust that men/women like me and think I'm good enough.
No one thinks I'm worthy. I don't deserve love.	Everyone thinks I'm worthy. I deserve love and respect for being who I am.
Men/women hate me.	Men/women love and accept me. Since I'm now willing to love and appreciate myself, others now love and appreciate me as well.
My opinion of myself is determined by men's/women's opinions of me.	I love and accept myself, regardless of anyone's opinion of me.
I reject men/women so that they won't get close to me.	It's safe to let men/women get close. It's safe to love men/women and allow them into my life.

Common Limiting Thought Pattern	New Thought Pattern to Integrate
I reject men/women so that they won't hurt me.	Love is safe. I no longer need to get hurt in love. Therefore, it's safe to allow men/women to get close and love me.

See also Pattern 3—Fear of Hurting or Being Hurt, Pattern 4—Fear of Abandonment, Pattern 8—Fear of Being Your Own Person, Pattern 11—Fear of Disapproval, and Pattern 17—Fear of Displeasing Others.

PATTERN 2

FEAR OF COMMITMENT

*"The big difference between sex for money and sex for free
is that sex for money usually costs a lot less."*
Brendan Francis

COMMON EXPERIENCES IN RELATIONSHIPS

- Having relationships with unavailable men/women (e.g., those who are married or live far away)

- Pushing your partner away or feeling pushed away by your partner

- Having affairs or attracting partners who have affairs

- Avoiding relationships or not finding someone you want to be with

- Being constantly "on the go" or committed to activities outside the relationship and never spending quality time with your partner (or having a partner like this)

- Breaking up with someone you love in order to alleviate feeling suffocated, burdened, or trapped

- Sabotaging a successful relationship by becoming interested in someone else or simply disinterested in your partner

- Avoiding relationships to avoid feeling burdened, trapped, etc.

- Having "on again-off again" types of relationships

- Attracting relationships that never last (so that you can have your freedom back/be yourself again)

- Attracting a partner who needs you, clings to you, can't make it without you (so that you can feel obligated/burdened/restricted)

- Attracting a partner who is jealous/possessive/demanding of your time

- Attracting men/women who won't commit to the relationship

- Avoiding intimacy in relationships
- Being unable to be intimate with your partner (or vice-versa)
- Creating superficial relationships
- Feeling afraid to ask for/do what you want in a relationship (since you believe you have to sacrifice yourself for your partner)

This pattern is based on the fear that once you get close to your partner, you will be obligated to him, and therefore trapped in the relationship. At a deeper level, you fear that being close to someone means that you will lose your freedom, your identity, or even your life! With this pattern, your basic belief is that relationships will take from you: your energy, your power, your money, your independence, etc. In essence, intimate relationships are to be avoided at all costs!

Ironically enough, you may say that you want to be in a relationship, yet nothing ever seems to work out for you. So, what is happening here? If you believe you will lose your freedom or have to sacrifice yourself for your partner, you will subconsciously sabotage your success in relationships in order to avoid that which you fear. You can't help but create a reality based on the beliefs in your subconscious mind!

However, in this case, your reality reflects an attempt to avoid the reality you fear creating because of your subconscious beliefs. In other words, you fear relationships will take away your freedom. So, you create relationships that don't work out for you, thus avoiding the issue of having your freedom taken away.

Appearances can be totally deceiving with this pattern, and you could easily avoid taking responsibility for a relationship's demise and deny having the pattern at all. For example, you may be in a good relationship already but attract a new person into your life who sweeps you off your feet, causing you to want to leave your current partner. "It's not my fault," you explain to your unhappy mate. "It just happened." The circumstances certainly seem beyond your control, and it's apparent that the new person is your destiny calling you forth. How can you possibly resist?

The **fear of commitment** is powerful. It is very likely, in this scenario, that your current relationship had become good, steady, and the bond between you had grown stronger over time. This brought your fears of commitment to the surface, and you unconsciously began to seek a way out. Enter your "dream-come-true," your ideal match—a perfect excuse to leave your current relationship. However, until the pattern is healed, your new partner will lose all his (or her) charm, once the relationship starts to get serious and your "fear of commitment" pattern rears its ugly head once again.

The negative pattern may appear in either you or your partner. That is, you might have a fear of commitment that you are unable to perceive in yourself, but you can see it clearly in your partner. What you perceive in those around you, particularly in your "significant other," is always a reflection of the patterns that you have inside. You actually project your negative patterns onto your partner in order to see them more clearly!

MARK'S FEAR OF COMMITMENT

Mark loved women. At least, he acted as if he did—until things got too serious. Then Mark ran the other way. Mark had received a heavy dose of programming from his mother that men are responsible for women's happiness and must do whatever women want. Consequently, Mark was always doing what he could to please women—but with great resentment. Mark felt obligated to do whatever women wanted him to do and felt guilty for doing what he wanted to do. He actually hated women for the control they exerted over him.

Because of his intensely conflicting feelings toward women, Mark continually created fiery, passionate, short-lived relationships. In fact, whenever a woman would fall for Mark's charming ways (he had gotten the art of pleasing women down to a science!), she would inevitably start wanting more of a commitment from him. At that point, Mark always found an excuse to break off the relationship—often another woman.

Mark's fear of commitment was so great, he could not stay in a relationship very long. It was bad enough to feel so obligated and responsible for women for a short period of time. But, forever? No way!

Although not the "marrying kind," Mark had managed to get married earlier in life. But shortly after the marriage, he started having frequent affairs on the side with a variety of women. Two years and two children later, Mark and his wife finally divorced. Mark has gone from woman to woman ever since, balking at any hint of commitment and leaving each relationship before it was "too late."

ARLENE'S FEAR OF COMMITMENT

Arlene is twenty-eight years old. She has had four serious relationships in her life—which she ultimately ended—because none of the men felt like someone she wanted to marry. "Actually," Arlene explained rather matter-of-factly, "I just lost interest over time. None of them were ambitious enough for me. I want someone who's going someplace."

Arlene said that she had gotten close to what she wanted in the third relationship, in that he was ambitious and wanted to have nice things in life. However, according to Arlene, he was kind of selfish, and since he was ten years older than she was, they didn't have that much in common. "Sex wasn't good either," Arlene admitted ruefully.

When she met her fourth partner, Joel, he seemed like a lot more fun. But after spending several months with him, she felt uncomfortable because he liked her much more than she liked him. Then, more time passed, and her feelings toward Joel began to change. Her interest perked up, and she felt as if she was becoming more serious about him. But then, as "fate" would have it (or as Arlene unconsciously "created" it), a job offer came from out of state and Arlene accepted it, moving half a country away from Joel. Shortly thereafter, she got involved with a local man, but didn't communicate it to Joel, who was still calling her once or twice a day.

"I don't want to bum my bridges, you see," Arlene quickly pointed out. Then, in a sudden burst of true confession, Arlene admitted to having had a boyfriend on the side during each of her past three relationships.

"I think I'm just afraid of not being able to get out of the relationship if I have to," Arlene shrugged, offering a possible explanation for her behavior.

Arlene's parents had separated early in their marriage, and Arlene's mother was very bitter and hurt about the relationship's rapid demise. She had warned her daughter for as long as Arlene could remember not to get married before she was thirty-five, because it probably wouldn't work out if she did. Arlene had always resented her mother for the advice, but had apparently absorbed it unconsciously and was afraid to commit to a relationship—in case it didn't work out.

In addition, Arlene's mother was an extreme disciplinarian and would always order her around and punish her frequently for all sorts of "wrong-doings." Her father travelled for his work and stayed away from home the majority of the time. The only love Arlene had experienced while growing up was forceful, controlling, and suffocating. As a result, Arlene also developed **a fear of love (Pattern 7)**, which clearly impacted the quality and duration of her love relationships.

HEALING YOUR "FEAR Of COMMITMENT" PATTERN

Acknowledging that you have this pattern is the first step, and often most difficult step, toward healing it. Often, when it seems to be the other person's fault that the relationship isn't working out, you need to swallow your pride and tell the truth about *your* contribution to the situation, rather than blame your partner. Once you acknowledge the truth of your pattern, you can begin to work on yourself (and even thank your partner for showing you what you need to work on!).

Although your partner may have the same pattern as well, the only effective way to begin to change your experience of the relationship is to work on yourself. Then, as you change your patterns, you will undoubtedly perceive changes in your partner, too. Even if you are not in a relationship, changing this pattern will transform your ability to feel safe getting close to others and allow you new possibilities for sustaining long-term, mutually-supportive, loving relationships.

Common Limiting Thought Pattern	New Thought Pattern to Integrate
Men/women suffocate me. I don't have the space to be myself in a relationship.	Men/women allow me the space I need to be myself and to feel good in relationships.
I have to please others. I have to sacrifice myself for the men/women I love. I have to be there for others. I have to do what others want. I have to be there for the men/women I love.	It's safe to please myself and take care of my own needs first. The men/women I love support me in doing what I need to do for myself. The more I please myself and take care of my own needs first, the better I feel and the more supportive I can be to my partner. I can now support the men/women I love in a way that works for me.
I lose myself in relationships.	Relationships support me in being myself. I can now maintain my identity and sense of self-worth while having successful relationships in my life. All my relationships support me in being true to myself.
Relationships cost me my freedom. I can't be free in relationships. I'm trapped in relationships. Relationships burden me/weigh me down/keep me from being free.	Relationships support my freedom. I now attract partners who support me in having life the way I want. My partner understands and accepts my need to be free. My relationships support me in feeling light and free.

Common Limiting Thought Pattern	New Thought Pattern to Integrate
I'm obligated to the men/women I love. I have to take care of the men/women I love. I'm responsible for my loved ones. I'm a slave to the men/women I love.	I now create mutually beneficial relationships in which my partner and I enjoy supporting each other in getting our needs met. I am now able to support my partner in a way that frees me and feels good for me as well. In allowing my partner (or loved one) to be responsible for/take care of himself (or herself) the better he (or she) feels, and the better the relationship works for both of us. Relationships now support my freedom and sense of self-worth.
Love traps me. Love enslaves me. Love destroys me. Love kills me. Love is a burden. Love keeps me from having what I want. I can't be free in love.	Love frees me. Love enlivens and uplifts me. Love always enhances my life. The more I let love in, the more I have what I want in my life. Love is a blessing.
Relationships destroy me. Relationships kill me.	Relationships uplift and enliven me. Relationships always enhance my well-being. Relationships support me in being fully alive and feeling good about myself and my life.

Common Limiting Thought Pattern	New Thought Pattern to Integrate
Relationships take away my power. Relationships drain me.	Relationships always enhance my personal power and support me in feeling in charge of life. I can now stay in my power while maintaining a harmonious, balanced, loving relationship. Relationships always uplift and energize me.
Relationships drain me financially.	Relationships support me in creating and maintaining financial abundance. I can now thrive financially in my relationships. Having a partner now enhances my financial success.
Men/women want me for my money.	Men/women want me for who I am. I forgive myself for believing that my money is the only attractive thing about me. Men/women enjoy my presence whether I have money or not.

See also Pattern 3—Fear of Hurting or Being Hurt, Pattern 8—Fear of Being Your Own Person, Pattern 18—Fear of Being Misunderstood, Pattern 19—Belief in Separation From Love, Pattern 21—Fear of Losing Control, and Pattern 26—Fear of Dying from Love.

PATTERN 3

FEAR OF HURTING OTHERS OR BEING HURT

"Where there is love, there is pain."
Spanish proverb

COMMON EXPERIENCES IN RELATIONSHIPS

- Having relationships with unavailable men/women (e.g., those who are married or live far away)
- Having relationships in which you push your partner away or he/she pushes you away
- Being unable to find someone with whom you want to have a relationship
- Being constantly "on the go" or committed to activities outside the relationship and never spending quality time with your partner (or having a partner who does this)
- Avoiding relationships altogether
- Getting "dumped"
- "Dumping" others
- Engaging in hurtful behavior (e.g., not showing up, not keeping agreements, not communicating honestly, having affairs, ignoring your partners, etc.)
- Having your partner engage in the above hurtful behavior
- Avoiding intimacy In relationships
- Being unable to be intimate with your partner (or vice-versa)
- Creating superficial relationships
- Feeling afraid to ask for/do what you want in relationships (since you're so afraid of hurting your partner)

With this pattern, you are afraid that your love will eventually hurt those you love, or that you will be hurt, somehow, when someone loves you. This pattern often comes from early life experiences, particularly with parents, when love became equated with being hurt or hurting others. Since, as a child. you learned to expect such negative experiences regarding love, you will continue, as an adult, to attract partners who respond to you in a similar fashion.

In the name of "loving" you, your parents may have forced you to do things that you didn't want to do, or prevented you from doing things that you wanted to do. They may even have abused you emotionally or physically as well. As a result of any of these experiences, you felt hurt. Supposedly these people loved you. Yet, you felt misunderstood, emotionally neglected, and perhaps abused at times. In your subconscious mind, such experiences became equated with "being loved," since that was your experience of being loved by your parents.

Conversely, as young children, you loved your parents. They were your caretakers and source of nurturing and love. When they got angry or upset with you, you often blamed yourself: "Something must be wrong with how I love them. It must be my fault that they are unhappy." When they couldn't be there for you or give you the attention that you wanted, you often concluded (subconsciously, of course), that "My love must be pushing them away," "There must be something wrong with my love," or "My love hurts people."

There is a tendency, with this pattern, to take responsibility for how the other person (your partner, in relationships) feels. Thus, this pattern, particularly for the one who "does the hurting," is often accompanied by excessive guilt. Guilt is what you might call a "double whammy." When you hurt someone, you feel bad and blame yourself for what you did, i.e., for creating some kind of separation or loss of love between you. That is your first dose of guilt. Then, because you feel responsible for your partner's feeling hurt, you also blame yourself for that. Thus, you get a double dose of pain from guilt. With this pattern, the one being hurt might also experience guilt, often in the form of self-blaming thoughts about attracting another hurtful partner.

When your parents acted in extremely hurtful ways toward you as a child, you probably (and understandably) developed a **fear of being hurt**. However, as an adult, you may exhibit hurtful or aggressive behaviors toward others, as a way to try and hurt them before they have an opportunity to hurt you, since, deep down, you fear that they will.

CARL'S FEAR OF HURTING OTHERS

Carl was a large man, and when anyone commented on his size, he was quick to report how guilty his mother made him feel for having hurt her at birth. Carl had been an extremely large baby and giving birth to him had been quite painful—an experience his mother never let Carl forget. Throughout his childhood, she continued to use guilt to manipulate Carl. Whenever she got mad or upset with him, she would make him feel responsible, and as a result, Carl continually blamed himself for his mother's unhappy state.

In his relationships with women, Carl was always very charming and pleasant, as he wanted to make sure they were happy. However, he would prevent each relationship from going beyond friendship, breaking it off before the woman got too serious about wanting to be with him. Although he always tried to avoid hurting women (his biggest fear), several of the women he dated did feel extremely hurt at the unexplainable breakup of their relationship or of Carl's sudden loss of interest in dating them. So, in this way, Carl managed to avoid any serious commitments until he was forty-six, when he met Linda, and decided that he would really enjoy being married to her.

Shortly after they married, however, Linda began drinking excessively, much to Carl's dismay, and became quite unbearable to live with. She began to do everything she could to sabotage Carl's life—from trying to turn his friends against him to constantly forcing him to do things that he didn't really want to do. Carl always went along with her requests in order to avoid hurting her and to keep himself from feeling guilty in the process.

They have been married now for over a year, and Carl is miserable. He admits to having to sneak out of the house just to get together with friends for breakfast. He complains of how bad his relationship is with his wife, but he refuses to do anything about it. His friends knew the woman wasn't right for him from the outset and had warned Carl about the possible mistake he was making.

Now, Carl knows that his friends were right, but he is so afraid of hurting women (and of the guilt he would feel as a result) that he just can't break it off with her. Consequently, Carl is spending longer hours at work and focusing his total attention on his business. He is avoiding resolving his unhappy home life and dealing with his fear of hurting his relationship partner—which attracted this situation to him in the first place!

BLAKE'S FEAR OF BEING HURT

Blake's parents divorced when he was only five years old, and Blake was extremely unhappy growing up. He began drinking at fourteen years old, and started using heroin and cocaine several years later. Highly romantic in the relationship arena. Blake would always fall "head over heels" in love, only to be destroyed when the relationship would suddenly come to an end. This happened to Blake twice during his first two years of college.

Each time Blake fell in love, he was certain that it would last forever. He would convince himself that this was to be the beautiful woman with whom he would spend forever, the future mother of his children. With his first girlfriend, happiness abounded, and life was simply perfect— until she dropped out of school and disappeared completely. Blake was shocked by the relationship's sudden and unexpected demise. He felt unbelievably hurt by the unexplained turn of events and had great difficulty accepting that such a thing could have happened.

Eight months later. Blake met a new girl, for whom he also fell "head over heels" in love. (Blake also had **Pattern 15—Being in Love with Love**.) He was absolutely sure that he had finally found his true love. Nothing could separate them now. They were totally happy together, elated at having found each other, and spent a blissful three months fantasizing about their rosy future. Then came the proverbial "straw that broke the camel's back."

Cindy, his girlfriend, announced to him one day that her ex- boyfriend was back in her life and that she couldn't see Blake anymore. Blake couldn't believe his ears. Surely this couldn't be happening to him—again! Their love had been so beautiful, so ideal, exactly what he had sought for so long. Surely she had felt that way, too. How could she be doing this? Blake couldn't understand.

Totally crushed and destroyed by Cindy's sudden and callous departure, Blake decided that he would have nothing more to do with relationships. They were far too painful, far too destructive. So, Blake quit dating or even thinking about being with a woman for the next twenty years. His **fear of being hurt** again was so deep, he didn't even want to risk trying to get close to a woman.

Consequently, Blake felt lonely and unloved for most of his life. At age forty-three, he is now feeling empty and alone, and afraid that love is never going to work out for him (**Pattern 5—Fear of Being Alone**). He is now, once again, looking for that "special someone" with whom to share his life, but is greatly concerned because of his past relationship experiences. Fortunately, Blake is very committed to facing and working through his relationship issues, and has decided to participate in counseling on a regular basis to help him through this period in his life.

HEALING YOUR "FEAR OF HURTING OTHERS OR BEING HURT" PATTERN

You must work on re-programming yourself about the nature of love. You must begin to believe that love is positive, safe, and nurturing—even though that has not been your experience to date. Furthermore, guilt never helps. It just adds "insult to injury" and increases your suffering. Be willing to clear your patterns that make you hurt others or attract being hurt. Do your best, in every moment, to be as loving as possible (even though sometimes you get caught in old subconscious patterns), and trust in your inherent innocence.

Realize that you are not responsible for what another person experiences. It is his (or her) own thoughts, attitudes, and beliefs that determine how he (or she) will react. If you choose to leave a relationship and your partner feels hurt, you must understand that his (or her) hurt is not your responsibility. The person will react however he (or she) does, based on his (or her) own programming about love and relationships. So, it is important for you to accept that you are innocent for doing what you need to do.[1] Relationships don't have to cause suffering in your life—unless, of course, you believe they do!

Common Limiting Thought Pattern	New Thought Pattern to Integrate
Love hurts. Love is painful. Being in love leads to being hurt.	Love uplifts me. Love is pleasurable. Love is safe. Being in love is safe and joyful.
I'm afraid of love. I'm afraid of being hurt.	I can now relax and feel safe in the presence of love.
I am hurt by the men/women I love. Men/women destroy me with their love. Men/women suffocate me with their love.	I am nurtured and uplifted by the men/women I love. Men/women support me and enhance my well-being by loving me.
Men/women abuse me. Men/women destroy me.	Men/women treat me with love and kindness. Men/women respect me and enhance my sense of aliveness and well-being.

1. However, if you continually engage in activities that are physically abusive or damaging to another, it is imperative that you seek help and work diligently on clearing your side of the pattern. Yes, the deepest truth is that you are innocent—just for being alive. Nonetheless, you cannot justify and perpetuate hurtful behaviors toward another by lightly proclaiming your innocence. You must work on believing that you are innocent with every fiber of your being. Only then will your actions reflect a level of love, kindness, and respect that was previously impossible for you.

Common Limiting Thought Pattern	New Thought Pattern to Integrate
Love destroys me. Love kills me. I push love away to avoid getting hurt.	Love is safe. Love supports me in feeling wonderfully alive. Since love nurtures and uplifts me, I now welcome love into my life.
When I love men/women, I always get hurt.	It's safe to love men/women. I now receive joy and pleasure when I love men/women. I can now win in love. Loving men/women always feels good.
When men/women love me, they always hurt me.	It's safe to let men/women love me. I am always uplifted and enlivened when men/women love me. Love always feels good.
I don't want love. It hurts too much.	I now choose to let love in and experience pleasure and joy. I now feel comfortable having love in my life. I forgive myself for thinking love has to be painful.
Love hurts so much. I will never be able to love again.	Since I am now safe in the presence of love, it's easy to allow myself to love again.
Love never works out for me. I always get hurt.	I am now safe with love, and create a reality in which love works out for me. I now create a positive, uplifting experience of love in my life.

Common Limiting Thought Pattern	New Thought Pattern to Integrate
I hurt the men/women I love. My love hurts. My love destroys men/women. My love pushes men/women away. My love suffocates men/women. I can't let men/women get close... I don't want them to get hurt.	Men/women are safe in the presence of my love. My love uplifts and enlivens the men/women I love. My love attracts men/women. My love heals men/women. Men/women feel good in the presence of my love. It's safe to let men/women get close. My love nurtures and uplifts the men/ women I love.
I abuse men/women.	I now treat men/women with kindness and respect. Men/women always feel well-treated and well-cared for in my presence.
I am responsible for how my partner feels. I am responsible for my partner's happiness. I am guilty for hurting my partner.	I now support my partner as best I can, without taking responsibility for his/her happiness. I forgive myself for my hurtful behavior toward my partner. I am innocent, just for being alive. My partner is responsible for how he/she feels.

See also Pattern 1—Fear of Rejection, Pattern 2—Fear of Commitment, Pattern 4—Fear of Abandonment, Pattern 6—Fear of Being Intimidated, Pattern 10—Being Victimized by Love, Pattern 11— Fear of Disapproval, Pattern 12—Fear of Being Dominated, Pattern 22— Fear of Being Manipulated/Taken Advantage of/Conned, and Pattern 26—Fear of Dying from Love.

PATTERN 4

FEAR OF ABANDONMENT

"To jealousy, nothing is more frightful than laughter."
La Rochefoucauld, *Maxims*

COMMON EXPERIENCES IN RELATIONSHIPS

- Feeling afraid that your partner doesn't love you

- Fearing that your partner will leave you (even when you're in a successful, committed relationship)

- Imagining that your partner is interested in someone outside the relationship—to validate your fear that he/she will leave you

- Having your partner become interested in someone else—to validate your fear that he/she will leave you

- Feeling that you aren't okay in others' eyes, and therefore not allowing them to be nice, kind, or loving to you

- Feeling that you can't have love here, and therefore resisting getting to know people who are kind and loving to you

- Finding a reason to sabotage your present relationship so that you can leave him/her before he/she leaves you

- Having affairs or attracting partners who have affairs

- Having your partner leave you for another man/woman

- Staying in a non-supportive, even unhealthy relationship just to have someone who will stay with you

- Attracting a partner who is extremely jealous/possessive (now you can relax since he/she obviously won't leave you!)

- Attracting a needy partner who "can't make it without you" (then surely he/she won't leave you!)

- Suppressing your own needs and desires for fear that if they are expressed, the other person will leave you

- **Feeling afraid to ask for what you want from the other person or do what you want in the relationship**

This pattern is very powerful. No matter how beautiful, loving, or giving you are, if you fear being abandoned, you will inevitably attract that experience to yourself. When you fear being abandoned, you are afraid that love won't be there for you, and that you will be left—at some point—unloved, uncared for, unwanted. The basic assumption here is that you need someone outside yourself to provide you with a sense of being cared for and loved.

Because of your deep fear of being abandoned, you will either attract relationship partners who actually leave you, or you will fear this happening, which will cause you to constantly distrust your partner. Even if you are in a successful relationship, part of you is already bracing yourself for the time when your partner will leave, and this can only create friction between you. When this pattern is operating, it is difficult for you to feel at peace in your life.

Sometimes you may play a defensive role In relationships and leave your partner first, as an attempt to abandon him (or her) before he (or she) can do it to you. Somehow that helps you feel safer and more in control. However, this behavior, born of your fears, certainly doesn't produce the lasting, satisfying relationships you seek.

You may also feel abandoned whenever you are judging yourself harshly or treating yourself unkindly. In this case, you are abandoning yourself! If you resist loving yourself, you'll find it difficult to receive love from others. If you are not there for yourself, you will have trouble experiencing that others are there for you, either.

This pattern can develop when a parent leaves home or even dies when you are young. It could develop simply from feeling that your parents weren't there to take care of your needs and wants when you were a child. Even one experience of feeling abandoned will often set the stage for a lifetime of re-creating that early experience.

KATY'S FEAR OF ABANDONMENT

Katy had such a strong **fear of abandonment** that she would put up with terrible treatment by men and stay in unhealthy relationships long after she realized how bad they were for her. Even though she didn't really love him, she thought that the first man she married, when she was twenty-five, was a nice guy. However, he became horribly abusive to her and would beat her frequently. She was so fearful of being alone and afraid that he would leave her that she kept trying to do whatever it took to please him, hoping to salvage the marriage. In the meantime, she also found out that he was having affairs on the side.

Finally she managed to get up the courage to leave, and then found another man only three months after her divorce who asked her to marry him. She didn't really love him, but decided it was better than nothing. Unfortunately, his drinking binges increased dramatically and he, too, became physically abusive to her. This husband was insanely jealous, and would scream and holler if she came home late, feeling sure that she was cheating on him. It turned out that he was actually having affairs on the side. She stayed with him for a year, and by the time she divorced him, she had a new man waiting in the wings.

She is now married again, for the third time, and this time, it is her husband who is playing the role of the one who does the abandoning. Every time they have an argument or a disagreement, he says, "This isn't working, I want out...," or, "I'm leaving." After many such scenarios and many potential break-ups, they had decided to get married—thinking that this would cement their relationship and commitment to one another. Then, during their fights, he would say, "I think I made a mistake, we shouldn't be married. I want a divorce." He even filed for a divorce at one point, which drove Katy crazy, and she pleaded with him to stay, even making him feel guilty for wanting to leave. She succeeded in her plea, and they are still together, doing their best to work through their issues with one another in counseling.

Shortly after Katy was born, her father was sent overseas to World War II and didn't return until Katy was four. She was raised by her mother for those four years, and then, upon her father's return, was given to her grandmother, who raised her through elementary school. She had felt abandoned not only by her father as a child, but also by her mother who left her at her grandmother's house.

Even during junior high school, when she rejoined her family, Katy's mother continually manipulated her by actually threatening to abandon her. One time, Katy had gotten a "D" on a report card, and her mother threatened that if she ever got a "D" again, she would take Katy to a convent and leave her there. Katy was petrified of the possibility of such abandonment and made sure she didn't get below a "B" from then on. (She also developed **Pattern 17—Fear of Displeasing Others**, as a result.)

Although Katy's father had returned from the war overseas, he was gone all the time, working seven days a week as a truck driver. "My father never went on picnics with the family," Katy recalled wistfully, "and he was never there for Christmas either," The one story Katy remembers her mother telling about her father was that he was busy having an affair with someone else the night she was delivering Katy at the hospital. Her mother never trusted men, and Katy had apparently (although probably unconsciously) adopted her mother's attitude.

BOB'S FEAR OF ABANDONMENT

Bob is forty-five years old and very lonely. He is convinced that he is simply a victim of "bad luck" in relationships. He has no clue that his two strongest fears—that of being abandoned and that of being rejected— are wreaking havoc on his love life. When women really like Bob and want to be in a relationship with him, he always finds something wrong with them—not pretty enough, body not perfect enough, hair too short, hair too long, hair not blond enough—and he rejects them. The women he wants to be with are never interested in him and reject all of his overtures, often making him appear foolish for his relentless pursuit of them.

When Bob did manage to get into a relationship, he would always sabotage it by being too demanding, overly critical, and expecting perfection from his partner. Bob believed that his partner should make sacrifices in the relationship to show how much she loved him, and insisted on such behavior with regularity. Inevitably, the woman would leave him, often for another man. By sabotaging all his relationships in such ways, Bob (unconsciously) ensured the outcome of each relationship that he feared the most: that he would get abandoned.

Bob was an only child and a real "Mama's boy." His father grew jealous of his wife's attention to the boy and became extremely disapproving of Bob as a result. He remained distant from his son and never available for him emotionally. Bob felt both rejected and abandoned by his father throughout his life, which proved to have a major impact on his love relationships. Bob had grown up feeling unwanted and unloved by the person he cared about the most, and these feelings continued to permeate and affect the outcome of his relationships with women. Ironically enough, it was Bob's overly critical and demanding behavior—which he (unconsciously) copied from his father—that ultimately sabotaged his relationships and caused women to leave him.

HEALING YOUR "FEAR OF ABANDONMENT" PATTERN

The lesson here is to learn to love and care for yourself, to treat yourself the way you want others to treat you. Ultimately, you must realize that love is always present inside you, that you are, in a sense, your own source of love. No one can take love away from you by leaving you or by not being there for you. Yes, it is a wonderful experience to share love with someone, but you can't be attached to that person being the source of your love.

Your attachment is the real cause of your suffering. You must, instead, learn to give yourself the love you want. Then, ironically enough, you will feel more love from others than you had ever experienced before! If you can't love yourself, it will be very difficult to truly receive love from other people. Loving yourself and trusting that love will always be there for you are the keys to healing this pattern.

Ultimately, a "Higher" way to view life is this: if a person leaves your life for some reason, it is no longer "right" for them to be in your life. Your life is no longer served by having them present, and apparently, they can best learn their own lessons somewhere else. Although our ego would balk at such a statement, our "Higher" self is capable of acknowledging such a truth.

Trust that people stay in your life as long as their presence is for your "Highest good." When it is time for them to move on, for whatever reason, surrender to the ultimate perfection of it all, even though you may feel emotional hurt or pain in the aftermath of their departure. True peace within your soul can be achieved only by such a deep surrender and trust in the process of life.

Common Limiting Thought Pattern	New Thought Pattern to Integrate
Men/women leave me. Love abandons me. The men/women I love, don't stay with me. Men/women don't want to stay with me.	The men/women I love, stay with me. No matter who comes and goes in my life, love always stays with me. When a man/woman is right for me, he/she loves me and wants to stay with me.
I am unwanted. I am unloved. No one wants to be with me.	I am wanted and loved. Men/women love me and want to be with me.
There is no love here for me.	Love is always here for me.
The men/women I love, die. My love kills men/women.	The men/women I love, enjoy a healthy and long-lasting life. The men/women I love, thrive and prosper from my loving presence. My love always enhances the well-being of those I love.
I can't stay with the men/women I love.	It's safe to stay with the men/women I love. I now enjoy being with the men/women I love on an ongoing basis.

Common Limiting Thought Pattern	New Thought Pattern to Integrate
If I express my needs and desires, men/women will leave me.	It's safe for me to express my needs and desires to those I love.
If those I love knew the real me, they would leave.	The men/women I love respect my needs and desires and enjoy how I express myself.
	Those I love accept the real me and enjoy being with me.
	It's safe to stay with the men/women I love.

See also Pattern 5—Fear of Being Alone or Lonely, Pattern 10—Being Victimized by Love, and Pattern 13—Fear of Emotional Dependency/Fear of Being Incomplete Without Another.

FEAR OF BEING ALONE OR LONELY

*"One may have a blazing hearth in one's soul,
and yet no one ever comes to sit by it."*
Vincent van Gogh

COMMON EXPERIENCES IN RELATIONSHIPS

- Choosing or staying in a non-supportive, unhealthy, or unhappy relationship to avoid being alone/lonely (e.g., "settling for less")
- Having co-dependent relationships
- Staying in a relationship that is no longer right for you/staying past the time it feels over
- Feeling unhappy when you don't have a relationship
- Feeling as if your partner pulls on you or drains your energy in some way (or your partner feels this way about you)
- Suppressing your true needs and desires in relationships
- Begging and pleading with someone to be in/stay in a relationship, even when it's not really what you want (or someone doing this to you)
- Sacrificing your needs and wants in a relationship in order to please your partner so he/she will stay with you
- Being shy/withdrawn in your interactions with others
- Being a bachelor, widow/widower, or loner
- Feeling lonely
- Acting reclusive or antl-social
- Being alone a lot
- Wanting to be in a relationship, but not finding anyone who wants to be with you or who you want to be with

This pattern stems from some basic beliefs you have about yourself which make you think that people don't like you and want to stay away from you. Because of this, you're afraid that you will wind up being alone or lonely. Since your fear of something happening will often draw that very thing to you, your fear of being alone or lonely will produce exactly what you don't want—feeling lonely, or being alone. If you believe that people don't want to be with you, you will attract experiences to validate your belief and prove you are right.

Sometimes you are the one who doesn't want to be around others, because you have judged yourself as not being "good enough" to be in their presence. You then project your judgment of yourself onto them and start believing that they don't want to be with you, that they think you're not good enough to be with them. In actuality, it is your judgment of yourself creating the separation from others. Conversely, you may project your "I'm not good enough" judgment onto them and choose not to associate with them, deciding that they are not good enough to be with you. In both cases of "projection," you will inevitably experience the same result: you being alone or lonely!

Many people will say "yes" to what they don't want in relationships, simply to avoid being lonely or alone. Unfortunately, by saying "yes" to what you don't want, you block what you do want from coming to you!

MARGARET'S FEAR OF BEING ALONE

Margaret is thirty-nine years old. When she was young, her parents would frequently hit her and send her to her room. Margaret remembers spending a lot of time alone in her room. Extremely afraid of getting hurt, Margaret made a decision to do whatever she could to avoid such a painful recurrence. As a result, she became a people-pleaser and learned to do whatever anyone wanted in order to make them happy (**Pattern 17—Fear of Displeasing Others**).

The oldest of four girls, Margaret was always made to be an example to her younger sisters. As a result, Margaret made sure she did things "right." Afraid of getting in trouble, she was careful to be good, to do things the way her parents wanted them done. The problem was that her sisters always resented her being good; it made them look bad.

"I never felt loved or nourished at home," Margaret winced at the painful memories. "I always felt like an object; there was never any emotional connection between me and the rest of my family."

In her twenties, Margaret dated off and on, nothing serious. She really didn't know how to handle someone being interested in her—that was such a foreign experience. Margaret would always cut a person off before anything serious could develop. Sometimes she would cancel a date at the last minute with some flimsy excuse. Then, she met Ben. "The only reason the relationship happened," Margaret explained, "was because he persisted. And I finally gave in."

She and Ben lived together for three years. Although he was a kind man, Ben kept to himself much of the time, and Margaret felt isolated from him. He seemed far away, unavailable emotionally. As time passed, Ben grew more and more aloof, and Margaret became more and more needy. She began to demand a greater commitment from Ben, and Ben responded by pulling away further.

Finally the relationship ended, and Margaret went into a severe depression, getting fired from her job and moving in with her parents because she couldn't afford her own apartment. After six months of on-going depression and not being able to find a job, Margaret's parents kicked her out of their home. Margaret felt unbearably alone at that time. In the years that followed, Margaret had only a few relationships, mostly "one-night stands" during times when she felt physically or emotionally needy. Sometimes she would get her hopes up that things would work out with the man, and then he would somehow disappear (Margaret also had **Pattern 4—Fear of Abandonment**). Margaret desperately wanted much more than "one-night stands," but her unconscious fears of being alone and isolated continually attracted relationship situations that kept her feeling that way most of the time.

PATRICIA'S FEAR OF BEING ALONE OR LONELY

Patricia described her mother and father as "absentee parents"—they were physically present, but not there for her emotionally. Neither of her parents were verbally or physically demonstrative of any love or affection, and indeed, on Patricia's twenty-first birthday, her mother said that she was sorry for never telling Patricia "I love you." Patricia's father had left when she was thirteen years old, to get back together with his college sweetheart.

Patricia dated from age sixteen through twenty-four and then got married. She married a man who was equally unfamiliar with love and expressing his emotions. He hardly ever told her that he loved her, which was fine with Patricia, because whenever anyone told her that, it actually made her sick. She gave and gave to her husband, wanting to please him to make sure he would stay with her. She even stopped pursuing her goals and her career, in order to support him in being successful. Despite all this, it seemed as if she couldn't do enough, and the marriage came to an end when her husband wanted out, three years later.

Patricia dated twenty people the first year after her divorce. In fact, over the next thirteen years, she dated men constantly, each relationship lasting about two to four months. She fell in love with each of them—"probably to justify sleeping with them," Patricia suggested. (She also had **Pattern 15—Being in Love with Love**.) She was so afraid of losing each one, that she was too giving, too needy. Thus, Patricia (unconsciously) pushed the men away from her and ensured that they would leave.

She would always make inappropriate choices in men, choosing men who were never right for her, e.g., men who were less educated, men who were from a different social class, or men with whom she had nothing in common. In short, she selected men with whom the likelihood was very slim, right at the outset, that the relationship would last long-term. Often, men would leave their current relationship to be with Patricia. They would claim to be interested in her, sleep with her, and shortly thereafter, go back to the person with whom they had been before. It was incredibly painful for Patricia each time this happened. (She also had **Pattern 4—Fear of Abandonment**.)

Patricia dated anyone and everyone who would think that she was pretty. In fact, she slept with everyone to make them happy, and to hopefully ensure that they would stay with her. She dated over seventy men during that thirteen year period following her divorce, experiencing unhappy endings again and again. Finally, three years ago, Patricia began to go to therapy and actively work on healing her patterns.

She has recently met a man who seems different from the others. They've been together about a year now, and Patricia is excited to have finally met "someone who didn't leave me." Because both of them are actively working on healing their subconscious relationship patterns, there is a far greater probability of this relationship working out for her than any of those in her past.

HEALING YOUR "FEAR OF BEING ALONE OR LONELY" PATTERN

Trust that you can have what you want in relationships. Trust is the opposite of fear. Fear pulls in what you don't want; trust allows what you do want to come to you. Trust requires an attitude of openness and receptivity. It encompasses the belief that you deserve to have what you want and that life can work for you.

You do not have to be alone in life. However, you must be willing to love yourself enough to enjoy life, whether you're alone or not. If you hate being alone, you will always settle for less than you want in relationships, since being with anyone is better than being alone (in your mind). Or, you will simply find yourself alone and unhappy.

Trust that you have all the love you need deep within you, from your connection to your Higher self. As you fill yourself with love from within, you will approach relationships from a place of wholeness rather than emptiness. You will be able to share your love with others, rather than try to get love from them.

Begin to make peace with yourself and appreciate who you are. If you can't love and appreciate yourself, you won't believe others when they express those feelings for you. When you can treat yourself the way you would like others to treat you, you will be ready to experience your ideal loving relationship. As your feelings of self-love and self-worth grow, you will continually experience greater harmony and satisfaction in all your relationships—and in all other aspects of your life as well.

Common Limiting Thought Pattern	New Thought Pattern to Integrate
I don't fit in. I don't belong.	I fit in. I belong.
No one likes me. No ones wants to be with me. Men/women don't want to be with me. I'm not good enough for men/women.	Men/women like me and want to be with me. I now experience how likeable I am. Others like me here. Men/women who are right for me want to be with me. I am good enough for men/women. Men/women welcome and enjoy my presence.
I am alone here. I am lonely.	I am whole within myself and happy to be alive, whether I have a man/woman in my life or not. The more I fill myself with love from within, the happier I feel, and the more I find men/women who want to be with me. I am always connected to the love I have within me. My inner happiness always attracts wonderful men/women to me who want to share my love.

Common Limiting Thought Pattern	New Thought Pattern to Integrate
Men/women don't understand me. Men/women don't hear me. Men/women don't want to listen to me.	Men/women understand me. Men/women hear what I am saying. Men/women enjoy listening to me and find my contribution worthwhile.
I am separate. I am isolated. I can't get close to men/women.	I feel a part of life. I am connected to all of life. It's safe and easy for me to get close to men/women.
I am unloved. I am unwanted. I am doomed to be alone.	I am loved and wanted. Men/women love being with me and appreciate the value of my company. Men/women want to be with me and choose to be with me often. I am always in the presence of Love.
I am separate from love. I am separate from the ones I love.	I am always at one with Love. I am always connected to the ones I love.
I have to do it all myself. No one is there for me.	Men/women are always there for me to support me in having my needs met. It's safe to let in the support I need.
I'm never wanted here.	I am always wanted, wherever I am. My presence is always valued.

Common Limiting Thought Pattern	**New Thought Pattern to Integrate**
I can't be loved.	I *am* loved. I am ready to experience how lovable I really am. I *can* be loved.
I don't want to be around men/women. I don't enjoy myself around men/women.	It's safe to enjoy myself around men/women. Since I now know how lovable I am, I can be with men/women and enjoy myself completely.
I hate being alive. I don't want to be here. I don't care whether I live or die.	I'm now ready to love being alive. Since I now feel loved and wanted here, it's safe to choose life and enjoy being here.
It's not okay to be by myself. I don't enjoy myself when I am alone.	I now enjoy being by myself. I now enjoy myself fully whether I am with others or not.

See also Pattern 4—Fear of Abandonment, Pattern 10—Being Victimized by Love, Pattern 13—Fear of Emotional Dependency/Fear of Being Incomplete Without Another, Pattern 19—Belief in Separation From Love, and Pattern 24—Not Getting Your Needs Met/Unwillingness to Care.

PATTERN 6

FEAR OF BEING INTIMIDATED

"Nobody can make you feel inferior without your consent."
Eleanor Roosevelt

COMMON EXPERIENCES IN RELATIONSHIPS

- Having partners who intimidate you

- Having partners who are afraid of you or feel intimidated by you

- Tending to avoid relationships altogether

- Acting like a "wallflower"/uncomfortable about meeting new men/women/feeling shy

- Suppressing your true needs and desires in relationships

- Allowing your partner to talk you into doing things that you don't want to do (e.g., going on a vacation to the lake when you want to go to the mountains)

- Being afraid to tell the truth or share your real feelings with your partner

- Being pretentious or bragging about yourself (to hide feelings of inferiority)

- Always trying to put your partner down or vice versa

- Developing a "second class citizen" mentality (often accompanied by a lot of anger at being treated as inferior, which sometimes leads to feelings of wanting to get even)

- Feeling as if you aren't okay in others' eyes, and therefore, not allowing them to be nice, kind, or loving to you

- Feeling as if you can't have love here, and therefore, resisting getting to know people who are kind and loving to you

Intimidation is a tool that some people use to manipulate others to get what they want. They make others feel inferior or "less than" in some way—physically, mentally, emotionally, intellectually—in order to appear more powerful, more in command. People who feel intimidated have difficulty standing up for what they want and so offer little resistance to the other person getting his or her way.

In personal relationships, this pattern is clearly destructive. One partner always wins at the other person's expense, generating hostility and resentment in the "losing" partner. True communication cannot exist when people play out the "Intimidation Pattern." With this pattern, love—which is always generated by true communication—is virtually absent.

The **fear of being intimidated** probably comes from your childhood experiences with your parents. Due to their own negative programming, some parents need to feel superior, and they belittle their children and make them feel stupid. They do not respect the child or allow for any mistakes or failures as part of the child's learning and maturing process.

As a child, suppose you didn't achieve the grades that your parents expected of you. You might have gotten the message from them that you were stupid, inadequate, or inferior, that you should have done better. The people who loved you made you feel bad about yourself. Then, you grow up and re-create this behavior in your partner, who "loves" you in a similar way.

With this pattern, you're always comparing yourself to another person to determine your sense of self-worth, since you've learned that, in each interaction, one person is "better" than the other. With such an attitude, you will continually struggle for love and never really feel okay about yourself.

GARY'S FEAR OF BEING INTIMIDATED

Gary was forty-seven years old and married to his third wife. Between marriages, Gary dated frequently, never allowing a relationship to last longer than a year—it was too uncomfortable for him. "I would change 'em out, just like a car," Gary explained. "I couldn't handle too much intimacy, too many good feelings... I had to keep moving on." (Gary also had **Pattern 12—Fear of Being Dominated** and **Pattern 18— Fear of Being Misunderstood**.)

In all of Gary's relationships, either he was intimidated by his partner or she was intimidated by him. His current wife continually acts like a "wallflower" around him, doing whatever he wants her to do, suppressing her true needs and desires in the relationship. Gary puts on airs of being superior to her and puts her down frequently for not knowing how to dress, for not being able to earn good money for herself, and essentially, for not being better than she is.

However, with his previous wife, Gary played the meek, "wallflower" role—the one who felt intimidated. "She wouldn't let me do what I wanted to do," Gary frowned, talking about his ex-wife. "And besides, you never knew what was coming," he shuddered with the memory. According to Gary, she would become monstrous whenever she got upset, so he was petrified of rousing her anger.

One time, his wife saw Gary talking to an ex-girlfriend whom he had accidentally bumped into at a shopping mall. She became so jealous that she went berserk and slashed the tires on Gary's new Mercedes, smashed his prized piano, and threw all his possessions out onto the front lawn. Whenever Gary would arrive home late from work, which he tried desperately to avoid doing, his wife would stay angry at him for at least a week. He felt totally intimidated by her and was terrified to do anything he really wanted to do, for fear of the repercussions that it would bring.

When Gary was growing up, his father was gruff and overbearing, and would lose control whenever he was angry. On one unforgettable occasion, Gary's father beat him mercilessly and uncontrollably for something he had done wrong. Gary was scared that if he ever did anything wrong again, his father would surely kill him. Thus, Gary learned to "tiptoe" cautiously around his father, trying not to upset or enrage him. When his mother wanted to control Gary, she would threaten to tell his father about his behavior.

Gary's father always made him feel inferior. Nothing Gary ever did was good enough. Even when he got good grades in school, it was never good enough. Gary never got any praise for his accomplishments, only criticism. Petrified of doing anything wrong, Gary stopped communicating with his parents altogether. Since Gary's father worked the graveyard shifts, leaving for work at two o'clock in the morning and always feeling tired, he was never in the mood, anyway, to hear anything from anyone. Predictably, Gary grew up keeping everything inside and not sharing himself with anyone—and feeling horribly misunderstood as a result.

Gary grew up feeling totally intimidated by his parents and unhappy about never being okay or acceptable in their eyes. He then adopted pretentious ways, in his adult relationships, of acting superior to everyone to hide his truth: that he really felt inferior. He also treated many of his relationship partners in the same controlling way that his parents had treated him, dominating them, taking all the power and authority in the relationship, and not letting them do what they really wanted to do.

LEE'S FEAR OF BEING INTIMIDATED

Lee is so afraid of being intimidated that he lets people walk all over him. He won't communicate his true needs and desires, and allows whomever he is with to dictate the terms and direct all interactions between them. Lee hates women for running his life, but he never does anything to change his circumstances. He refuses to stand up for himself because he is so afraid that his partner will humiliate him. For Lee, it's not even worth trying.

During his childhood, Lee's father mercilessly humiliated and belittled him—often in front of others. He was quick to point out his son's flaws, and always made Lee feel that his way of doing things was inferior and inadequate. As a result, Lee continually cringed in fear, as his father would lash out at him unexpectedly, and for no apparent reason.

When Lee was fourteen, he would go to his father's architecture firm and help him in his office. One day, while Lee was at a drawing table, drafting some plans that his father had given to him, his father suddenly walked over to the table, grabbed the sheet of paper, ripped it off the drafting board, and proceeded to yell at Lee in front of all the other workers. After screaming that he was doing it all wrong, his father stormed out of the office, slamming the door behind him. All of his co- workers immediately approached Lee to offer their sympathy and support, but the incident absolutely devastated the boy, nonetheless.

Lee's father continued to humiliate him throughout his entire life, always making him feel inferior, stupid, and no good. As a boy, Lee constantly sought his father's approval, but his father never gave it to him. Hoping to please his father, Lee followed in his footsteps and became an architect. But, ironically enough, Lee never received the approval that he so desperately wanted.

At twenty years old, Lee married a young woman who turned out to be an intimidator—just like his father (and who, interestingly enough, his father hated). She would go into fits of rage and scream at him in public, humiliating him terribly each time. He offered no resistance to her attempts to belittle him, and he began to withdraw, refusing to communicate his thoughts or feelings. (He also developed **Pattern 24— Not Getting Your Needs Met/Unwillingness to Care**.) She completely dominated and controlled his life. He let her have her way all the time and refused to ever stand up for himself and his needs. He stayed with her for seventeen years, then finally left, unable to tolerate any more abuse.

About a year later, Lee married again. This woman seemed much nicer, but Lee's patterns were so deeply ingrained that he began to react to her in similar ways—as if she were going to intimidate him! When she would tell him what she wanted, he would start to withdraw and not share his real feelings. Then, she would get mad at him because he didn't seem to be listening to her.

Her demands grew louder and stronger. Lee would retreat even more into his own world and just nod to whatever she wanted. He had simply learned to give up doing anything the way he wanted—since he had always been made to feel that his way was wrong, inferior, and not acceptable. Consequently, Lee has let each one of his partners have all the power in the relationship, leaving him to feel downtrodden, oppressed, unhappy, and resentful, as a result.

HEALING YOUR "FEAR OF BEING INTIMIDATED" PATTERN

No one's sense of self-worth should be determined by how others think, feel, or act. You must learn to appreciate yourself for who you are, on your own merits, regardless of what is going on with the people around you.

Comparing yourself to another to measure your value is useless. To play the "better than/less than" game is a waste of time and energy; no one ever really wins. You can only feel intimidated by others if you believe that they are smarter, more powerful, or better than you in some way.

Everyone has a unique part to play in life. Everyone has a contribution to make. Get in touch with your good qualities. Focus on what you have, not on what you lack. You can still work on improving yourself, but accept yourself along the way.

Remember, the "Intimidation Pattern" always requires two sides to keep it running. If you let go of your beliefs that you are inferior or less than others, you will not attract partners who intimidate you, or if they do, you will not take it personally and react to them as you did before.

Common Limiting Thought Pattern	New Thought Pattern to Integrate
Men/women are smarter than I am.	I appreciate my own inherent intelligence. I no longer need to compare myself to men/women. I now feel good about myself in the presence of men/women.
I am weak/helpless in the presence of men/women. I lose my power in the presence of men/women.	I easily stay in touch with my power in the presence of men/women. I now experience equality and support in my relationships with men/women.

Common Limiting Thought Pattern	**New Thought Pattern to Integrate**
Men/women make me feel insecure about myself. I don't like myself in the presence of men/women.	Men/women support me in feeling good about who I am. I now view myself in high esteem in the presence of men/women.
Men/women intimidate me. Men/women make me feel stupid. Men/women degrade me. Men/women insult me. Men/women make me feel inferior. Men/women think I'm inferior.	Men/women support me in feeling powerful and capable. Men/women acknowledge me for my strengths and appreciate my presence. Men/women now treat me as an equal. with love, respect, and dignity.
I am inferior. Men/women are better than I am.	I am equal to others. I no longer need to put myself down by comparing myself to men/women. I now appreciate my individual uniqueness and find satisfaction in being myself. The more I appreciate myself for who I am, the more men/women appreciate me.
I don't want men/women to see how weak I really am.	I forgive myself for seeing myself as weak. I am now in touch with and acknowledge my strengths. It's safe to let men/women see the real me.
I am shy.	I no longer need to hold myself back. It's safe to let men/women know who I really am.

Common Limiting Thought Pattern	New Thought Pattern to Integrate
I don't know if I am the way that men/women want me to be. I'm not acceptable the way I am.	Men/women naturally like me the way I am. I am acceptable and pleasing to others just by being myself.
Love isn't here for me.	Love is always here for me.

See also Pattern 1—Fear of Rejection, Pattern 8—Fear of Being Your Own Person, Pattern 11—Fear of Disapproval, Pattern 12—Fear of Being Dominated, Pattern 17—Fear of Displeasing Others, and Pattern 25—Feeling Out of Control in Love.

PATTERN 7

FEAR OF LOVE

"I learned that love was the only dirty trick that nature played on us to achieve the continuation of the species."
W. Somerset Maugham

COMMON EXPERIENCES IN RELATIONSHIPS

- Avoiding relationships/not wanting to get involved
- Feeling abused/attracting abusive partners
- Leaving relationships when they get too good
- Feeling as if you're going to die because you are in a loving relationship
- Feeling as if you're aren't okay in others' eyes, and therefore not allowing them to be nice, kind, or loving to you
- Avoiding someone who is interested in you
- Pushing away men/women who love you
- Feeling as if you can't have love here, and therefore resisting getting to know people who are kind and loving to you
- Maintaining long-distance relationships or relationships with unavailable partners
- Not wanting to settle down with one person
- Avoiding intimacy in relationships
- Being unable to be intimate with your partner (or vice versa)
- Creating superficial relationships
- Being a bachelor or loner

This pattern clearly keeps relationships from working out for you. You might have a **fear of love** if the love you experienced as a child was mingled with threats to your safety in some way. For example, if your parents physically, mentally, or emotionally abused you, and that was your first experience of love, understandably, you may fear love or prefer to live without it. If your parents were overbearing, unreasonably demanding, or frequently made you do things you really didn't want to do, you may have felt overburdened, overpowered, or suffocated by love. If such was the case, you are probably inclined to resist love in any form.

The problem is that because of your negative programming about love, you are convinced that love is to be avoided at all costs. You are not truly open to creating a loving relationship with another, because you are so fearful of the consequences of being that close to someone again. Your early experiences with "loving" relationships taught you to stay away from them, as a way to ensure your survival and sanity. Sadly, however, such an attitude only sets the stage for unhappiness in life.

Often, with this pattern, you don't feel as if you deserve to be treated well, since you are so accustomed to being treated poorly by the ones who "loved" you as a child. Therefore, you often avoid people who treat you kindly and lovingly. Not only do you feel undeserving of such kind and loving attention, but such treatment is totally unfamiliar.

You may find yourself choosing pain over pleasure again and again, because the mind always gravitates toward the familiar. You've been programmed to expect poor, unloving, or abusive treatment by those who love you; your "inner computer" is "wired" to continually attract those same kinds of circumstances. Anything to the contrary would "blow your circuits," that is, be too unfamiliar to handle.

ANDY'S FEAR OF LOVE

Andy has been married three times and is currently in the process of divorcing his third wife. Understandably, Andy has reached the conclusion that love is just not for him. It is too complicated and causes too much pain. "Relationships are always such an emotional roller coaster for me," he explained rather matter-of-factly, "I'd rather not participate in them at all." Thus, Andy was bailing out—again! (He also had **Pattern 10— Being Victimized by Love**.)

In all of his relationships, Andy had done his best to keep himself busy, so that he would not have to deal with emotional intimacy. A true workaholic, Andy worked twelve to fourteen-hour days, and had little time, if any, to spend with his wife. Besides, Andy didn't like dealing with feelings—which always happened when he spent too much time with her.

Discussing feelings made Andy extremely uncomfortable and he avoided such discussions. In fact, Andy would remain silent whenever any of his partners would want to discuss things with him, and he would always complain about how much they all wanted to control him.

"Women drive me crazy," Andy rolled his eyes, exasperated. "They're always trying to tell me what to do." (He also had **Pattern 12— Fear of Being Dominated**.) Andy is convinced that relationships just aren't worth the trouble, yet he always seems to find someone new, shortly after each relationship ends.

Andy was raised by a domineering, controlling mother who always had the upper hand in family dealings and by an angry father with a violent temper. Andy's father beat him frequently, using a two by four or any other hard object his hands would fall upon during a fit of rage. His mother would hit him as well, but his father's beatings were far more intense and difficult to bear.

Andy could never express how he really felt as a child and had learned to shut his feelings off, almost as easily as turning off water from a faucet. He had made a decision that he didn't want to feel all the pain that was bottled up inside him. Besides, it made him feel too out of control—a feeling which he hated more than anything else.

Andy's first experience of being loved was so painful, he decided that he would be better off without it. Of course he would always be drawn into new relationships, since love is the true nature of life, yet his fear of love was so great that he would create only superficial relationships with women, wherein he would experience minimal love and therefore minimal pain, in his mind. Andy continually pushed his loving partners away by his distancing behaviors, until eventually each relationship would die, with no love to fuel it.

SALLY'S FEAR OF LOVE

Sally had a very challenging childhood, which caused her to develop a **fear of love**. Sally's mother was extremely critical and disapproving of her, dominating the entire family. Sally's father, an alcoholic, was extremely rejecting and abusive toward Sally and her two brothers. Her father, normally unaffectionate and physically aloof, would lose his temper periodically and beat Sally.

Because of such experiences, Sally learned that physical contact with the man she loved was unsafe and hurtful, and understandably, she developed a **fear of sex** (**Pattern 16**) later in life. Based on how she was treated as a child, Sally had terribly low self-esteem, and as an adult she would bend over backwards to please people, so that they would accept her. (She also had **Pattern 1—Fear of Rejection**.)

Sally eloped at age eighteen in order to get out of the house. Then, within the next three years, she became obese, her 5'8" frame carrying well over three hundred pounds. She hadn't been heavy at all when she first got married.

Several years later, her husband Matt had an affair, after which he and Sally separated for a year. During that time, Matt moved in with the other woman. Then, Sally and Matt decided to get back together and move out of state, in order to distance themselves from their unhappy memories. After two years, however, they returned to the same town, and a few years later, Matt had an affair with the same woman again. This time, when he moved in with her, he took their twelve-year old daughter along. Six months later, Matt decided that he didn't want to be with the other woman anymore, and at that point, Sally welcomed him back.

Sally's fears of love and sex certainly contributed to her gaining the excess weight, in an attempt to prevent love and intimacy from being a part of her life. Her husband leaving her for another woman, and even taking their daughter with him, also ensured the same outcome. As a side note, Matt also had this pattern—a **Fear of Love**, along with **Pattern 20—A Fear of Being Dominated**. Sally had dominated Matt throughout their marriage and always bossed him around. His "yo-yo" participation in their marriage clearly shows his conflicting feelings toward her, as well as his inability to resolve those issues.

HEALING YOUR "FEAR OF LOVE" PATTERN

Love is the essence of life. To resist love is to resist the true nature of life, and such resistance can only keep you limited and blocked. Letting love in is vital in order to harmonize with your true essence. Allowing yourself to love sets you free.

To feel safe and comfortable in love's presence, you must be willing to release your erroneous programming about the nature of love. Although you might have had a negative experience of love in the past, you can start to create a different, more positive experience of love from now on. Love, itself, can never kill you. Your beliefs about love, on the other hand, could!

Work diligently on "re-wiring" your "inner computer." You must change all your negative ideas about love, even though they may seem real to you. Take some time to visualize how it would feel to be treated with genuine love and respect. Since love is so unfamiliar to you, it is important to do all you can to create a sense of comfort and familiarity with love.

You will literally have to imagine how it would feel, to be genuinely nurtured and uplifted by love. If you can't picture this, it will be difficult to attract such experiences in relationships. Do your best to see and feel how you want your life to be. Then, you can truly manifest what you envision for yourself.

Common Limiting Thought Pattern	New Thought Pattern to Integrate
I will die if men/women love me. Love makes me feel like dying. Love destroys me.	It's safe to let men/women love me. Love always enhances my aliveness and well-being. Love inspires me to live fully and enjoy myself. Love empowers me and makes me feel whole.
Love overpowers me. Love hurts me. Love is too complicated for me.	Love is now easy and enjoyable for me to experience. Love is now easy and simple for me. I now trust love.
Love keeps me from being free. Love gets in my way.	Love supports my freedom in life. Love supports me in easily having what I want.
I don't want love in my life—it causes too many problems.	Love now brings a sense of clarity, peace, and simplicity to my life. It's safe to let love into my life.
Love is not for me.	Love is the true nature of life and relationships. Love is right for me.
I am not okay, and therefore, I don't deserve love.	I am okay, and therefore, I deserve love.

See also Pattern 2—Fear of Commitment, Pattern 3—Fear of Hurting or Being Hurt, Pattern 19—Belief in Separation from Love, Pattern 20—Fear of God, and Pattern 26—Fear of Dying from Love.

PATTERN 8

FEAR OF BEING YOUR OWN PERSON

"I was raised to sense what someone wanted me to be and be that kind of person. It took me a long time not to judge myself through someone else's eyes."
Sally Field

COMMON EXPERIENCES IN RELATIONSHIPS

- Being a "yes man," always saying "yes" to men/women in order to be liked (in either you or your partner)
- Feeling afraid to ask for what you want or do what you want/ giving up your power in the relationship
- Not being true to yourself in relationships
- Having low self-esteem and being moody/negative/withdrawn/ (in either you or your partner)
- Having a partner who demands that you wear the "right" clothes/go to the "right" social functions/follow a strict social etiquette in order to conform/be liked/prove that you're okay as a couple
- Having violent, unexpected outbursts of temper
- Acting self-destructively (excessive eating, smoking, drinking)

When you have a **fear of being your own person**, you feel pressure to conform to other people's ways. In order to be accepted by them, you think that you have to be just like them. You might project this fear onto the two of you as a couple and insist that you do the things that other couples do, fearful of the consequences of being unique or different as a couple. This pattern can also lead to an exaggerated desire to please people outside the relationship. You or your partner might find yourself constantly saying "yes" to other people's requests, which might cause either one of you to sacrifice time normally given to the relationship. If this happens excessively, it could create jealousy, separation, or hurt feelings between the two of you.

Another common result of this pattern is being afraid to ask for or do what you want in a relationship, in order not to "rock the boat," "make waves," or "upset the applecart." You're afraid to do anything that might displease others. As a result, pent-up hostility or anger may develop, which could lead to bouts of violent temper or self-destructive behaviors. By not being true to yourself over an extended period of time, you will invariably vent your frustration somehow—on your partner, yourself, or others outside the relationship.

This pattern can develop during childhood in several ways. First, if your parents had the pattern themselves, they might have modeled this behavior for you, in their own lives, of having to conform in order to be liked. Or, they might have simply insisted that you conform to a certain way of being in order to please them, or society, in general. You learned that you could not be your own person, but had to conform to others' standards in order to be accepted.

This pattern can also develop, or at least be heavily reinforced in your early experiences with your peers. Peer pressure to conform at school is enormous. Cliques and special groups, formed by the more "popular" students, often demand conformity. Because of your over-whelming desire to be liked and accepted, you can develop a **fear of being your own person** and doing things in a way that respects your own unique individuality. You learn to sacrifice being who you are in the hopes that others will like you because you are Just like them.

VICKI'S FEAR OF BEING HER OWN PERSON

When I first met Vicki, she was forever complaining of her husband's willfulness. "He always insists that we do whatever he wants to do. He tells me what to wear to social functions. I feel like I can't be who I am around him." Interestingly enough, however, Vicki never complained to him.

Vicki was afraid to ask for what she wanted in the relationship because she was convinced that her husband would say "no." So, she said "yes" to whatever he wanted. In a sense, she disappeared; she lost her identity. Vicki also lost touch with what she really wanted in life, because, in essence, she gave up her own will. (Vicki also had **Pattern 9—Fear of Being Unimportant**.)

Vicki became moody, despondent and withdrawn. She began to read more and more, in an effort to escape her circumstances. By believing that she had to give her power away in relationships, Vicki had created an extremely unhappy life for herself.

Vicki's parents had had very high expectations of her while she was growing up. They insisted that she get superior grades. They demanded top quality performance from her in all areas of life. The message that she got from her parents was that she was okay—as long as she lived up to their expectations. Vicki learned to do only what was expected of her, not what she really wanted to do. She became the ultimate "people-pleaser" (she also had **Pattern 17—Fear of Displeasing Others**), and her self-esteem plummeted.

Vicki lost all confidence in herself and her ability to succeed in life. She admitted that she no longer even knew what she wanted for herself. Still, she continued to resent her husband for insisting that she do all that he wanted of her. Because Vicki didn't value herself and her desires, none of her relationship partners ever did either.

GABRIELLE'S FEAR OF BEING HER OWN PERSON

Gabrielle is thirty-six years old. She got married at eighteen in order to escape an unhappy life with her parents, particularly her father, and the marriage lasted fifteen years. She has been divorced for four years now, feeling free for the first time in her life.

Gabrielle felt as if she had grown up in a prison. "I had to be careful so I wouldn't get in trouble," Gabrielle shared vehemently. "I was scared to death of getting my Dad mad at me." Gabrielle's father used to keep a paddle with her name on it, and would spank her with it regularly. There were times when he would slap her hard—in front of company—just for joking around with him. Life was all work in her father's household; having fun was never allowed.

Gabrielle's father, a severe alcoholic, was extremely controlling. She always had to do things his way—and, no matter how hard she tried, she never seemed to be able to do anything right. He insisted on controlling every detail of her life. She couldn't have friends visit, and she couldn't go out with them. If he gave her permission to go somewhere with them, she had to be home by a certain time or she would be punished.

Petrified of his anger, Gabrielle learned to accommodate his every wish; however, she resented it greatly. "If I didn't keep him happy, he wouldn't like me," young Gabrielle had reasoned. She had learned to do everything he wanted her to do, in order to have the best chance of getting the love and acceptance she craved. Of course, she never got that love and acceptance. She had simply learned to give her power away to men, and was totally unable to live life according to what was true or appropriate for her from within.

Charlie, the first man Gabrielle dated, drank a great deal. She was completely in love with him and put up with all kinds of abusive behavior. (She also had **Pattern 10—Being Victimized by Love**, and **Pattern 22— Fear of Being Taken Advantage of**.) Charlie was very irresponsible and owed money to many people. He borrowed large amounts from her to pay off his debts, and he never paid any of it back. Sometimes, when Gabrielle needed a lift home, Charlie would promise to pick her up, but often he would arrive late, and sometimes not at all.

Then Gabrielle met Hank and married him. At first, he seemed very kind and loving. Shortly after they got married, however, Hank began to be mean and argumentative. It seemed as if she could never do what she wanted or else she would anger Hank. She enjoyed lounging around and reading the paper on Saturday morning, but Hank wouldn't let her. He would accuse her of being lazy and wasting the day. And, to make matters worse, Hank didn't like anybody and wouldn't let her get together with her friends. Gabrielle stayed in this second "prison" for another fifteen years before she finally divorced Hank.

Four years later, Gabrielle, extremely wary of relationships, is still guarding her precious freedom. She is enjoying being her own person and having the freedom to do whatever she wants in life. However, she has recently started dating a new man, Barry, and Gabrielle feels confused, because she is so used to being there for men and doing whatever they want her to do. But, Barry is different.

Fortunately for Gabrielle, Barry understands what's going on and really wants her to be her own person. "He really wants me to have interests outside of being with him," Gabrielle explained in amazement. "He encourages me to do things without him and do what I really want to do."

Sometimes Gabrielle finds herself trying to sabotage the relationship because Barry isn't trying to control her. She thinks that he must not like her anymore, since he isn't treating her the way she is used to being treated. Sometimes she does things to make him angry, as if to test him, such as announcing that she wants to date other men. Until Gabrielle releases this pattern, it will always seem unfamiliar, and therefore, somewhat threatening, to be with a man who supports her in being who she really is.

HEALING YOUR "FEAR OF BEING YOUR OWN PERSON" PATTERN

Love and respect yourself for who you are! The more you do this, the more you will be able to love and appreciate the unique qualities that other people possess as well. This will allow you to create more satisfying relationships, in which both partners enjoy the freedom of self-expression. It is much more fulfilling to be loved for being who you are than to be loved for conforming to someone else's expectations of you.

Acknowledge the truth—that being who you are is more important than anything else in life and that to deny yourself this birthright can only perpetuate unhappiness and suffering. Choose to be true to yourself, and trust that people will like and respect you for doing so. By being true to yourself, you give the people around you the opportunity to be true to themselves as well. When this happens, relationships can become a source of harmony and joy, wherein both partners feel honored and respected for being who they are.

Common Limiting Thought Pattern	New Thought Pattern to Integrate
I'm not okay if I don't do what men/women expect of me. Men/women won't like me if I don't do what they want me to do.	Men/women support me and approve of me for doing what I want. I am okay whether I do what men/women expect of me or not. Men/women like me no matter what I do.
I can't be who I am. If I do, men/women won't like me.	I can be who I am. Men/women like me for being who I am. Who I am is naturally pleasing to men/women.
Men/women won't like me if I'm different. I'm afraid to be myself. Men/women don't want me to be different from the way they are. I can't be different around men/women.	Men/women like me for being the unique individual that I am. It's safe to be different and still receive men's/women's approval. Men/women support me in being just the way I am. It's safe to be myself around men/women.
I'm not good the way I am. If I'm like other people, maybe they will think I'm good.	I am good the way I am. I no longer need to be like others in order to be good. Men/women think I'm good just the way I am.
I don't know who I am. I don't know who I am when I'm around men/women. I'm not anyone worth knowing.	I know who I am when I'm around men/women. I am someone worth knowing. Men/women enjoy knowing me and being with me. I know who I am.

See also Pattern 1—Fear of Rejection, Pattern 4—Fear of Abandonment, Pattern 11—Fear of Disapproval, and Pattern 17—Fear of Displeasing Others.

FEAR OF BEING UNIMPORTANT

*"When a girl marries, she exchanges the attentions of many men
for the inattention of one."*

Helen Rowland

COMMON EXPERIENCES IN RELATIONSHIPS

· Avoiding or retreating from others/being a "wallflower"

· Feeling as if you aren't okay in others' eyes, and therefore not allowing them to be nice, kind, or loving to you

· Having "know-it-all" partners (who don't need or want your opinion)

· Having partners who demean or humiliate you

· Having partners who take control/make decisions for you (without asking)

· Giving your power away/turning to your partner to make decisions for you

· Feeling loneliness and often resentment (toward your partner for treating you the way you are subconsciously asking to be treated!)

· Not believing a partner when he/she reassures you of your importance

· Feeling unloved/unappreciated in relationships

· Ignoring your partner (or being ignored by your partner)

As with all subconscious patterns, your beliefs create your reality. If you believe that you are unimportant, you will experience being treated that way by other people. Someone in your life may continually reassure you of how much you mean to him (or her), but it is likely that you will have a hard time believing it. Also, you are sending out the *subconscious* message: "I'm unimportant. Don't respect me. Don't notice me." Your thoughts go out to others as decrees on what you expect from your world and the people in it. As a result, people respond accordingly (although they are unaware of doing so) and give you what you (unconsciously) request to experience as your truth. That's why it is so important to "clean up" your negative subconscious programming—so you can stop telling others to treat you in ways that are no longer in harmony with your conscious desires.

This pattern generally develops as a result of how you were treated early in life. Perhaps you were born "last in line" in a family of many children and literally weren't noticed or got "lost in the shuffle." Perhaps your parents were extremely busy, even self-absorbed, and didn't solicit much input from you. Whatever the scenario, you decided that somehow you were unimportant, not respected, or ignored by the people around you.

With this pattern, it often appears to be the other person's fault. "He doesn't treat me with respect. He should treat me better." And often: "If it weren't for him, then I'd be happy, feel important, be someone, etc." Thus, it is easy to get stuck in blame and continually resent the people around you for making you feel the way you do. In such a state, you may never take responsibility for having this pattern, in which case, you will be at its mercy your entire life.

JANICE'S FEAR OF BEING UNIMPORTANT

Janice is the sixth of seven children, and by the time she was born, her parents never had much time for her. Janice never got the attention she wanted and always felt as if the people she loved the most ignored her and didn't really care about her. As a married adult, Janice continues to project those same feelings onto her relationship with her husband Pete and constantly demands more attention from him. In order to keep the peace, Pete finds himself compromising far more than he really wants to, and after sixteen years of marriage, he feels extremely resentful of the control his wife exerts over him.

Sometimes Pete wants to go play cards or shoot baskets with a few friends, and this causes Janice's **fear of being unimportant** to surface. So, she always insists that he do something with her instead, and he begrudgingly complies. When Pete wants to visit his family with whom he is very close, Janice feels threatened and insists that he be with her and their own family instead. Pete is starting to feel very uncomfortable about having to do what she wants all the time and he is even pondering leaving the relationship.

Fortunately, though, Pete really loves Janice and wants to work it out with her, but Janice's strong-armed tactics are still pushing Pete away. If Janice continues in the same way for much longer, it is quite possible that Pete will leave. If this happens, Janice's life will reflect another subconscious pattern she has—the **fear of abandonment**. Luckily, Janice has become aware of the need for self-reflection and self-healing, and is open to working on herself to heal subconscious negativity from her past. As I discussed Pete and Janice's situation with them, much of the old hurt and resentment on Pete's part began to dissolve (he had never discussed "any of his feelings with his wife before this), and Janice became aware of her behaviors which were pushing Pete away. Their commitment to each other is strong, and it is likely that, in time, they will work through these issues and choose to be together, but in a more loving, mutually supportive way.

BILL'S FEAR OF BEING UNIMPORTANT

Bill was so afraid that his partner would discover that he was unimportant and had no value, he would bend over backwards doing things for her, trying to please her and show her how important he really was. However, Bill suffered greatly in his relationships with women. He continually sacrificed himself in the name of love, yet deeply resented his partners for not loving him back in the same way.

Because he felt so unloved and devalued, Bill blamed his partners incessantly for the unkind way they treated him. No matter what his partners would tell him or how much they would reassure him of their love, Bill was convinced that he was not getting the love or respect he deserved. In fact, he was certain that women just wanted to use him for what he could do for them (**Pattern 22—Fear of Being Manipulated/ Taken Advantage of/Conned**), and he was furious at women for taking advantage of his kind-hearted nature.

Bill's friends would warn him that he was doing too much for his relationship partner and that he should be more wary, demanding some kind of compensation for his efforts. Not realizing that his friends were feeding back to him the very fears and negative beliefs already in his subconscious mind, Bill would believe them, and use their words of advice as ammunition against the woman.

"I knew you were just using me," Bill would shout at his girlfriend. "My friends are right. You really don't think I'm important. You don't really love me!"

What Bill didn't understand was that as long as he continued to believe his negative programming and project his own fears and doubts onto his partner, he would never be able to resolve his dilemma and let love in. He would continue to feel victimized by his partner (he also had **Pattern 10—Being Victimized By Love**), and believe her to be responsible for his lack of self-worth.

While Bill was growing up, both of his parents were professionals and highly devoted to their careers. Both worked full-time outside the home, and brought additional work home as well. Bill, the oldest child, got pushed aside and ignored in favor of their other priorities. In fact, the only time Bill ever got attention was when he did something wrong, and he seemed to get in trouble rather frequently. Bill felt unnoticed and unloved by his parents and grew up feeling estranged from them.

As a result of his upbringing, Bill also developed a deep **fear of love (Pattern 7)** since love had always been so unfamiliar to him. Therefore, it was easier for him to play the role of "giver of love" in relationships and then blame his partner for her inability to return that love. Yet, it was actually Bill's unconscious unwillingness to receive love and attention that prevented him from experiencing what he truly wanted with his partner.

Once Bill was able to identify the source of his troubles—his own subconscious programming and not his partner—he was able to experience greater love and satisfaction in his relationship than ever before in his entire life. Letting go of blaming his partner for his negative feelings was crucial to this process.

HEALING YOUR "FEAR OF BEING UNIMPORTANT" PATTERN

Accept that no one is to blame for your negative feelings about yourself. The pattern starts with you and the message you're giving out to other people about how to treat you. That is why it's imperative that you work on changing both your conscious and subconscious attitudes and beliefs.

As you change your beliefs about yourself, people will necessarily treat you differently and give you more of what you really want. It is also possible that you will choose to change some of the people in your life! Whatever happens, your life will always improve as a result of your willingness to "clean up your inner act."

You will need to forgive the people in your life—probably your parents—for not treating you the way you wanted to be treated. Trust that they did the best they could. You see, if they could have done it better, they would have. Let go of your old hurts and resentments toward them in order to make more room in your heart for love and self-acceptance.

Common Limiting Thought Pattern	New Thought Pattern to Integrate
I'm stupid.	I forgive myself for thinking I'm stupid. I am now in touch with my innate wisdom and intelligence.

Common Limiting Thought Pattern	New Thought Pattern to Integrate
Men/women don't respect me. I get no respect here.	I deserve respect. I now attract men/women who respect me and treat me the way I want to be treated. I now respect myself. The more I respect myself, the more men/women treat me with respect.
No one knows I'm here. Men/women don't notice me. I don't exist.	Men/women are aware of and appreciate my presence. Men/women notice me. I exist; I have value.
Men/women don't think I'm important. Men/women don't care if I'm alive. I'm not important.	Men/women care about me and want me around. The men/women in my life think I am important and treat me with love and respect. I am important.
I must not be okay, since everybody treats me that way.	I am okay, and everyone treats me that way. Men/women now treat me with the love and respect I deserve.

See also Pattern 8—Fear of Being Your Own Person and Pattern 24—Not Getting Your Needs Met/Unwillingness to Care.

BEING VICTIMIZED BY LOVE

"He who loves the more is the inferior and must suffer."
Thomas Mann

COMMON EXPERIENCES IN RELATIONSHIPS

- Avoiding relationships to avoid being overwhelmed/distracted by love
- Feeling a loss of identity/an inability to be, do, and have what you want in relationships
- Co-dependent relationships
- Loving others who don't feel the same way— "unrequited" love
- Feeling abused/attracting abusive partners
- Having melodramatic relationships (stormy breakups, violent quarrels, etc.)
- Attracting partners who have affairs
- Attracting partners who don't keep their agreements
- Feeling overwhelmed or incapacitated while in a relationship
- Feeling unloved in relationships
- Not feeling as if you have any choice when in relationships (e.g., you have to say "yes" because your partner wants to, or your partner wants to end the relationship and you don't, etc.)
- Feeling lovesick and obsessively thinking about the person you love
- Being preoccupied with being in love
- Looking for a partner to "save" or "rescue" you
- Looking for a partner who needs "saving" or "rescuing"

With this pattern, your basic attitude toward love and relationships is "woe is me," and you probably love to complain and be dramatic about how bad life is for you in matters of love. With this pattern, you can't win. You are out of control and unable to achieve the "happy endings" you desire.

You may have developed this pattern out of a strategy (unconscious, of course) to gain love and approval. Think of how many people's shoulders you can cry on when love doesn't work out for you. Your "drama queen" or "tragedy queen" role could get you attention that you might not get if your life were peaceful and smooth (if that's what you believe!).

As a child, you may have gotten more approval when something went wrong (such as when you fell down and got hurt, when someone at school called you names and made you cry). You learned that drama has its rewards. Perhaps you even had parental role models of love not working out or not being mutually fulfilling. As a result, you began to unconsciously play out a similar scenario in your own life, adding the "woe is me" sentiment to ensure that you would get some love or attention for your unhappy state.

When this pattern is operating, you are often subconsciously "calling out" to be "rescued" from your plight. Thus, you attract "savior" type partners. Such a partner would be unable to love you the way you want to be loved, i.e., for being who you are. He (or she) would merely be playing the game that you (unconsciously) have asked him (or her) to play, called "to love me is to save me."

This form of love (whether you play the "savior" or the one "needing saving") is highly unfulfilling. It does not support either partner in taking responsibility for his (or her) own life and happiness. It is not based on mutual sharing, respect, and cooperation—the basis for a successful relationship—and requires that one partner be a "victim" in order to keep the game going.

Often, with this pattern, you will make the other person into "God" and the source of your love, which is not based on the ultimate Truth. When you think that he (or she) is your source of love, you start to become needy, addicted to having him (or her) in your life, and horribly crushed if he (or she) leaves for any length of time. Basically, you create tremendous unhappiness for yourself, and the love you feel for the other person is tainted, in a sense, because it wreaks havoc on the rest of your life. In this pattern, **"being victimized by love,"** a dichotomy exists between having love and having what you want in life. Often the attitude is, "I can't have what I want, but at least I have love."

GEORGIA'S PATTERN OF BEING VICTIMIZED BY LOVE

Georgia is now forty-two years old and has been divorced for seventeen years. Her first boyfriend died. Her ex-husband committed suicide about five years after the divorce. Many of her boyfriends over the years have lived in distant cities and would spend only weekends with her. She said, however, that she enjoyed long-distance relationships because she felt less distracted from her work. Besides, a faraway boyfriend was enough proof for her that somebody cared about her, without interfering with her lifestyle.

Throughout her adult life, Georgia never pursued men. They all chose her. Nonetheless, she often felt that she had no choice but to take what she could get. Most of her relationships lasted about two years, then would suddenly and traumatically crumble.

"I was never wined and dined," Georgia shook her head sadly. "No man has ever really taken care of me or supported me in any way." She had always felt that she needed to be a "trooper" and stay strong, never letting her partner see her as anything less than a perfect model of love and understanding.

A relationship was top priority for Georgia, and as a result, she would put a tremendous amount of effort into it, even to the point of losing her own sense of self. Her own needs were never met because she was so focused on taking care of her partner. She would become addicted to him and feel at a loss as to what to do with herself—if it wasn't an activity that related to him.

Georgia would lose herself in relationships to such a great extent that she finally isolated herself from them completely, moving to a remote part of the country and living in a small isolated farmhouse, all alone. At least, that way, she could re-connect with herself once again. At times, however, she wished that a man would appear to rescue her and "make it all better."

For Georgia, relationships always seemed painful, unrewarding, and too much effort. She has been avoiding them for many years now. Although Georgia's primary pattern is **being victimized by love**, she also has **Pattern 25—Feeling Out of Control in Love, Pattern 22—Belief in a Punishing God**, and **Pattern 19—Belief in Separation from Love**.

While Georgia was growing up, she watched her mother sacrifice herself in order to make her father happy. Her mother never seemed to be happy unless she succeeded in making her husband happy. Georgia's role model was one of a woman whose entire sense of self-worth depended upon her relationship with a man. In addition, Georgia's father never seemed to appreciate her mother or all her efforts to make him happy, and Georgia's mother would constantly complain in his absence.

For Georgia, relationships appeared to be a "no-win" situation, in which the woman's only purpose in life was to support her man in every way possible. The only possibility for her to gain any love or attention was by complaining about how unappreciated and unloved she felt. No wonder Georgia felt inclined to avoid relationships altogether.

MARCIA'S PATTERN OF BEING VICTIMIZED BY LOVE

Marcia's life had a strong resemblance to a soap opera—complete with violent quarrels and other intensely melodramatic episodes. She got pregnant at sixteen while still in high school, and decided to marry the father of the child. Her husband, a strong, body-builder type, appealed to Marcia because of his physical strength and the feeling of security that gave her, but he was totally uncommunicative, stoic even, and Marcia felt terribly unloved in the relationship.

She would complain all the time to her friends about his ill treatment of her and what a terrible time they were having as a couple. She felt that she loved him far more than he loved her, and she began to criticize and antagonize him in order to get even. (She also had **Pattern 6—Fear of Being Intimidated** and used criticism to put him down and overcome her own feelings of insecurity and inferiority.)

After three years, they had a violent fight in which he pushed and shoved her, and everyone—including her husband's father—got involved in a screaming, yelling brawl. Marcia decided to leave in order to sort things out, and she proceeded to move two thousand miles away. During this period of "sorting things out," she immediately had an affair with another man and began calling her husband to accuse him of sleeping with other women in her absence.

Six months later, she decided to go back to her husband, who was agreeable to the plan. However, she and her new lover decided that he would call her regularly, but simply hang up if the husband answered the phone. Marcia was obviously setting herself up for more trouble.

Marcia's mother married at seventeen, when Marcia was born, and divorced her husband the following year. Then, a few years later, she remarried a man who was terribly abusive to Marcia. "He was a real slave driver," Marcia spoke of him through clenched teeth. "If I didn't clean the house perfectly, he wouldn't let me have dinner." She grew up hating her stepfather, and their fights grew so intense that she finally left home at age thirteen to live with her grandparents.

Marcia, the unwanted stepchild, always felt intimidated by her stepfather, who criticized her endlessly and made her feel inferior—and Marcia has continued to feel this way throughout her adult life. Because of the intensity of her upbringing and the many negative subconscious patterns that she developed as a result, Marcia continually creates intense melodrama and strife in her relationships with men and is unable to sustain anything resembling true love, nurturing, support, or caring for another.

HEALING YOUR "BEING VICTIMIZED BY LOVE" PATTERN

Being in love can absolutely include having the rest of your life work for you! You do not have to give up anything that you want in order to have love in your life. Love doesn't demand sacrifice... unless of course you think it does!

The ultimate truth about love is that it resides deep within you, at your core. It is your essential nature, once you strip away the mass of negative programming that you have accumulated over the years (or lifetimes). Instead of another person being your "source" of love, he (or she) is actually stimulating the love that is already inside you. In a sense, the person is mirroring back to you the parts of yourself that you love and adore. Remember, what you see in your partner is always a reflection of some part of you!

The key here is to love yourself fully, creating that sense of love within you, whether you have a partner or not. Then, once you are in a relationship, you can truly enjoy the love you share with your partner—without being overwhelmed by, addicted to, or desperate for it!

Common Limiting Thought Pattern	New Thought Pattern to Integrate
Love is too much for me. Love overwhelms me. When I'm in love, I can't concentrate on anything else.	I can easily accept love. Love feels good to me. Love supports me in being effective in all aspects of my life.
I have to do what my loved one wants—I am a victim of being in love.	Being in love supports me in feeling in charge of my life. My loved one always supports me in being true to myself and doing what is right for me.
Being in love means I'm incapable of doing what I want. Being in love means I can't have what I want.	Being in love supports me in doing what I want. Being in love supports me in having what I want.
The men/women I love don't love me.	The men/women I love appreciate me and love me in return.
Men/women don't love me the way I love them.	Men/women love me in a way that feels good to me. I now accept and enjoy the way men/women love me.

Common Limiting Thought Pattern	New Thought Pattern to Integrate
When I love someone, I am overwhelmed (i.e., it's too much for me, I can't handle all that it entails, etc.).	Relationships *can* work out for me. Loving someone always supports me in feeling happier, more alive, and more effective in my life.
I get attention for the drama I create in my life. People notice me when I am unhappy.	I now feel loved and cared for as I create peace and harmony in my life. I feel loved and cared for here, even when I am happy. It's safe to be happy.

See also Pattern 1—Fear of Rejection, Pattern 3—Fear of Hurting or Being Hurt, and Pattern 25—Feeling Out of Control in Love.

FEAR OF DISAPPROVAL

"I'll have to marry a virgin. I can't stand criticism."
From the movie, *Out of Africa*, 1985

COMMON EXPERIENCES IN RELATIONSHIPS

- Feeling ashamed or embarrassed about yourself in relationships
- Feeling afraid to express yourself/let your real feelings show (in you or your partner)
- Not being true to yourself in relationships
- Attracting authoritarian/domineering partners
- Attracting critical or judgmental partners
- Doing whatever your partner wants you to do (or feeling guilty when you don't)
- Feeling abused/attracting abusive partners
- Looking to your partner as the authority
- Resenting your partner for controlling your life (or your partner resenting you for the same)
- Saying "yes" when you mean "no" /sacrificing your own needs and desires so your partner will get what he/she wants (giving away your power)
- Feeling afraid to ask for/do what you want in relationships
- Feeling unhappy, unloved, or insecure in relationships
- Feeling guilty when your partner isn't happy with you/feeling responsible when anything goes wrong in the relationship
- Feeling uneasy in your partner's presence—afraid he/she will find fault with you for something
- Attracting a partner who excessively blames you for what's wrong in his/her life

• Attracting or staying in relationships that are negative or abusive (thus validating your belief that you are "bad and not loved by the ones you love")

The **fear of disapproval** will always attract what you don't want: disapproval! With this pattern, you basically believe that you are bad and unlovable, and as a result, you will generally find partners to validate your viewpoint in no uncertain terms. Often, you will attract partners who blame you and find fault with you incessantly. On the other hand, you may have this pattern but project it onto your partner. In this case, you would blame or find fault with him (or her) incessantly as a way to ensure that he (or she) won't have the chance to do it to you.

With this pattern, you are always so afraid of your partner's negative judgment of you that you continually feel self-conscious and fearful of being true to yourself. Still, because of your basic belief that you are bad for being who you are, you cannot help but evoke a critical response from your partner. No matter how "good" you are or how much you sacrifice your own needs and wants, you can't seem to stop your partner from disapproving of you, and naturally, this makes you feel terrible.

One problem with this pattern is that you often have it "wired" in your subconscious mind that "love = being disapproved of." When you were young, the people who loved you also disapproved of you. Therefore, to you, love equals disapproval. You hate the disapproval, but you think that you'll die without the love. So, since "love = disapproval," you continually attract disapproval to "ensure your survival." It makes you unhappy, but subconsciously you feel safe, because it is so familiar.

When you think you need love and approval from someone else to survive, you will put up with just about anything to get that love and approval. Suffering can easily become the norm in your interactions with your partner, and abusive behavior an accepted part of daily life. Relationships born out of this pattern can only produce unhappiness and ill-feelings between two people.

RAY'S FEAR Of DISAPPROVAL

Ray was commonly known in his circle of friends and acquaintances as a "womanizer." Everyone warned Marianne about that when she started dating him. She looked at him as her veritable "knight in shining armor" (**Pattern 15—Being in Love with Love**), and was unable to see anything but perfection. He looked at her (and every other woman who crossed his path) with lustful desire and Ray's friends began to bet that his relationship with Marianne wouldn't last more than six months. His current record for lasting relationships was only two months. Ray also had a strong **fear of commitment (Pattern 2)** and never seemed to be able to stay with one woman for very long.

Ray and Marianne began living together a month after they first met. However, their "honeymoon" lasted only five days. After that, Ray began to feel criticized by Marianne, even though she tried to be loving and accepting of him. Ray began to feel unworthy, bad, not good enough, unloved—all the same feelings that he had experienced with his mother while growing up.

Ray's mother had been extremely critical of him, and after years of such treatment, he hardly felt that he could do anything right in his relationships with women. He had also learned to sacrifice his own needs and desires to make women happy and began resenting Marianne for not appreciating all that he had done for her. His **fear of disapproval** from women was enormous, and it began to surface soon after his relationship with Marianne began.

As a result of feeling so criticized, Ray began to pull away from Marianne, withdrawing from the "critical mother" that he perceived in his partner. He began to look at other women with desire. Two months later, he announced that he was interested in dating other women.

In spite of a great effort on Marianne's part to try and hold the relationship together, they finally parted ways three months later. Unfortunately, subconscious patterns won out over love once again. Ray's (unconscious) need to experience disapproval actually elicited that response from Marianne. Then, the negative feelings that surfaced in him fed into his fear of commitment, and Ray, once again, bolted.

TANYA'S FEAR OF DISAPPROVAL

Tanya always did the right thing. Rather, she always tried very hard to do the right thing. Unfortunately, however, it never seemed to work. She was never good enough, as far as her mother was concerned, and Tanya received endless criticism for all that she did. Tanya's mother was a perfectionist and expected the absolute best from her daughter at all times. Her mother believed in living life by the rules, and she had plenty of them for every possible circumstance.

Tanya was so busy trying to follow the rules and please her mother that there was no room for enjoying life or having a good time. With such a fear of her mother's disapproval, Tanya was willing to sacrifice everything in order to get it. Sadly, she never succeeded.

Tanya grew up unhappy. She had learned to live life according to her mother's expectations, never veering from what was expected of her. She learned to smile when she felt bad inside, and to say "yes" when she meant "no." Consequently, no one around her ever really knew how Tanya felt inside; she had learned to mask it so well. Furthermore, Tanya resented the people around her for not letting her be herself.

Tanya married right after high school and immediately turned over her power, previously held by her mother, to her new husband. Then, she began a career of trying to please him, live up to his expectations, and be a good wife, just as she had been a "good girl" for her mother—all of this, in the hopes of being loved. Tanya was so convinced that the only way to be loved was to be the way others wanted her to be, she was petrified to be her own person (**Pattern 8**) and terrified to let her real self show.

Because of Tanya's inability to let go and enjoy herself, she never experienced having an orgasm or receiving pleasure while making love. To Tanya, sex was a chore and an obligation, and she did it obediently, to please her husband—with a smile on her face, but resentment in her heart. She always said "yes" to the trips that he planned, when in truth, she really wanted to stay home and have some time to herself. Tanya was simply too afraid to live life the way she wanted and to be true to her own feelings and desires. In a sense, she had been programmed to "disappear," to sacrifice herself for the good of others, to take care of everyone else's needs but her own—just the way her mother had done.

When Tanya was asked what would happen if she were to allow herself to be who she is, no matter what other people expected of her, her answer was this: "I'm afraid that I might find out that I'm really no one, that I have no importance or value... that I'm really nothing." Interestingly enough, underneath Tanya's other subconscious patterns, she also had a deep **fear of being unimportant (Pattern 9)**. Tanya didn't want to risk being her own person for fear of finding out more bad news about herself—that she was really unimportant and not worth much.

Tanya had been married twenty-eight years before she started consciously working on changing her negative patterns. The results have been interesting. On one hand, Tanya is finding that, as time goes on, it is becoming easier to be true to herself and take care of her own needs, which is increasing her happiness and self-esteem. On the other hand, her husband continually expresses his dissatisfaction with her and complains that he wishes he had "the old Tanya" back again. He misses the totally subservient housewife who would do whatever he wanted her to do, the one he could easily dominate and control. Tanya considered leaving the relationship but decided against it because she was too scared to be on her own. Now, her husband is having to adjust to life with "the new Tanya."

HEALING YOUR "FEAR OF DISAPPROVAL" PATTERN

First and foremost, trust that you don't need to suffer in life, and you don't need to put up with abusive behavior. You must work on loving yourself and knowing that you are okay. Once you can hold your head high and feel good about being who you are, others will respond to you positively as well. It all starts with you approving of yourself. If you truly love and accept yourself, you will radiate such energy to others, who will then "obey" your positive thoughts about how you want to be treated. This is how you create your reality!

Accept that you're innocent for being who you are. Honor yourself by surrounding yourself with loving, caring people. Again, the more you treat yourself in such a manner, the easier it will be to find others who truly love and care for you. As you heal this pattern and learn that you are a good person and deserve to be treated with love and respect, the quality of your relationships will definitely improve.

Common Limiting Thought Pattern	New Thought Pattern to Integrate
I can't be myself. Men/women don't like me. Men/women don't want me to be who I am. I'm not okay the way I am. I am afraid to be me. Men/women don't like who I am.	I can now be myself. Men/women like me and support me in being who I am. It's safe to be myself and trust that I am okay the way I am.
I can't do what I want to do.	Since men/women accept me for who I am, they now support me in doing what I want.
Love doesn't exist for me. I am unlovable. I am alone.	Love exists in my world. I am lovable. I now allow myself to feel connected to others through love. I always feel connected to the source of love within.
Life is against me.	Life supports me. I now win in life. Life now gives me what I want.

Common Limiting Thought Pattern	New Thought Pattern to Integrate
I want men/women to approve of me so that I will feel loved.	I no longer need approval from outside myself in order to feel loved. I now allow myself to feel love from within, whether men/women approve of me or not. The more I love myself, the more men/women naturally love and approve of me.
Men/women destroy me by not liking me.	I am likeable. It's easy to feel good about myself, no matter what the men/women around me think. I now easily attract men/women who like me and enjoy me for who I am.
I will die without love. I need love to survive.	I am always connected to an Infinite Source of Love deep within me. Since I always have love within me, I am always safe.
I must do what others want me to do so they will approve of me. I will do anything I can to make men/women approve of me.	Since I now have all the love I want within me, I no longer need to sacrifice myself to get others' approval. Men/women naturally love me and approve of me, just for being who I am.
When men/women love me, they disapprove of me.	Men/women who love me now approve of me. Men/women who love me support me in feeling good about myself and having what I want in life.

125

See also Pattern 1—Fear of Rejection, Pattern 8—Fear of Being Your Own Person, Pattern 17—Fear of Displeasing Others, and Pattern 25—Feeling Out of Control in Love.

FEAR OF BEING DOMINATED

*"When we fear someone, it is because
we have given this someone power over us."*
Herman Hesse

COMMON "FEAR OF BEING DOMINATED" EXPERIENCES

- Avoiding relationships to avoid being dominated
- Feeling abused/attracting abusive partners
- Dominating your partner
- Attracting strong-willed/controlling/inflexible/domineering partners
- Attracting weak/helpless partners that look to you as the authority
- Giving up your power in the presence of your partner (letting your partner make all the decisions, tell you what to do; not trusting your intuition to know what's right for you)
- Suppressing your own needs and desires in relationships
- Feeling afraid to ask for what you want from your partner and do what you want in relationships
- Complaining about or blaming your partner behind his/her back
- Being rebellious in relationships/excessively unwilling to compromise or conform to what your partner wants
- Desire to dominate your partner
- Broken spirit in relationships/giving up all desires for yourself in despair
- Developing some physical illness (because of your suppressed anger, resentment, etc. toward your partner)
- Feeling as if you aren't okay in others' eyes, and therefore not allowing them to be nice, kind, or loving to you

• **Feeling as if you can't have love here, and therefore resisting getting to know people who are kind and loving to you**

When you fear being dominated in a relationship, you will often attract an inflexible, controlling type of partner who dominates you, thus validating your fear. Sometimes you will attract the exact opposite: a weak and helpless partner who is (unconsciously) asking you to dominate him (or her). Both situations will probably drive you crazy; both represent flip sides of the *same* pattern. In the second case, you create a partner that you can dominate as a way to ensure that you won't be the one who gets dominated.

The "domination" pattern is often created by over-controlling parents who don't allow a child much freedom of self-expression. Such parents make all the decisions for the child, who learns not to trust his own ability to know what is right for him. Because he doesn't learn how to make choices for himself, he will often turn to a partner (a substitute parent in this case) to make choices for him.

The problem is that letting someone else run your life *never* feels good and usually creates bitterness and resentment on both sides. No one else really wants to be responsible for your life, even though they might comply with your request for direction. Since subconscious patterns always match, of course, you will probably attract a person with beliefs such as: "Relationships burden me" or, "I am responsible for the people I love." So, these people will begrudgingly take on the burden of telling you how to run your life.

Sometimes, if you are forced, as a child, to swallow all decisions handed down from your parents, you will rebel, resisting *any* type of advice or hint of direction that a partner might give you. In fact, you might do the exact *opposite* of what your partner suggests. Because of your rebellious nature, you could be very difficult to get along with. Or, your partner could be very difficult to get along with, if you experience this pattern by projection.

In truth, the "domination" pattern is never one-sided. No one is "doing it to you." Your partner might look like the "bad guy," but inevitably it is *your* subconscious thoughts that are creating your experience of the relationship. If you didn't have any beliefs about men or women dominating you, you either wouldn't attract that type of person to you, or, if your partner tried to dominate you, you'd probably laugh, dismiss it as a joke, and not be bothered at all.

CARLA'S FEAR OF BEING DOMINATED

Carla grew up in a home where her mother ruled the roost and dominated everyone in the family. Her mother would continually make disparaging remarks about Carla throughout her childhood, and really quashed any chance her daughter ever had of developing self-esteem. Her mother's constant mental abuse, coupled with her father's intermittent physical abuse, truly broke Carla's spirit in relationships, and she gave up believing that she knew what was best for herself. She simply turned to her parents to tell her what to do and how to be. Inwardly, Carla gave up all hopes of ever being able to be herself and do what she really wanted to do.

At twenty-nine, she married Joe, a man who was unrefined, uneducated, unmotivated, and penniless. Carla educated him, polished him, and pushed him to become successful and make something of himself. Joe was unappreciative of her efforts and treated her with great hostility. He didn't like her relating with anyone else, so Carla simply gave up all her personal friends and stayed home, occupying her time with cooking and cleaning the house. Angry at her dominating ways, Joe became physically abusive with her, even to the point of pushing her down the stairs, which required that she have extensive face surgery to repair the damages she sustained. Another time, when Carla was pregnant, he punched her in the stomach and caused her to miscarry the child.

While she was in the hospital, Joe began having affairs, and contracted a sexually-transmitted disease. Needless to say, throughout all of this, Carla developed a tremendous distrust of men and a **fear of being conned** by them (**Pattern 22**). After seven years of putting up with great abuse, Carla filed for a divorce.

Out of a sense of low self-esteem and unworthiness, Carla decided to get a breast augmentation operation to make herself more attractive.

She seemed to feel that a good-looking body was that all she had to offer. Having overeaten for most of her life, she reversed directions with a vengeance, and began to diet and work out with a body-builder. She now spends hours a day doing her make-up, hair, and nails. She still feels extremely insecure and unsure of herself, having given her power away to others for so long, and she is trying to overcome these fears by making herself more appealing physically.

Carla has met another man and has been in a relationship with him for several months. He is already trying to control her life, telling her what she should and shouldn't do. Predictably, Carla is already "walking on eggshells" (**Pattern 17—Fear of Displeasing Others**), trying not to do anything that would upset him. They have "dynamite sex," according to Carla, apparently content with her success in that area. Carla really needs to develop the confidence to make it on her own in order to break the pattern of allowing others to dominate her life. However, because she also has **Pattern 5—Fear of Being Alone or Lonely**, and **Pattern 13—Fear of Being Incomplete Without Another**, she is unwilling to work on herself to such an end. Having the confidence to make it on one's own doesn't imply that one will necessarily be alone; yet, for Carla, just the thought of being on her own is too scary to entertain.

PATTY'S FEAR OF BEING DOMINATED

Patty grew up in a home where "Father Knows Best," that is, her father always had the final word, and her mother meekly kowtowed to whatever he wanted. Patty's father was actually the silent type who didn't share much of what he was thinking or feeling, but whenever he put his foot down, his word was law. No one was allowed to dispute or disagree with him. Her father was always right, no matter what.

Patty learned, from an early age, that men had power over her. Although she grew up quite interested in the opposite sex, as most young girls are, deep in her heart, she feared men because of the power they held over her.

Because of the inequalities and lack of love she perceived in her parents' relationship, Patty was convinced that she would never marry. In and out of several relationships over the years, Patty remained single until age twenty-eight, when she met Dan, a man who was seventeen years her elder. When they first met, Dan actually reminded Patty of her father since he seemed so old.

Dan decided that he wanted to marry Patty within hours of meeting her and proceeded to court her heavily. Dan was determined to make her his wife, and Patty finally acquiesced to his charms, accepting his invitation of marriage only five months after they met. The week prior to the marriage, Patty noticed herself wondering if she really loved Dan. However, she quickly dismissed such thoughts. The plans had already been made and the path was set. Surely her doubts were unfounded.

Dan, indeed, had been very kind and loving to Patty during his brief and exciting courtship of her. However, shortly after they were married, the proverbial honeymoon came to a rapid close and old negative patterns began to surface for both of them. Dan, who had a strong **fear of rejection (Pattern 1)**, began to unconsciously push Patty away sexually to prove that he wasn't okay in her eyes and that she really didn't love him for who he was. Then, instead of acknowledging the true cause of his unhappiness, Dan became angry and screamed at Patty for not wanting to make love with him more.

The more Dan screamed, the more Patty shriveled in fear, for she was terribly afraid of Dan and the power he had over her. The more Patty withdrew in fear, the less love and intimacy they were able to experience with one another. Dan's anger was volatile, and Patty never knew when he would explode. It could be over the least little thing, and Patty lived in terror, trying to avoid any possible triggers to Dan's anger. Sometimes, when Patty went to bed before Dan, she would lie in bed at night, her heart pounding in fear, afraid of the demands that he would make once he got into bed next to her. She was also afraid of what might happen if she refused him. There was no way that Patty could experience loving Dan because her fear of him was too great.

Their marriage lasted five years, and Patty remained fearful of his domination and control the entire time. Also, since she believed him to be the ultimate authority in her life, she was sure that he must be right—that *she* was the one with the problem and that it was all her fault that their marriage was in such terrible straits. Patty blamed herself the entire time they were married for not being good enough to please Dan (**Pattern 17—Fear of Displeasing Others**). In the end, she finally realized that they both were contributing to the outcome of the marriage, although this knowledge alone wasn't enough to "save a sinking ship" or clear the subconscious patterns each of them had.

Patty had two significant relationships in the fifteen years that followed her divorce, and both of the men she attracted were volatile, hot-tempered individuals who could "go off" at the drop of a hat. They both seemed kind and loving at first, eager to please and to win her over. In both cases, once they won Patty's heart, each man began to dominate and control her and make demands of her that made Patty quake in fear. She wanted to please them; she wanted each relationship to work out. Unfortunately, her fear of each of the men was so great that the possibilities for true intimacy could only dwindle over time. Inevitably, the relationships ended, both sides feeling wounded, misunderstood, and betrayed by the opposite sex yet another time. Subconscious patterns strike once again!

HEALING YOUR "FEAR OF BEING DOMINATED" PATTERN

When you have this pattern, you need to learn to stand up for your-self and realize that no one has any power over you—unless, of course, you give it to them. You must begin to take responsibility for your own life and trust in your own ability to know what is best for you. The more you treat yourself with the respect you deserve, and the more you honor your own needs and wants, whatever they may be, the more others will treat you as the equal that you are. No one is better than anyone else. You must begin to appreciate yourself for who you are and let go of your need to compare yourself to others.

The only type of relationship that *really* works is one in which both partners respect each other for their own individual uniqueness and support each other in being themselves and taking charge of their own lives. There must be a willingness and a commitment on both sides for each individual to experience winning in the relationship. If either person is unwilling for his (or her) partner's needs to be met, the relationship, at best, will have a shaky foundation.

Common Limiting Thought Pattern	New Thought Pattern to Integrate
Men/women control me. Men/women have power over me. Men/women know more than I do. Men/women know what is right for me. Men/women have authority over me.	I am my own authority. I now easily stay in touch with my own power in the presence of men/women. It's safe to trust in my natural ability to know what is right for me. I no longer need to let men/women control me or have power over me.
I have to obey men/women. I have to do whatever men/women want.	Since I know what is right for me, I need only turn to myself to decide what to do. I no longer need to obey men/women. I am free to do what I choose.
I can't do what I want in the presence of men/women. Men/women don't approve of me doing things my way.	Men/women now support me in doing what I want. Men/women now support me in doing things my way.
Men/women are stronger than I am. Men/women are smarter than I am.	I am strong in my own way. I no longer allow others to dominate me. I am smart enough in my own way. It's safe to stand up for who I am.

Common Limiting Thought Pattern	New Thought Pattern to Integrate
Men/women dominate me. I am weak/helpless in the presence of men/women. I'm not in control in the presence of men/women.	I now experience myself as equal to men/women. I am now able to maintain my power in the presence of men/women. I remain centered, calm, and in control in the presence of men/women.
I can't be myself in the presence of men/women.	All my relationships now support me in being who I am. I can now be myself in the presence of men/women.
I don't have any rights in the presence of men/women.	I am entitled to the same rights men/women have. I now easily stand up for myself in the presence of men/women. Men/women now support me in being true to myself.
I'm not important in the presence of men/women.	I am important in the presence of men/women. Men/women support me in getting my needs met.
I can't trust myself to take care of my needs.	I trust myself to take care of my needs.
I'm not okay compared to others. Therefore, I don't deserve love.	I am okay the way I am, and therefore, I deserve love.
Love doesn't exist for me here.	Love is real and plentiful for me here.

See also Pattern 3—Fear of Hurting or Being Hurt and Pattern 22—Fear of Being Manipulated/ Taken Advantage of/ Conned.

(For people who dominate others in relationships, their behavior is most commonly based on Pattern 12—Fear of Being Dominated, Pattern 22—Fear of Being Manipulated, or Pattern 21—Fear of Losing Control.)

PATTERN 13

FEAR OF EMOTIONAL DEPENDENCY/ FEAR OF BEING INCOMPLETE WITHOUT ANOTHER

*"Sometimes, only one person is missing,
and the whole world seems depopulated."*

Alphonse De LaMartine

COMMON EXPERIENCES IN RELATIONSHIPS

· Avoiding relationships altogether to avoid feeling dependent on your partner

· Having co-dependent relationships

· Denying your desire to be with someone (pretending that you don't want to be in a relationship)

· Denying the truth about what you really want (saying "yes" to a person when you really want to say "no" or vice versa)

· Feeling unhappy when you don't have a relationship

· Clinging/holding on tightly to a partner

· Feeling lost/confused/helpless when your relationship ends

· Feeling insecure and needy (in or out of relationships)

· Not being true to yourself in relationships

· Getting "dumped" because your partner feels burdened by you (or you "dump" your partner because you feel burdened)

· Preoccupation with your partner (talking about him/her, being overly concerned with him/her, etc.)

· Putting the rest of your life on hold (which might be forever) until you get relationships handled

- Having an ongoing fear that your partner will leave you/die/fall in love with someone else

- Staying in a relationship past the time it feels over

- Choosing or staying in a relationship that really doesn't give you what you want

- Being in a relationship and fooling yourself that you are very independent and self-sufficient

- Feeling as if you aren't okay in others' eyes, and therefore not allowing them to be nice, kind, or loving to you

- Feeling as if you can't have love here, and therefore resisting getting to know people who are kind and loving to you

This pattern is dualistic in nature and can present a real "Catch-22" situation. Here, a person is afraid of being emotionally dependent on another, while simultaneously being afraid that he/she is not complete without the other's presence. With this pattern, you might avoid relationships altogether in order to avoid feeling emotionally dependent on another person. At the same time, however, you will feel uneasy, fearful, insecure, because you are not with someone. In other words, you lose either way, whether you're in a relationship or not!

Sometimes, when you have this pattern, you will pretend to be okay/have it all together/be independent, while holding onto a relationship as a security blanket. Being in the relationship gives you a sense of self-confidence that isn't real, because it wouldn't be present if you were on your own. If such a relationship comes to an end, you will invariably feel crushed, broken, and lost—perhaps even dead—until you can heal the negative beliefs that caused those feelings.

Often, with this pattern, you find yourself in a relationship that is not very satisfying for either partner. You will tend to choose someone for a partner whether he (or she) is able to give you what you want or not—since, according to this pattern, *someone* is better than *no one*. Generally, you don't want to risk being without someone, even though this might be necessary for a time, in order to find a more ideal partner.

KIRK'S FEAR OF EMOTIONAL DEPENDENCY/FEAR OF BEING INCOMPLETE WITHOUT ANOTHER

When Kirk called me, he was totally distraught. His wife wanted a divorce and he couldn't bear the thought of her leaving him. He desperately wanted to save the marriage. Kirk loved his wife very much, and even though they had already been separated for two years, he just couldn't deal with the thought of finally ending their marriage. As he shared his story with me, Kirk made a telling remark that clearly indicated one of his primary subconscious patterns: **Fear of Emotional Dependency/Fear of Being Incomplete Without Another.** "Somehow, I tend to self-destruct when things get really good in my life. Yet, if I only had that special relationship, I know I could just conquer the world."

Kirk was convinced that a relationship with a woman would ensure his success in life. Unfortunately, though, such a relationship always seemed just beyond his reach. Whenever he had wanted to get close to his wife physically, she would freeze and shut down at his touch. When he would pull away in frustration and keep his distance from her, she would call and want to get together. Not only did Kirk feel incomplete without his wife, but he also felt totally **victimized by love (Pattern 10)**. He never felt that he had any choice about the outcome of the relationship. His wife was clearly in charge of their fate. He never felt as if she loved him the way he loved her, and yet he couldn't get her off his mind.

Kirk's mother had used guilt to manipulate him, and Kirk became somewhat of a puppet, jumping to his mother's demands in order to ease his guilty conscience. Although he hated and resented such control over him, he never really learned to break away and be free from a woman pulling his strings. Also, he never learned that love with a woman could work out for him in a way that produced satisfaction and harmony.

JEFFREY'S FEAR OF EMOTIONAL DEPENDENCY/FEAR OF BEING INCOMPLETE WITHOUT ANOTHER

Jeffrey was an actor. Jeffrey was also a real lady's man, falling in love with every leading lady who happened to be working with him at the time. Jeffrey was actually married, but "heading for divorce," he said. Interestingly enough, he had been in this position—having numerous affairs while heading for divorce—for a number of years. Jeffrey said that he and his wife had an understanding and that he was free to do what he wanted, whenever he wanted.

It turns out that Jeffrey was deeply afraid of feeling dependent on his partner, and as a result, he avoided spending time with her, even pretending that he didn't want the relationship. However, notice that he wasn't able to end it. He also had a deep sense of insecurity, which would overtake him at the thought of ending the marriage.

It was as if the marriage—even though he *acted* like he didn't want it—was a security blanket for him, and thus, he unconsciously clung to it tightly, for dear life. He was also choosing to stay in a relationship that really didn't give him what he wanted, but he was too afraid to let it go. Jeffrey was able to act very independent and self-sufficient because the relationship gave him the security to do so.

STAN'S FEAR OF EMOTIONAL DEPENDENCY/ FEAR OF BEING INCOMPLETE WITHOUT ANOTHER

Stan is twenty-eight years old and prides himself on being very independent. At the same time, Stan loves being in relationships—until they become too confining and burdensome. Stan has a pattern of finding a girlfriend, dating her briefly (for three months), ending the relationship, and then avoiding intimate contact for the next six to seven months. This same cycle continually repeats itself again and again in Stan's life.

After each three-month stint with a woman, Stan's negative patterns would kick in, and he'd start to feel uncomfortable, confined, and suffocated in some way. (He also had **Pattern 2—Fear of Commitment**.) Although he didn't know it, Stan would start to feel emotionally dependent on the woman, and as a result, he'd choose to avoid relationships for awhile, in order to avoid such feelings. All Stan knew was that his relationships would end after three months "for some strange and unexpected reason." Stan was totally unaware that he was "creating" this reality based on his negative subconscious patterns.

When Stan met Mary, he apparently was more ready to "settle down" than he had previously been, although marriage was still the furthest thing from his mind. He answered an ad for a "roommate wanted" and moved into the house where she was already living with a group of students from the local university. Stan and Mary hit it off shortly after Stan moved in and have been dating steadily since that time, for almost two years now. They seemed to be harmonious as a couple, yet Stan would always bring his gripes about her to our therapy sessions.

"I've got to break up with Mary," Stan would complain at the outset of each session. "It's just not working. It's just not what I want." When asked about his biggest problem with Mary, he vehemently replied, "She's way too needy! She clings too much! I'm much more independent than she is!" Stan said that he could easily spend time on his own, listening to music, entertaining himself, whereas Mary *needed* to be with him so much more. This really bothered him.

The problem was that being in the relationship made Stan feel secure. Although he professed to be "independent," Stan also *needed* the relationship in order to feel complete, but was not in touch with his own neediness or dependency on the relationship. In fact, it was not okay for Stan to feel needy or dependent on anyone, so he projected those feelings onto Mary and criticized her for feeling that way. In reality, he was "looking in the mirror" and making himself wrong for what *he* was feeling. He blamed Mary instead and wanted to leave the relationship as a result.

Because Stan had seen such positive changes in his life from our work together, he encouraged Mary to work with me as well. Ironically enough, after a short time, Mary began to complain about seeing a side of Stan that she had never seen before—where he seemed needy and dependent. She referred to his behavior on an overnight rafting trip they had taken together. Mary had had a great deal of experience in wilderness activities, while Stan, a total novice, appeared to be weak and uncertain, turning to Mary constantly for direction and guidance. "He seemed so immature and clingy," Mary exclaimed. "I don't know if I really want to be with someone like that."

At once, it became crystal clear—both Mary and Stan had this same pattern, "**Fear of Emotional Dependency/Fear of Being Incomplete Without Another**," and they took turns playing out each side of the pattern. Neither of them could see their own neediness and fear of being dependent on the other. They were only able to see it in their partner. Both continued to share their desire to get out of the relationship, yet neither ever acted on that desire, because both felt secure in the relationship.

The good news here is that Stan and Mary are now aware of their subconscious patterns and are working avidly to release them. When both members of a couple are committed to healing their negative patterns, tremendous strides can be made. They both understand that if they leave the relationship without doing the necessary work on themselves, they will, at some point, experience the same negative feelings in the next relationship they attract. So, both of them are committed to clearing their patterns here and now.

Although committed to clearing his patterns, at the end of Stan's last therapy session, he was still in the mode of "This isn't what I want; I want to end the relationship." However, I got an intuitive "message" for Stan: because we were addressing and releasing the main negative pattern that was blocking the couple, Stan would soon experience a shift in his relationship with Mary and in another month, would start to see her differently. He admitted to feeling dubious about the prospects, but reluctantly agreed to wait and see.

Here's the amazing part: When Stan called for his next session a month and a half later, we talked about everything BUT his relationship with Mary. When I finally asked him how that was going, he said, "Oh, things are going well with our relationship. You were right... I *am* seeing her differently." We then proceeded to discuss other subjects that he felt were more pressing. Every prior session had included his complaints about the relationship. Once Stan was freed from the negativity of this subconscious pattern, the relationship no longer felt problematic as it once had.

HEALING YOUR "FEAR OF EMOTIONAL DEPENDENCY/ FEAR OF BEING INCOMPLETE WITHOUT ANOTHER" PATTERN

It is not the "Highest Truth" that you need someone so that you won't die (a common fear accompanying this pattern). This is a belief that often develops in infancy and is never reversed. When you're a baby, you *will* die without someone to take care of you. When you're an adult, this is no longer true. Your basic assumptions about yourself and your life must be changed!

It is important to develop a sense of confidence and security in being who you are, and a trust in your ability to make it in life. You don't have to avoid relationships to avoid feeling dependent on them, nor do you have to settle for less than you want in order to avoid feeling alone or "incomplete." Work on feeling whole and complete within yourself. Then you can create wonderful, loving relationships that enrich your life and support you in being powerful and capable as an individual.

And, remember this truth: There's really "no one else out there." IT'S ALL YOU! Whatever you see in another person is some reflection of something in you. Any time you criticize or judge someone, ask yourself how it could relate to something in *you*. The more you take responsibility for everything you see "out there," the more rapidly you will learn about yourself and get the lessons your Higher Self is trying to teach you.

Common Limiting Thought Pattern	New Thought Pattern to Integrate
I need a man/woman to survive. I am dead without a man/woman in my life.	I forgive myself for thinking I need a man/woman to survive. It's safe to be on my own and know that I can easily survive. I now allow myself to receive love and support from a man/woman without thinking that I need him/her to survive. I can now be in a relationship and experience that I am whole and complete within myself.
I can't make it without a man/woman in my life. I can't make it unless I have a man/woman to help me. I need what men/women give me in order to succeed. I can't succeed without a man/woman in my life. I'm a failure without men/women. I'm incapable without a man/woman in my life.	I can easily make it in life, whether I have a man/woman to help me or not. I have all that I need within me to succeed in life. I am capable on my own. I am a success in life, whether I have a man/woman with me or not. I now perceive my inherent strengths and capabilities, which allow me to easily succeed on my own. I can now receive love and support from a man/woman without feeling as if I need him/her to succeed. I am secure within myself.

Common Limiting Thought Pattern	New Thought Pattern to Integrate
I am lost when I'm not with a man/woman.	I know who I am, whether I'm with a man/woman or not.
	I am now motivated from within to succeed in my life, whether I have a man/woman with me or not.
	I can now find meaning and purpose in my life, whether I'm in a relationship or not.
	I can easily make it in life, whether I'm with a man/woman or not.

See also Pattern 5—Fear of Being Alone, Pattern 9—Fear of Being Unimportant, Pattern 21—Fear of Losing Control, and Pattern 25—Feeling Out of Control in Love.

PATTERN 14

FEAR OF BOREDOM

*"Until you make peace with who you are,
you'll never be content with what you have."*
Doris Mortman

COMMON EXPERIENCES IN RELATIONSHIPS

- Sabotaging relationships after a short time so that they come to an end
- Breaking off your relationship after a short period of time (you or your partner)
- Meeting a new person more interesting than your partner (or meeting a new person you're interested in—just when things were starting to get really good with your partner!)
- Being interested in dating more than one man/woman at a time (you or your partner)
- Attracting "shallow" men/women who wind up boring you after a short period of time
- Avoiding intimacy in relationships
- Being unable to be intimate with your partner
- Creating superficial relationships

Often, when you are afraid of being bored in a relationship, you are afraid to get to know *yourself* in a deeper way. What happens is this: The more time you spend with a person, the more that person will reflect back parts of yourself to you—since your partner is always a mirror of what's going on inside you. So naturally, as time goes on, you might start seeing things in the other person that you *don't* want to see, particularly if you haven't cleared much of your own negative programming. As the person reflects back to you these deeper parts of yourself that need healing, it could easily trigger anger, sadness, resentment, and other negative feelings in you. Rather than feel any of these, it's easier to "numb out" and become bored. And suddenly, that person isn't fun to be with anymore.

When you have this subconscious pattern, you are doing your best to "skim the surface" of life. You want to have fun, be light; you probably party a lot! But as relationships deepen over time, the happy-go-lucky fun and lightness of the early stages often give way to a different kind of feeling. Your subconscious "buttons" start getting "pushed," and your old programming starts to "come up for review."

If you decide at this point that it's time to change relationships, it is doubtful that you will ever heal yourself of the negative programming that makes you want to leave the relationship in the first place. It is doubtful that relationships will ever work out for you. If you are never willing to look inside yourself for the real cause of your desire to leave your partner, you will never be able to find a relationship that lasts for very long.

NEIL'S FEAR OF BOREDOM

Neil says that he wants a deep, meaningful relationship in his life, yet he continually meets people whom he perceives to be shallow and superficial. He says that he wants to get to know people. He says that he wants people to open up to him and get to know him in a deeper way, but people keep boring him and he finds that he doesn't want them around for too long. What he perceives is that he is truly interested in getting to know people, but they seem to be hiding from him. What he cannot see is that he is actually afraid to get to know himself better and is, therefore, projecting this fear onto those he meets.

Neil often finds himself dating more than one person at a time. His explanation is that he often finds different qualities he likes in different people, and no one person has all that he really wants in a partner. However, he does admit to getting bored when he is with only one partner at a time. In his relationships, Neil frequently finds a person he wants to be with for a short while, and then finds someone else who interests him more, causing him to break off his first relationship. His resistance to looking more deeply within himself keeps him from wanting to be with one person for any length of time.

Neil did confess that each time he would break up with someone, he would feel guilty and wonder if he had done the right thing. Maybe the woman wasn't as bad as he thought she was. Maybe he could have done it differently. (Neil also had **Pattern 3—Fear of Hurting Others**.) In any case, he just didn't want to be bored. "Boredom—" Neil proclaimed emphatically, "that's *death* to me!"

In discussing his past, Neil laughs and says that he is exactly like his mother when it comes to getting bored easily. She was a school teacher for a while and then became bored with that. So, she became a dental hygienist. Then she got bored with that and became a hairdresser. Whenever she got bored, she would go back to school and learn another trade. Neil had certainly absorbed her restlessness and short attention span, as far as his relationships were concerned.

MIMI'S FEAR OF BOREDOM

Mimi grew up in a household where her father was emotionally distant, and she never felt as if he loved her. Mimi was close to her mother, however, and paid careful attention to all the advice her mother gave her. Concerned about all of the teenagers who went steady throughout high school and then married at a young age, Mimi's mother was determined to set her daughter on a different course. She impressed upon Mimi the importance of dating around and "not putting all your eggs in one basket." She did all she could to make sure Mimi wouldn't make the mistakes so prevalent of children her age.

"Maybe I followed her advice too well," Mimi admitted ruefully, forty years later, looking back at how her love life had unfolded. "It was so hard to settle down and stay interested in one person. I just seemed to get bored so easily with all the guys I met." Mimi couldn't seem to find someone who held her attention for very long, and she dated a number of men until, at age eighteen, she met Rob.

Mimi and Rob shared an intense and passionate romantic interlude of six weeks, followed by two years of writing letters and maintaining their connection via the U.S. mail. Rob seemed to be everything Mimi wanted. She felt sure that he was her "soul-mate"—the veritable man of her dreams.

When Mimi was twenty years old, Rob asked her to marry him and live with him in Hawaii. At first his offer sounded like everything she could possibly want from life, a true opportunity to experience paradise. However, Mimi began having doubts. "Gee," she thought to herself, distressed, "if I marry him, I'll be so happy that, in a few years, I'll be bored." Thus, amazingly enough, Mimi refused the proposal and thereby ended the relationship.

Mimi had no conception of allowing the loving connection with a significant partner to grow deeper and more meaningful over time, as the two people get to know each other. Mimi's definition and experience of love was having the profound happiness and joy right away, and then the only place to go from there was downhill. In other words, after a while, boredom would necessarily set in, and Mimi was petrified of this happening.

As time went on, Mimi tended to create relationships characterized by greater turmoil and struggle at the outset, so she could work at making the love happen. If "paradise" happened too quickly, Mimi was afraid that she would lose it equally as quickly—to the inevitable boredom that would take over her mind and heart.

Mimi did, however, meet a man, Geoffrey, shortly after she finished college, and they got married when she was twenty-two. They loved each other, Mimi felt sure, but then, as they began to live together, the relationship started going downhill rapidly. Mimi found herself taking care of her husband, cleaning up after him, and doing whatever she could to see that his needs were met. She began feeling more like Geoffrey's caretaker and mother, not his wife and lover. (Mimi also had **Pattern 10—Being Victimized by Love**, in which the tendency is to "save" or "rescue" others and **Pattern 21—Fear of Losing Control**, in which the tendency is to jump in and dominate or control the situation when it isn't the way that you want.)

Then, struggles ensued as they realized that each of them had different desires for their life paths. Mimi wanted to stay in the city and go back to school. Geoffrey was convinced that country living was the way to go and wanted to move as far away from the city as possible. Unable to resolve their differences, Mimi rapidly grew bored with Geoffrey, complaining that she was tired of hearing him tell the same old stories and jokes all the time. They decided to end the marriage.

The dating continued, and after a few years, Mimi married again. She stayed with this man for five years, but because of her pattern, she grew weary of the familiarity and repetition of being with the same person all the time. Boredom was at Mimi's doorstep once again, with the possibility of yet another divorce looming ahead.

At that point, Mimi began a quest for greater understanding and clarity about her situation. She read every self-help book she could find, attended personal growth workshops, and sought the guidance of a counselor. She finally realized that something had to change within her, in order for her to experience the happiness and satisfaction she had so much trouble finding in her relationships with men.

HEALING YOUR "FEAR OF BOREDOM" PATTERN

You must understand: it's safe to look inside yourself and find out which negative beliefs from the past cause you to experience relationships in the way you do. Remember, you are not "bad" for what you believe, nor are your thoughts "bad." Whatever thoughts you consider "bad" are simply conclusions you drew about yourself and life, at some point in the past, based on what seemed true at the time. You simply "bought into" a reality that wasn't based on the "Highest Truth," one that did not support you in creating a positive experience of life and relationships.

Now the time has come to discover which of those *past* beliefs need to be changed so that you can fully enjoy all aspects of your life. Remember, just because a negative belief is subconscious (i.e., out of your awareness), doesn't mean it isn't affecting you. The fact is, *all* of your beliefs, both conscious and subconscious, are creating your experience of life. Therefore, make it safe to explore your subconscious mind—since whatever is in there is controlling your life anyway!

Be willing to tell the truth about your subconscious beliefs, and work on changing them. Then, and only then, will you be free from their negative influence. Your willingness to face and heal your negative, subconscious beliefs about yourself and your relationships will allow you to experience a richness, depth, and duration to your relationships that would otherwise have been impossible.

Common Limiting Thought Pattern	**New Thought Pattern to Integrate**
I get bored when I am with the same man/woman for more than a short period of time. Men/women are no longer interesting to me after I'm with them for a short period of time. Being with the same man/woman for a long period of time makes my life become boring.	The longer I stay with a man/woman, the more stimulating and interesting he/she becomes for me. Having a lasting relationship with a man/woman supports me in maintaining a sense of interest and excitement in life. The longer I stay with a man/woman, the deeper I get to know him/her and the richer my life becomes.
Relationships never work out for me the way I want them to.	Relationships now easily work out for me the way I want them to. Relationships always support me in feeling fulfilled within myself.
Relationships never last. Men/women leave me after they get to know me.	Relationships last for me. Men/women enjoy staying with me and getting to know me over time.

Common Limiting Thought Pattern	New Thought Pattern to Integrate
Men/women get bored with me after they've known me for a short time.	Men/women grow more interested in me the more they get to know me. Men/women appreciate me more, the longer they know me.
I don't want to see anything bad about myself. I'm afraid of what I might find in the depths of my mind.	It's safe to examine my deep attitudes and beliefs that are creating negativity in my life. By my willingness to look inside myself, I am now able to create the joy, excitement, and freedom I have been seeking in all my relationships. It's safe to explore the depths of my mind.

See also Pattern 1—Fear of Rejection, Pattern 2—Fear of Commitment, and Pattern 24—Not Getting Your Needs Met/Unwillingness to Care.

BEING IN LOVE WITH LOVE

"To be in love is merely to be in a state of perceptual anesthesia—
to mistake an ordinary young man for a Greek god
or an ordinary woman for a goddess."

H.L. Mencken, *Prejudices*

COMMON EXPERIENCES IN RELATIONSHIPS

- Not seeing a person as he/she really is

- Not knowing who your partner really is/thinking that your partner is someone whom he/she is not

- Projecting "God-like" qualities onto your partner (putting him/her on a pedestal which eventually comes crashing down)

- Selecting incompatible partners because you are "in love with love," not with the person

- Not seeing the inherent flaws in a relationship, so not working on the relationship to keep it together

- Not understanding why a relationship broke up/fell apart when you thought it was so good

- Continually forgiving your partner for repeated destructive behavior, without discussion, and insisting that the relationship is wonderful

- Thinking that you are in a loving relationship but actually spending very little time with the other person

- Ignoring a potentially decent relationship because the person falls short of your high expectations (isn't "perfect" enough)

- Feeling disappointed in love

- Looking for a partner to "save" or "rescue" you

- Looking for a partner who needs "saving" or "rescuing"

"**Being in Love with Love**" is a subtly deceptive pattern. It would be easy to think that since love feels good, there's nothing wrong with being in love with love. The problem here, however, is that the loving connection between the two partners is based on delusion. The love here does not stem from a true appreciation of each other's being, a mutual admiration and respect for who each one is and what they mean to one another. Rather, it is a contrived state, a trumped-up feeling that temporarily helps a person overcome an otherwise unhappy reality. With this pattern operating, you often expect the other person to be your "savior" and rescue you from yourself and the problems of life.

Once in love, however, you discover that you are the same person and that life still has many of the same problems. As a result, you become disappointed and blame your partner, or love, for being inadequate. Your expectations of how your partner *should* be in order to make you happy are unrealistic. You seek perfection in your partner, demanding that he/she live up to your inner idea of god/goddess. You are not willing to accept the scars and problems your partner has, which are simply part of being human.

This pattern can develop as a result of your attempt (albeit unconscious) to overcome the unhappiness or lack of love you might have experienced early in childhood. Growing up, you learned from our culture (via television, movies, etc.) that the "prize" and the goal of life (*especially* for women) is being in love. "Ah... *that* will make me happy," you decided somewhere deep inside you. Fulfillment through love and romance became your dream, and you began to project your romantic pictures of love onto the men (or women) you met, hoping to find that wonderful love, which would indeed make you happy forever.

The problem is that this kind of love never lasts; it doesn't have its basis in Truth. In the state of "being in love with love," you often fool yourself about what you want in relationships. It is common to say "yes" to what you don't want in a partner and get involved with someone who is incompatible with you. You cover up the truth by pretending to be in love with the person. In reality, however, you are "in love with love" and not really experiencing the person as he (or she) is. Since the beliefs underlying this kind of love are often: "Love eludes me," and "Love is impossible," it is highly unlikely that the relationship will be fulfilling over any length of time.

MORRIS' PATTERN OF BEING IN LOVE WITH LOVE

Morris was always in love—because Morris was in love with love. Whenever he was in love with a woman, it was always "head over heels" in love; Morris never did anything half way. He was always very demonstrative of his love, showering his partner with attention, affection, gifts. However, Morris never felt that he got much of that in return. In fact, Morris always felt disappointed in love.

Morris would give and give, and then, somehow, his relationships would fall apart. He just couldn't understand why. (He also had **Pattern 10—Being Victimized by Love**.) Morris was so loving and giving, and the women he loved always seemed so perfect for him. "Beautiful, wonderful women," Morris proclaimed, "women who deserved to be put on a pedestal!" There was no reason, in Morris' mind, that the relationships shouldn't last.

His first relationship ended because his girlfriend's parents decided their daughter and Morris were too young to be serious. They were still in high school. Morris felt very victimized by *their* decision to end *his* relationship, because he felt totally in love with the girl.

When his second significant relationship ended, Morris was heartbroken. Although a gorgeous model (according to Morris), his partner had been having trouble finding work, so Morris stepped in and took her portfolio to New York in order to help her find a job. She was soon called for work and left to go to Europe for a few years, which ultimately ended the relationship. Morris had worked so hard to help (save?!) her and couldn't believe that she then, in turn, left him.

His third significant relationship became his wife, and that lasted nine years. She was very intellectually stimulating, and Morris felt that they made a good team. When she decided to change careers, they had to move to a different city in order for her to finish her degree. The relationship started to sour at that point.

"We started growing apart," Morris explained, shrugging his shoulders helplessly. "Our priorities were different." Apparently, his wife started to want more outside social contacts, as well as to focus more on her career. Morris wanted more attention paid to their relationship and to their family—they had two children. As the distance between them grew, they decided to open their relationship, and Morris had an affair with someone else. He thoroughly enjoyed himself, but then decided to re-commit to his wife and to working things out between them.

Morris began to put a great deal of energy into the relationship to make it work, but apparently it was like trying to bring a dead horse back to life. His wife had already decided that their relationship was over. He wanted them both to go into therapy. She just wanted to leave. He couldn't believe it. He really thought they could pull the relationship back together. He was clearly in denial of the reality of the situation.

For Morris, love was always so important to him, because he never felt as if he received enough from his parents when he was young. Morris was the seventh of nine children and grew up in a household where he watched his parents fight much of the time, yelling and screaming as well as hitting each other. Both of them were alcoholics and their relationship, according to Morris, was quite destructive. They each would threaten the other with divorce on a regular basis, and the energy between them was extremely emotional and dramatic. With five brothers and four sisters, there was lots of rivalry and competition for love and attention, and the older boys began using drugs as a way to escape an unhappy home life.

Morris claimed to have felt loved while growing up; however, an examination of his subconscious patterns indicated that he really didn't. He didn't want to tell the truth about his childhood. It was too painful. Deluding himself about the love that was available to him as a child at least gave him memories of feeling loved. His need to feel loved was so strong that he had to pretend it was true for him. And thus, the roots of this pattern developed.

BETSY'S PATTERN OF BEING IN LOVE WITH LOVE

Betsy viewed her relationship partners through veritable "rose-colored" glasses. Every man she attracted was perfect, just what she wanted. Every time she entered a new relationship, it was because she felt certain that he was "the one"—the man with whom she was destined to spend the rest of her life. However, Betsy was never able to see her partners clearly and acknowledge the truth of their circumstances in life and what that meant, as far as getting involved with them was concerned. Because she was so in love with love, she ignored the facts about each partner, idealistically proclaiming that she had found her perfect match, her veritable soulmate.

For example, one of her partners was the proverbial "starving artist," a young man who was barely able to pay his bills each month. Another had been sick for several years, and doctors were unable to determine the cause of his ailment. Consequently, he lived on welfare and was fairly dysfunctional in life, unable to participate in a relationship of any kind in a normal way. A third partner was a divorced father of three who never paid any child support, had bad credit, and went from job to job, living at a subsistence level.

Betsy, of course, made good money, and in the name of love, freely opened her wallet to these men. They happily took from her. (She also had **Pattern 22—Fear of Being Taken Advantage of**.) Still, Betsy kept getting dumped, time and time again. (She also had **Pattern 4—Fear of Abandonment**.) The men would stay with her for a certain period of time—some longer, some shorter—and then would leave her, often for another woman. Betsy just couldn't understand. She had loved each of the men so much, she just couldn't imagine why the relationships didn't work out. The reasons would be obvious to any on-looker, yet Betsy was oblivious, so blinded was she by being in love with love.

When Betsy was young, she had never felt loved. Her mother was extremely disapproving and her father was silent, aloof, and emotionally unavailable. Betsy never really believed or experienced that love was there for her, and as a result, she learned to create an unreal version of love in order to get her needs met. Of course, ultimately, this never worked for her, and relationships became an endless source of frustration and disappointment in her life.

HEALING YOUR "BEING IN LOVE WITH LOVE" PATTERN

To have successful relationships, you need to accept and love *all* aspects of the other person. This is called "unconditional love." It does not require a person to change in order for you to love him (or her). Ultimately, the key is to love yourself in this way.

If you accept and love yourself unconditionally, you won't project your judgments onto your partner and criticize him (or her) when he (or she) falls short of your "standards of perfection." As you learn to love and accept yourself for who you are, you will begin to realize that you don't need to be loved by someone *outside* yourself in order to feel love *inside*. At this point, you will be able to share true love with another—a love which reflects the joy and satisfaction you have discovered within yourself.

Common Limiting Thought Pattern	New Thought Pattern to Integrate
I'm not able to know what love is. I don't understand love. Love confuses me. I don't know how to love.	I am now able to know what love is. I now surrender and let love in, whether I understand love or not. Love brings me satisfaction and peace of mind. I naturally and effortlessly know how to love.
Love isn't real. It never works out for me. Love never lasts.	Love is real for me. I now experience love working out for me. I now create a reality in which love lasts for me.

Common Limiting Thought Pattern	New Thought Pattern to Integrate
Love is impossible. Love never works out the way I want it to. Love disappoints me.	It's safe to be optimistic about love. Love now works out for me in new and satisfying ways. Love now supports me in feeling fulfilled within myself.
Love isn't here/doesn't exist for me. I am always without love. I can't have love the way I want it. Love eludes me.	Love is here for me. I always have love in my life. I can have love the way I want it. The more I love myself, the more love I naturally experience in my life.
Something always goes wrong when I love someone. I can't understand why. Love always feels good at first, and then something goes wrong.	The more I get to know my partner for who he/she is, the more our love for each other grows. I can now create mutually supportive, loving relationships that get better with time. I now attract men/women with whom I share a love that is real.
Love makes me feel happy. I love men/women so that I can feel love and happiness.	I no longer need to create a false sense of love in my relationships. I now love men/women for who they really are. I now create relationships in which the love is genuine. The more I love myself, the happier I feel. I now feel happy being who I am, whether I'm in love or not.

Common Limiting Thought Pattern	New Thought Pattern to Integrate
Men/women don't love me. I'm not able to hold onto love. No one enjoys being with me.	Men/women love me for being who I am. Love lasts for me. Men/women enjoy being with me.

See also Pattern 4—Fear of Abandonment, Pattern 5—Fear of Being Alone or Lonely, Pattern 10—Being Victimized by Love, Pattern 19—Belief in Separation from Love, and Pattern 25—Feeling Out of Control in Love.

PATTERN 16

FEAR OF SEX

*"All this fuss about sleeping together. For physical pleasure,
I'd sooner go to my dentist any day."*

Evelyn Waugh

COMMON EXPERIENCES IN RELATIONSHIPS

· Avoiding sex in relationships

· Having quick or unfulfilling sexual relationships (also using prostitutes)

· Avoiding relationships in order to avoid sexual experiences

· Being a "workaholic" and therefore, having no time for relationships/sex (or attracting this trait in a partner)

· Feeling guilty or ashamed about sexual experiences

· Feeling guilty, ashamed, or embarrassed about your body

· Having sexually-related illnesses or disorders (diminishing the likelihood of sexual contact)

· Feeling shy around others/exhibiting "wallflower" behavior

· Feeling unloved, unattractive, or inadequate in relationships

· Experiencing impotency or performance anxiety in sexual relations

· Faking orgasms

· Sexual abuse or sexually abusive partners

The **fear of sex** can result from a variety of circumstances in life. You might have low self-esteem and feel undeserving of love. Therefore, having sex may be viewed as a threat to the self because it increases and intensifies feelings of love. You may have "bought into" the social programming that says you should look a certain way (e.g., like the beautiful models always shown in ads) in order to be acceptable to others. Then, when you compare yourself to these externally-imposed social standards and find yourself lacking, you convince yourself that others find you lacking as well. As a result, you fear getting close to others because you don't want them to discover your "lacks." Sexual intimacy would obviously activate this fear of getting close, and thus a specific **fear of sex** could develop.

Any traumatic sexual experience you may have had as a child could also cause a fear of sex. If you were sexually "explored" or even molested by a parent, relative, sibling, or other child, you may understandably fear sexual encounters of any kind. These early sexual experiences are not always bad (e.g., many kids who "play doctor" or other sexual exploratory games grow up to have healthy attitudes towards sex), but the stigma—the shame and guilt—surrounding these experiences often gets stuck in your consciousness.

When the older person involved feels guilty or ashamed of his behavior (or even thoughts) towards you, you "pick up" the feelings and internalize the guilt and shame. Often, the older person will say things, such as, "Don't tell anyone about this," or might even threaten you: "You better keep quiet about this, or else..." Thus, you are stuck with a heavy emotional charge around the issue, for which there is no apparent hope for release. Feelings of fear stay with you and make you afraid of future sexual encounters.

Another source of negative programming that contributes to the **fear of sex** is the "Hollywood" image of lovemaking so often portrayed in the media. Many people attempt to live up to the "perfect" lovemaking scenes they witness, in which the lovemaking occurs flawlessly, each partner totally thrilled with every move the other person makes. There is no room for dialogue, sharing feelings, or discussing the process, if, for example, one partner has a request or suggestion.

As a result, many people have unrealistic expectations of sexual encounters. When the lovemaking experience doesn't happen the way you *expect* it to (which usually occurs when you are being flexible, spontaneous, and in the moment), you judge yourself and/or your partner for doing something wrong or being inadequate. This could result in impotence on the man's part or simply feeling turned off to one's partner sexually. Finally, you may have received negative programming, contributing to the **fear of sex** from your parents and from your religious training. Perhaps, as a child, you were taught that sex was bad, dirty, wrong; that it was bad to touch yourself (and others!). You might have learned that God doesn't approve of you receiving sexual pleasure.

A true devotee of God, it seemed, would be willing to take vows of celibacy and leave sexuality behind forever, in order to ensure a spiritual life. It often seemed, somehow, that sex and God were at opposite ends of the spectrum and mutually exclusive. You couldn't be loved by both God and man simultaneously! Sex, when necessary, was for the purpose of procreation, not pleasure!

Obviously, if you want to please God and do what is "right" (according to what you've been taught), you could easily develop a fear of sex. You don't want to allow yourself to feel good in a way that will go against God's wishes for you. If you were raised to believe that God is a cruel, punishing God who demands obedience to rules that are difficult or unpleasant to follow, you will respond to life in fearful ways. As a result, you may well deny yourself sexual pleasure and the joys of sexual intimacy as an attempt to appease God's wrath. If you believe that your sexuality makes you bad or unworthy in God's eyes, then it is quite understandable that you would either want to avoid sex completely or feel terribly guilty for enjoying it.

BARBARA'S FEAR OF SEX

Barbara developed this pattern, **fear of sex**, as a result of some bizarre and unfortunate circumstances in her early family life. Barbara was adopted as an infant and had a history of sexual abuse by her adopted father from a very early age. He started by cutting a hole in the wall in order to watch her get undressed, and then began having sex with her on a regular basis from the time she was twelve. Barbara loved her father and was afraid that if she didn't let him have his way with her sexually, he wouldn't love her (She also had **Patterns 1, 11, & 17—Fear of Rejection, Fear of Disapproval, and Fear of Displeasing Others**).

Finally Barbara's mother found out what was going on and divorced her husband. Barbara, totally rejected by her mother, went to live with her father who continued to have sex with her on a regular basis until he remarried during Barbara's senior year of high school. At that point, he cut Barbara off completely, insisting that she live in her own apartment, so that his new wife wouldn't find out what had been going on. Barbara was crushed because suddenly, it seemed, her father didn't love her anymore, and she felt totally confused about all that had transpired between them. She began to distrust love, and thus also developed **Pattern 23—Fear of False Love**.

By the time she met and married Stuart, she had trouble believing that anyone could love her or care for her on an ongoing basis. Stuart had to work hard to convince Barbara that he really loved her and wanted to be with her. She often became jealous of other women in whom she was convinced Stuart was interested, even though there was no reality to her suspicions. Since Barbara's father was unfaithful to her mother, Barbara began to suspect all men of such infidelity. Often Barbara would withhold sex from him, but couldn't explain why. She had actually come to fear sex because of all the unpleasant and hurtful feelings it had caused in her relationship with her father.

Barbara did stay with Stuart, however, and gradually learned to trust his love and caring. Eventually, although it took awhile, she was able to relax and enjoy herself sexually with him. Barbara was indeed fortunate to attract such a man who had the patience and perseverance necessary to make the relationship last.

VICTOR'S FEAR OF SEX

Victor is thirty years old, single, and lives with his parents. A self-employed consulting engineer, Victor is a veritable workaholic, working seven days a week, often late into the night. Victor is quite self-conscious about his looks, having wrestled with bad acne and an overweight condition during his formative years, and has never felt attractive to women. Living at home is "safe" for Victor because it helps him to avoid relationships entirely and not have to deal with the possibility of sexual rejection.

(Victor also has **Pattern 7—Fear of Love**.) In fact, Victor avoided dating altogether until he met Jeanine, with whom he fell totally "head over heels" in love.

They met at a conference in her home town, Atlanta, Georgia. Victor had flown in from his home in Concord, New Hampshire. They both described each other as "the love of my life." They pursued this long-distance relationship for nearly three and a half years, primarily via telephone, visiting each other every couple of months. After six months, they began to sleep in the same bed, but only cuddling, never having sex.

Since it is common to attract partners with similar patterns, it turns out that Jeanine also felt unattractive and had a similar fear of sex. As a result, they continued relating in this way, never having sex during the entire three and a half year period. However, Jeanine finally reached a point of wanting more from the relationship and was no longer willing to settle for cuddling as their only form of sexual intimacy.

One day, she announced to Victor that she had met another man who lived in New York with whom she was madly in love and that now, *he* was the love of her life. "And, by the way," Jeanine added emphatically, "we are having sex as part of our relationship." After three and a half years of giving in to her fears, Jeanine finally broke through and wanted to have sex, whereas Victor still wasn't interested. So, she went somewhere else to get what she wanted. (Interestingly enough, the new love of her life was married and lived out-of-state—essentially unavailable and, therefore, still "safe" to a great degree.)

Victor was an only child, raised by parents who were very prim and proper. His parents gave him very little affection when he was a child and displayed almost none between themselves. Victor received the subconscious message that physical touch was an unnecessary part of life and in fact, was to be avoided as much as possible. When Victor was eight years old, his parents listened at his door on several occasions, and when convinced that they heard the boy masturbating, scolded him severely, telling him that it was very bad of him to do that, and warned him never to do it again. Needless to say, Victor has been afraid of any kind of sexual contact ever since.

HEALING YOUR "FEAR OF SEX" PATTERN

There are no "rules," no "right" or "wrong" way to make love. What is important is that you are willing to take responsibility for your own experience and not blame your partner for what you feel (or don't feel). It's okay to communicate your needs and desires to your partner— contrary to the popular belief that "talking breaks the romantic mood and diminishes the pleasure of the experience." Share your feelings! Stay present with your partner and be willing to share love.

Sharing love is far more important than "technique." If you focus only on the physical pleasure, you will often lose the loving connection you have with your partner. Keeping your hearts flowing in love will allow you to experience a deeper level of intimacy and satisfaction with one another. Loving your partner for who he (or she) is, not for what he (or she) does, will allay many of the fears regarding sex for both partners and create a more fulfilling, rewarding experience of lovemaking.

If you've been influenced negatively by your religious programming, you may need to re-think your concept of God and the role God plays in your life (see also **Pattern 20—Fear of God**). Although contrary to what you may have been taught, you could choose to believe in God as a source of Infinite Love and Goodness in your life. You could be *thankful* to God for the love you are able to share with others, *including* sexual love.

Since you can choose what you want to believe, you could simply trust that life is meant to be lived joyfully and lovingly, accepting all the pleasures that the human experience entails. In truth, you *deserve* to enjoy all aspects of your life. You deserve fulfillment in life. To be able to enjoy full sexual expression is a blessing. God supports you in enjoying yourself fully.

Remember, whatever you choose to believe will determine how you experience your life. If you believe in the need to suffer, you will create sexual experiences (or the lack thereof) that will cause you to suffer. If you have unresolved guilt about sex, you will always (although unconsciously) attract some form of punishment—even to the point of contracting a sexual disease.

If you release your past programming regarding sex, you will free yourself to find greater peace, joy, and satisfaction within yourself and your relationships. You will be able to trust the process of life and feel safe in your sexual encounters. As you do the inner work necessary to release your negative programming, you will better be able to hear the voice of your intuition and Higher Self, who will guide and support you in being in the right place at the right time—in order to be maximally safe and protected.

Finally, if there was actual physical pain or brute force involving sex when you were a child, you have reason to fear sex later in life. The fear is that the same experiences will be repeated. They do not, however, *need* to be repeated. As an adult, the fear can be released and a new sense of safety and trust in love, and consequently, in sex, can be integrated into your consciousness.

The feelings associated with earlier traumatic sexual experiences are often buried so deeply within the subconscious mind that they will surface only with extensive "inner work." Be patient as you work on changing your old beliefs. Also, know that it may be appropriate, at some point, to seek professional assistance to support you in "healing the scars" from the past.

Common Limiting Thought Pattern	New Thought Pattern to Integrate
Love isn't right for me. Sex isn't right for me.	Love is right for me. It's safe to let love in. Sex is right for me. It's safe to enjoy the natural expression of my sexuality.
Sex is bad. Sex hurts people.	Sex is safe. Sex is innocent and natural. Lovemaking is always safe and pleasurable.

Common Limiting Thought Pattern	New Thought Pattern to Integrate
I am afraid when I let men/women love me. I am out of control when I let men/women love me.	I feel safe when I let men/women love me. Letting men/women love me is easy and pleasurable. It's easy for me to let go and enjoy men/women loving me.
I am not the way men/women want me to be. Men/women don't want me the way I am. I am not what men/women want.	Men/women enjoy and appreciate me the way I am. Men/women accept me naturally and want me just the way I am. I now attract men/women who want me the way I am.
Men/women find me unappealing.	I now attract men/women in my life who enjoy my appearance and find me appealing the way I am. The more I love and accept myself the way I am, the more others love and accept me the way I am.
Men/women don't want what I have to give them.	I now attract men/women who appreciate me and all that I have to give them.
My body is unacceptable to men/women.	I forgive myself for thinking there is something wrong with my body. Men/women are now attracted to me who like my body the way it is.
Love passes me by. I have no love in my life.	Love is here for me. I now have the love I want in my life.

Common Limiting Thought Pattern	New Thought Pattern to Integrate
I am not right in God's eyes because of my sexuality. I am not worthy in God's mind because of my sexual desires.	God loves and accepts all parts of me, including my sexuality. I am completely innocent for my sexuality and sexual desires. I am worthy in God's mind and deserve to enjoy my sexuality.
I have to please men/women by doing what they want in sex. I'm not good enough to please men/women in sex.	I can now support my partner in enjoying himself/herself without feeling obligated to please him/her. I am free to do what feels right for me in sex. The more I'm willing to enjoy myself, the more my partner naturally enjoys himself/herself. I am naturally able to please men/women in sex, just by being who I am and sharing my love.

In truth, the area of sex and sexuality encompasses all the other patterns. A "Fear of Sex" can develop as a result of Pattern 1—Fear of Rejection, Pattern 3—Fear of Hurting or Being Hurt, Pattern 11—Fear of Disapproval, or Pattern 21—Fear of Losing Control. If you examine each of these other patterns, you will notice that they could contribute, in some way, to a person developing a "Fear of Sex."

FEAR OF DISPLEASING OTHERS

*"I don't know the key to success, but the key to failure
is trying to please everybody."*

Bill Casaba

COMMON EXPERIENCES IN RELATIONSHIPS

· Saying "yes" when you mean "no" to your partner
(or having your partner do that to you)

· Always putting your partner's needs and wants before your
own—not being true to your own needs, desires, and values (or
attracting partners who always put their needs before yours)

· Feeling afraid to really be yourself with your partner (or attracting
partners who are afraid to be themselves with you)

· Attracting authoritarian/domineering partners

· Attracting partners who look to you as the authority (or vice
versa)

· Resenting your partner for being in control of you/for not letting
you be yourself (or attracting partners who resent you for the
above)

· Feeling insecure in relationships (like you're "walking on
eggshells"— always afraid that your partner isn't pleased with
you/doesn't love you/will find fault with you)

· Suppressing your own needs, desires, and values in relationships

· Avoiding relationships altogether to ensure that there will be no
one to be displeased with you

· Finding fault with or feeling displeased with your partner
(being critical or judgmental)

· Having partners who find fault with or are displeased with you

· Faking orgasms

· Feeling abused or attracting abusive partners

With this pattern, you think you're unacceptable to others the way you are. As a result, you feel a strong need to modify your behavior in order to be liked. While you were growing up, the people you loved probably found fault with you and expressed displeasure at your behavior. They failed to let you know that they still really loved you, even though they may not have liked what you were doing.

Identifying with your actions, you began to assume that because they were displeased with what you *did*, they must not like who you *are*. These people (usually your parents or caretakers), would often reinforce this idea by deliberately withdrawing their love when they didn't approve of your actions. You began to feel unlovable, unwanted, and pressured to please them in order to get love. Eventually, you learned to suppress your natural expression of who you are in order to make them happy. You decided that the real you was definitely not okay and must never be seen again!

Frequently, if there is early religious training in the family, you will extend this feeling of being displeasing to others to include God. Either that will be communicated to you directly (e.g., "You won't go to Heaven if you keep doing that..."), or you simply conclude that since you're displeasing to the people you love, God must be displeased with you as well. Believing that God is displeased with you often creates tremendous guilt for being who you are, coupled with a sense of hopelessness about life ever giving you what you truly want. If you truly believe that God is displeased with you, you may find yourself attracting "punishment" in some form (such as relationships not working out for you, partners who abuse you, etc.), and you will have difficulty finding satisfaction in your life.

KAREN'S FEAR OF DISPLEASING OTHERS

Karen always tried to please everybody, but felt that no one was ever happy with anything she did for them. Relationships were extremely frustrating for her, because the harder she tried to please her partner, the less he seemed to be pleased with her. The happier she tried to make him, the unhappier he became. Karen always put her partner's needs and desires before her own.

"My needs never mattered," Karen admitted ruefully. "I always had to do everything for the other person." Karen even dressed to please her partner, often feeling uncomfortable and out of place, as a result. She would do *anything* to try to make her partner happy.

While making love, Karen would pretend to enjoy herself—even when it hurt—in order to make her partner feel good. She would fake orgasms at times because she wanted her partner to think that what he was doing felt good to her. Karen found herself doing anything and everything she could to please her relationship partners. Unfortunately, it never worked. Men would always leave her. Karen found herself alone—far more than she wanted to be. She also, understandably, developed a **fear of rejection (Pattern 1)** and a **fear of being alone (Pattern 5)**, which reinforced her lack of success in relationships.

Karen was the second daughter in her family and always felt as if her older sister was the "apple of her parents' eye"—the one who could do nothing wrong. Karen, on the other hand, never seemed to do anything right. No matter what she achieved—the musical talent she displayed, the good grades she made in school—it was never good enough. Her parents simply weren't impressed. They never seemed pleased about anything she did that was good. As a result, Karen began to believe that there was no way anyone would ever be pleased with her, and no way she could ever make anyone happy in life.

Interestingly enough, Karen's father never seemed to be pleased with her mother, who continually bent over backwards in an unsuccessful attempt to make him happy. Thus, Karen had a strong role model for such behavior in loving relationships.

LUCILLE'S FEAR OF DISPLEASING OTHERS

Lucille is twenty-five years old and married. Her father is an ex-military, overbearing type who always demanded perfection and tried to control his relationship with Lucille's mother, as if it were an extension of military life. When things weren't exactly the way he wanted, he would get angry and scream at her, causing tremendous dissension in the family while Lucille was growing up. Lucille hated all the fighting and, over time, learned to go to any lengths to avoid such confrontations.

With her current husband Martin, Lucille gives in all the time and, like a puppet, does whatever he wants her to do. (She also has **Pattern 6—Fear of Being Intimidated**.) She will never say what she wants—even if it is something she wants badly. When Lucille and Martin go to a restaurant, Martin won't let her order, but selects which food she should eat. He tells her if she isn't eating properly (according to his standards), when she has had enough, and when she shouldn't order anything else. In short, he tells her what she wants and doesn't want. Lucille is so afraid of displeasing him and being true to herself, she just gives in, totally accepting that he is in charge.

Martin controls all the money in their relationship and won't allow Lucille to work. Although he makes good money, Martin is extremely tight-fisted and won't let Lucille buy anything. Martin always finds fault with Lucille and corrects everything she does, even pointing out her supposed "flaws" in public. Understandably, Lucille deeply resents her husband for being in control of her life, but since she is unwilling to acknowledge the truth about her feelings, Lucille, instead, suffers from severe migraine headaches.

HEALING YOUR "FEAR OF DISPLEASING OTHERS" PATTERN

As long as you *believe* you are unacceptable to others, you will be afraid to be yourself with them. Masking your true self to please others can only make you unhappy and uncomfortable, deep within your being. It is important to be who you are! You need to express your true self in order to feel good in life. Begin to accept the idea that you are pleasing to God and to everyone else—just by being yourself.

Pleasing other people can never give you a lasting sense of self-worth. As you learn to accept yourself and enjoy being who you are, you'll attract people who will appreciate and enjoy your sincerity and spontaneity. Forgive those in your past who seemed to be displeased with you. The key here is developing a fundamental trust that you are okay the way you are and that you are naturally pleasing to others, simply by being the *real* you.

Common Limiting Thought Pattern	New Thought Pattern to Integrate
Men/women don't like me for who I am. I am not okay the way I am.	Men/women like me for who I am. I am okay the way I am.
I am displeasing to others.	I am naturally pleasing to others just by being myself.
I am unacceptable to men/women.	Men/women naturally like me and accept me for who I am.
No one enjoys my presence. I can't get along with men/women. Men/women don't want me around. No one wants me.	Men/women enjoy my company and are pleased to have me around. I now easily get along well with men/women. I am loved and wanted here.
I am bad for being the way I am.	I am innocent for being the way I am. The more I accept myself, the more others accept me for being who I am.
I am displeasing to God. God isn't here for me.	I now accept that God loves me and is pleased with me for being who I am. I now accept that God is here for me.

Common Limiting Thought Pattern	New Thought Pattern to Integrate
Since I am displeasing to God, I have no hope of ever pleasing anyone.	Since I have God's total love and support for being who I am, I can now relax, be myself, and trust that I'm naturally pleasing to others.
Since I am displeasing to God, I have no hope of life ever working out for me.	Since God accepts me completely, it's safe to relax and allow life to work out for me.

See also Pattern 1—Fear of Rejection, Pattern 3—Fear of Hurting or Being Hurt, Pattern 8—Fear of Being Your Own Person, Pattern 11—Fear of Disapproval, and Pattern 20—Fear of God.

FEAR OF BEING MISUNDERSTOOD

"There is no worse lie than a truth misunderstood by those who hear it."

William James

COMMON EXPERIENCES IN RELATIONSHIPS

- Attracting non-communicative partners
- Either you or your partner being unemotional, apathetic, detached, or not interested in sharing life with the other person
- Feeling unappreciated or uncared for in a relationship
- Feeling isolated/separate from your partner in a relationship
- Suppressing your true needs, desires, and feelings in the presence of your partner
- Feeling hopeless regarding communication with your partner
- Misunderstanding your partner
- Feeling misunderstood by your partner

When you fear being misunderstood, you will attract that experience to you. If you have this pattern, you probably had parents, teachers, or other authority figures early in life who became impatient with you when you tried to explain yourself or communicate your feelings. These people would cut you off, somehow, before you could fully express yourself and make your point of view understood. As a result, you felt misunderstood, unwanted, and isolated. You often felt as if you didn't fit in or belong. The message you received was that they really didn't care about you or what you had to say.

In actuality, this may or may not have been true. These people possibly didn't realize that they cut you off and made you feel bad. Perhaps they were in a hurry or simply weren't paying close attention to the interaction between you. Still, since you felt misunderstood in your early experiences of relating to others, you tend to recreate a similar way of being treated in relationships throughout your life and continue the pattern of feeling misunderstood.

As a result of being misunderstood over time, you (or your partner, if you are experiencing the pattern by projection) might have learned simply to withdraw, not even attempting to communicate. Communication would be too risky, since you are risking the chance of being misunderstood. Feeling misunderstood often creates feelings of alienation and separation from others, which in turn can lead to frustration and a sense of hopelessness. Walls go up and love diminishes over time.

MELISSA'S FEAR OF BEING MISUNDERSTOOD

Melissa was unhappy growing up because she felt as if her parents never really listened to her. Any time she would try to communicate with them, they would accuse her of being "a little miss know-it-all" and dismiss whatever she said to them. "There was no two-way street," Melissa complained bitterly. "They just didn't want to hear what I had to say." Sometimes they would tell her that she was just trying to get attention by having problems. Melissa grew up feeling isolated and misunderstood.

In fact, life at home was so difficult because of this, Melissa actually ran away from home when she was seventeen. She borrowed money from friends and left, on a bus, for another city—where her grandmother lived. She wanted to be with someone who would listen to her and understand what she was saying. After that, of course, Melissa's parents were eager to talk with her, but Melissa still felt that communicating with them was a losing proposition; they didn't really care about her true feelings or want to hear her point of view.

Melissa had only two significant relationships in her life. Her first relationship was with a young man her own age, eighteen. They were engaged to be married. The relationship dissolved simply because Melissa went away to college. However, in thinking back upon it, Melissa realized that the man was extremely stubborn and would never listen to her when she talked. He was also unwilling to share his feelings or his experience, and this lack of communication continually frustrated Melissa.

At twenty-one, Melissa met and married Robert. Although they stayed married for eleven years, Melissa felt extremely frustrated in the marriage, because of the lack of good communication. "It was like pulling teeth to get him to communicate," Melissa grumbled. "He would make a joke of everything and never let me know what he was really feeling."

All she wanted from him was a willingness to talk about what was going on with them, so they could work things out. He would never comply. After a certain point, Melissa felt so misunderstood, she became afraid to even talk to him. It didn't feel worth the effort. She simply gave up trying. They finally divorced, eleven years and one child later.

After several years of working on herself to heal her negativity and bitterness toward men, and upon reading *Prince Charming Lives!* (*Princess Charming Does Too*), Melissa decided that she was ready for her ideal relationship. She sat down one day and announced "to the universe" that she was ready to attract someone who was highly compatible and who had a similar philosophy of life. Two weeks later, a friend introduced her to Mack, and Melissa was sure that she had found the man of her destiny. At first, she was afraid that it was too good to be true. But then she reminded herself to be open and trusting, and that it was okay to let love in. Her fears subsided and her happiness and joy have been growing ever since.

DANIELLE'S FEAR OF BEING MISUNDERSTOOD

Danielle has been married three times and has experienced a great deal of frustration in her communications with all three partners. "I get so frustrated when I'm trying to communicate," Danielle explained, frowning. "I put tremendous internal pressure on myself and struggle to find the exact words to get my message across." Danielle's **fear of being misunderstood** has created much tension in her attempts to communicate with her relationship partners.

In her first marriage, Danielle's husband was emotionally abusive to her. However, it was he who suddenly decided that he didn't want to be in the relationship. A true reflection of Danielle's difficulties in communicating, her husband was afraid to tell her of his decision. He, instead, began being mean to her in order to make her leave. "He would say all these terrible things about me—that I wasn't a likeable person and that my personality wasn't pleasing—until I thought I was really terrible," explained Danielle, appalled at how badly he had treated her. "I felt as if he wasn't understanding me at all!" Finally, her husband was unfaithful to her, and the relationship soon ended.

In Danielle's second marriage, she discovered that her husband was an alcoholic and that his whole life revolved around his job and socializing with his co-workers. He spent very little time with her, and she felt totally excluded from his life. (She also had **Pattern 9—Fear of Being Unimportant**.) That relationship lasted only one year.

When she met her third husband-to-be, she couldn't figure out if he really liked her, because he never told her how he felt about her. Danielle had even started dating other people, because he didn't seem to care much about her. Then, suddenly, he announced, "I think it's time we get married." There was no candlelight, no romance, no hint that he really cared, but Danielle accepted his proposal.

He did become more affectionate after they were married, but he still refuses to talk about himself or share his real feelings. Danielle continually feels frustrated about that and finds herself having to work hard to find out what's going on inside him. Also, whenever she begins to share her emotions, he shuts down and tries to run the other way. As a result, Danielle feels as if she has to hold herself back from expressing what she really feels in order to communicate with him.

Danielle's father was the classic Irish man—always jovial, the life of the party. He loved to tell stories, especially to non-family members. He was a very congenial, likeable man when he was out socializing with others, but, at home, he acted quite the opposite—aloof and withdrawn, like a stranger. Consequently, her mother felt as if she was never heard.

Danielle's father, who was unable to talk about his feelings, was actually hospitalized twice with clinical depression. Whenever Danielle was upset about anything, her father would tell her to go away, that he was too busy to take care of her. When she would go to her mother with her problems, her mother would also tell her to go away, that she couldn't do anything about it. Danielle grew up feeling terribly misunderstood and alone.

HEALING YOUR "FEAR OF BEING MISUNDERSTOOD" PATTERN

Obviously, it is imperative that you change your negative beliefs about being misunderstood in order to open yourself to experiencing good, satisfying communication with others. Real communication is a precursor to feeling love. If communication isn't there, it's challenging to experience love flowing between two people.

To heal this pattern, you must be willing to take the risk and open the door for communication to happen. Although it may feel uncomfortable at first, a willingness to communicate is the key here. Also, as you change your deep beliefs about not belonging and about being alone, you will start to heal the isolation caused by this pattern, and love—for yourself and for others—can be restored. Naturally, as you feel better about yourself, you will feel more comfortable expressing your thoughts and feelings to others, and this will pave the way for more loving, satisfying communication to take place between you.

Common Limiting Thought Pattern	New Thought Pattern to Integrate
Men/women don't understand me.	Men/women now easily understand me.
I can't make myself understood.	I can now easily communicate with others and make myself understood.
No one understands me.	I'm now willing to be easily understood.

Common Limiting Thought Pattern	New Thought Pattern to Integrate
I'm not wanted here. I don't belong here. No one wants me around.	I now experience being wanted here. I feel as if I belong here. Men/women enjoy my company and want to be with me.
I am alone here. Men/women aren't there for me.	I now easily connect with others and feel their support and understanding. Men/women are truly there for me.

See also Pattern 1—Fear of Rejection, Pattern 8—Fear of Being Your Own Person, and Pattern 9—Fear of Being Unimportant.

PATTERN 19

BELIEF IN SEPARATION FROM LOVE

"A man can be happy with any woman as long as he does not love her."

Oscar Wilde

COMMON EXPERIENCES IN RELATIONSHIPS

- Having relationships with unavailable men/women
- Pushing your partner away or he/she pushing you away
- Having affairs or attracting partners who have affairs
- Avoiding relationships or being unable to find someone you want to be with
- Being constantly "on the go" or committed to activities outside the relationship and never spending quality time with your partner (or having a partner who does this)
- Having long-distance relationships
- Feeling isolated and separate/feeling lonely both in and out of a relationship
- Creating conflict with a partner for no apparent reason
- Feeling an unexplainable need to leave a relationship or having partners that leave you for no apparent reason
- Having relationships that don't work out over time
- Not being attracted to those who are attracted to you
- Not finding what you want in relationships
- Either you or your partner being unemotional, detached, or uncommunicative
- Acting reclusive or anti-social
- Being a bachelor, widow/widower, or loner
- Abusing your partner/feeling abused by your partner

The **belief in separation from love** is probably the least apparent, yet most powerful reason for lack of success or lack of fulfillment in relationships. If you *believe* that you are separate from love, you will inevitably push love away (by sabotaging relationships, breaking up with your partner, etc.) to validate your belief. On the other hand, you may simply feel a sense of separation or isolation in the context of your relationships; that is, you will keep loving relationships in your life, but not really let yourself feel the love.

The **belief in separation from love** can come from early childhood experiences where touching, affection, or other loving behaviors were missing. It could develop in children whose parents were frequently away from home or too busy to be with them on a regular basis. Actually, any situation in which you felt unloved, unwanted, or unnoticed as a child could have caused you to believe that you are separate from love, that love doesn't exist in your life. In addition, whenever you found yourself on the outskirts of a crowd, feeling like an outsider, thinking that no one cared about you, a belief in being separate from love could have developed.

You may also create a belief in separation from love as a defense against possible abandonment. To avoid the risk of losing love and feeling the pain of its loss in the future, you decide that it's better to cut yourself off from love now. You think it's wiser, in the long run, to live life separate from love. You rationalize that if you don't experience love being there for you, you will never be vulnerable to losing it!

One problem with thinking that you are separate from love is that you then create a life in which love has no part; love becomes unfamiliar to you. As a result, you are unable to perceive love around you or receive love from others. In addition, we human beings always gravitate towards that which is familiar. We continually recreate old ways of thinking, feeling, and doing in our present circumstances. If love is unfamiliar to you, you will continue to reject all good that comes your way as a result of people loving you. You will continually shut love out, because it is unfamiliar to life as you know it.

In truth, your deepest connection to love is through the Creator. Therefore, it is possible that, just by being born, you may feel separate from that Great and Unconditional Source of Love. Many children feel a sense of separation from God, and hence, a separation from love, that even the most loving of parents cannot extinguish.

Some people have religious programming that says: the only way to be at one with God is through death; only then can you *truly* be united with your Creator. The challenge here is this: if you love God and yearn to be with Him, you will (*unconsciously*) attract experiences to give you the death you seek in order to fulfill your wish to be with God. The problem, of course, is that this may not match your *conscious* desires for your life!

TOM'S BELIEF IN SEPARATION FROM LOVE

Tom was so convinced that he was separate from love at the deepest levels of his being that he (unconsciously) did whatever he could to ensure that outcome in all of his relationships. On the surface, Tom had a very charming demeanor and seemed to win women over fairly easily. Then, as the relationship progressed, he would ask them continually, much to their surprise, "Will you ever leave me?" (He also had **Pattern 5—Fear of Abandonment**.)

At first, the women had no clue as to why he would say this. But, as each relationship became more serious (Tom married twice), another side of Tom emerged. He would begin to abuse his partner emotionally, and ultimately he alienated each woman. He always created some sort of conflict for no apparent reason, screaming and yelling at his partner for twenty minutes at a time, over extremely trivial matters, such as no more toilet paper in the bathroom, a poorly squeezed tube of toothpaste, or a mess of papers on the dining room table.

He even physically beat up his first wife, putting her in the hospital. In addition, he would have numerous affairs on the side, sometimes staying away from home at nights. His abusive behaviors inevitably made his partners want to leave, thus validating his belief that he is separate from love and that no one wants to be with him. (He also had **Pattern 25—Feeling Out of Control in Love**.)

Tom's mother had babied him and had done everything for him, never giving him any sense of responsibility in life. Thus, Tom learned that he was never accountable for anything that happened, and therefore, all of his problems must be someone else's fault. Tom blamed his partners constantly for anything that wasn't right in his life and would never acknowledge his own role in any conflict or disagreement. Tom's father was jealous of him because of all the attention his wife gave the boy—far more than she gave her husband and the other children. His jealousy and resentment fed his bad temper, and Tom's father began taking out his hostility on Tom.

He did everything he could to prevent the boy from getting close to him. He would refuse to take Tom fishing and always act grouchy and grumpy toward him. He talked to Tom in a negative, demeaning way and made it apparent that he wanted nothing to do with him. One time, when he was extremely angry, his father slammed Tom through a door, and on occasions, when Tom got a little older, they actually had fist fights. Tom learned to fear love—it just wasn't safe, and he grew up to behave in extreme and anti-social ways to ensure the absence of love in his life.

PAULA'S BELIEF IN SEPARATION FROM LOVE

Paula married a wealthy man when she was twenty-four years old. After she and her husband returned from their honeymoon, his mother called and asked that they come to see her. She lived about fifty miles away. Paula refused to go, so her new husband went without her. This pattern of separating herself from all sources of love continued throughout her life.

Shortly thereafter, her husband got a job in another city, and Paula decided that she didn't want to go with him. They lived in separate cities for a year and a half, while maintaining the relationship. Her husband wanted to have kids; Paula emphatically did not. Soon they divorced, and Paula found a new husband—with whom she proceeded to have four kids.

Her second husband, an alcoholic, had a bad period in his business and couldn't find a job for over a year. Paula fell out of love with him because he wasn't able to provide for her, and she turned off to him sexually and emotionally. They stayed in this unhappy state for another three years, at which point he finally moved out. Paula is now married to her third husband and will allow him to get close to her sexually only if he spends a lot of money on her and her children. Otherwise, she keeps him at a distance.

Paula received no love from her parents while she was growing up. They were too busy and involved with social activities to give her or her two sisters much attention. Also, Paula's parents showed very little affection toward each other. Their relationship seemed to be about the business of running a household and providing a roof over everyone's head and food for them to eat. The only form of love any of the children were shown was through infrequent presents on special occasions, such as birthdays and Christmas. The girls learned to fend for themselves, for the most part, and not have much to do with the parents, who frequently left housekeepers in charge of the family for extended periods of time while they were away.

Paula's parents were very strict with the children and gave them explicit rules to be followed in their absence. If the girls disobeyed, the threat of some terrible punishment would loom over their heads, and the girls always obeyed out of fear. Because of her parents' overbearing ways, the rigidity of their demands, and the threats of punishment, Paula learned to fear love (**Pattern 7**) and this, too (unconsciously), made her want to keep her partners at a distance.

MARIE'S BELIEF IN SEPARATION FROM LOVE

Marie's father was an alcoholic, and her parents fought all the time. Neither parent was ever physically demonstrative of their affection for her, and Marie grew up feeling alone, unlovable, and unworthy of love. No real love or intimacy was ever displayed during her upbringing, and Marie never felt close to anyone in her family. As a result, she developed a strong belief that she was separate from love, which continues to block her from experiencing the joy of intimacy with her husband—the first man she ever dated.

Marie has been married nearly fifteen years and has always felt that she and her husband never have enough time together. In fact, no amount of time that they spend together ever seems to alleviate the feelings of isolation and loneliness she feels. Plus, she always complains that her husband won't communicate with her and is too emotionally detached.

In the past few months, Marie's husband has actually been experiencing an unexplainable need to leave the relationship, and if he does so, it will only reinforce this pattern for Marie. As Marie works on clearing this pattern, however, it is likely that her husband's desire to leave the relationship will either greatly diminish or even disappear altogether.

HEALING YOUR "BELIEF IN SEPARATION FROM LOVE" PATTERN

Love is always here for you, although sometimes it may take unusual forms, as when a mother reprimands her child for crossing the street alone. She is doing this out of love, along with concern and fear for the child's safety. As a child, it's difficult to distinguish one motivation from another. However, as an adult, you can learn to recognize the caring in others' actions and attitudes toward you and filter out the rest: the anger, manipulation, fear, etc. The actual key here is learning to love and accept yourself! The more you are able to do this, the easier it will be to perceive love from those around you.

To change this pattern, you must start feeling comfortable with love, even though it is new for you. Continually remind yourself that love exists in your life. Envision a life in which love is the norm for you. See and feel yourself filled with love, experiencing love in all that you do. The more you can imagine feeling safe and comfortable with love, the more you will be able to experience love as an ongoing reality in your life.

Trust that God's love is always with you; you need only to allow yourself to experience it. Begin by believing it is there! As you change your negative subconscious beliefs that you are separate from God, you will begin to experience love always being here for you. Know that you can feel God's presence in life. You can absolutely feel at one with God and still be alive and well *in a physical body!*

Understand that no belief is right or wrong, and no one is trying to invalidate your religious upbringing. There are simply aspects of it that may be influencing you subconsciously and limiting the amount of love and joy you allow yourself to feel. In truth, you are free to believe as you choose! It's just that believing you can be at one with God *while being alive* gives you many more options for enjoying your life.

Common Limiting Thought Pattern	**New Thought Pattern to Integrate**
I am separate from love. Love does not exist in my life.	I am connected to love. Love is wherever I am. Love is always here with me.
I keep love at a distance. I separate myself from love.	It's safe to let love get close. It's safe to be at one with love. I now let love in.
I reject love because it is unfamiliar to me.	I feel an ever-growing safety and comfort in the presence of love. I now experience love in men's/women's behaviors toward me. It's safe to let men/women love me.
If I allow myself to experience love, it will disappear.	I trust that love will always be here for me.
I am separate from God. I am separate from God's love.	I am one with God. God's love is always present within my heart.

Common Limiting Thought Pattern	New Thought Pattern to Integrate
Being born means that I am separate from God. Having a body keeps me from experiencing God's presence.	Being born means that I am still totally connected to God. I am able to experience God's loving presence while being alive and well in my physical body.
I have to die to experience God's love.	God's love is here with me throughout my life. I forgive myself for thinking that I have to die in order to experience God's love.

See also Pattern 4—Fear of Abandonment, Pattern 7—Fear of Love, Pattern 9—Fear of Being Unimportant, Pattern 20—Feeling Abandoned by God, and Pattern 23—Fear of False Love.

FEAR OF GOD/
FEELING ABANDONED BY GOD/
BELIEF IN A PUNISHING GOD

*"I turned to speak to God
About the world's despair;
But to make matters worse
I found God wasn't there."*

Robert Frost

COMMON EXPERIENCES IN RELATIONSHIPS

- Having relationships in which there is suffering

- Having relationships with alcoholics, abusive partners, partners requiring a caretaker (where you can do your penance for God)

- Feeling stuck in relationships and unable to leave (because "it's a sin to divorce, to break up the family")

- Being widowed at a young age or with unusual frequency

- Having relationships where a strong sense of separation or isolation is felt

Negative programming from our early religious upbringing about our relationship with God (or lack thereof) influences our experience of relationships with others. Often, we project a sense of being abandoned by God or "kicked out of Eden" onto our human relationships, and create being abandoned or "kicked out" by our partner.

Some people subconsciously believe that God hates them, and therefore, they don't deserve to have what they want in relationships. Some believe that God wants them to suffer in life. This causes them to create either negative relationships, in which they suffer, or a *lack* of relationships, which also causes them to suffer.

Many people actually believe they deserve punishment in God's eyes and therefore keep relationships at a distance. On the other hand, they may think that God will punish them if life gets "too good." In a relationship, they often create conflict and struggle with their partner to make sure the relationship doesn't get "too good." Sometimes they will stay in an unhealthy or negative relationship to keep life itself from getting "too good." "Since man is a sinner, he doesn't deserve to be happy" is how the thinking here goes.

Many people are afraid of God because they believe that since death is inevitable, God, at some point, must want them dead. This kind of thinking is understandable when you believe that you are merely a victim of God's will (often an angry God, according to much of our religious programming). Remember, here we are dealing with the subconscious, and therefore most of these beliefs will be *out* of your conscious awareness—although they still affect you deeply in your everyday life!

SHIRLEY'S BELIEF IN A PUNISHING GOD

Shirley called herself "unlucky in love," because she always attracted abusive men who continually used her for her money and took advantage of her kindness. Eugene, her current live-in partner, didn't earn money on a regular basis, but managed to make a couple hundred dollars every few weeks or so. His monthly phone bill, which Shirley paid, was regularly about $2500. Eugene's ex-wife and son lived in Wales, and he spent much of his time talking to them and to other friends and relatives in both Europe and the U.S.

Soon after Eugene moved in, Shirley found herself making his child support payments ($1800/month) and giving him money to fly overseas to visit his son. Being forgetful, Eugene had a bad habit of losing plane tickets, and on several occasions, Shirley had to send him money to pay for a new ticket, so that he could return home. Friends couldn't believe that Shirley put up with such abusive behavior. Shirley wasn't happy about the situation, but she didn't feel she had any power to do anything about it. She simply accepted her caretaker role as a necessary part of being in the relationship. In the meantime, she had just lost her four children in a custody battle with her cruel and vindictive ex-husband, Sam. Sam hadn't really wanted the children, or the horses, or the dog, or Shirley's house, but had fought tooth and nail (and perhaps even paid off the judge) in order to win everything that belonged to Shirley, including forcing her to pay his $125,000 worth of legal fees. Unbelievably, all this happened in a state that normally awards everything to the wife and mother.

Her ex-husband has since starved her horses to death and "accidentally" lost the dog. He continually abuses the children—physically, emotionally, and even sexually, and there has been nothing that Shirley could do to stop him or get the children back. Shirley's experience indicates that she has both a deeply ingrained **belief in a punishing God**, along with **Pattern 26—Fear of Dying from Love**.

When Shirley was born, her mother had already had seven children. Experienced at dealing with newborns, Shirley's mother was struck by how upset Shirley was at birth. She later told Shirley that the expression on her face and the intensity of her emotions were so extreme that she felt that something really bad must have happened to Shirley before this life. Indeed, Shirley continued to experience extremely intense events throughout her life.

At age six, she was kidnapped and molested by a man while she was playing in front of her house. Another time, the same man came and grabbed her arm, but the boy with whom she was playing baseball started hitting the man with the bat, and Shirley managed to get away from him. Life was never easy for Shirley.

Her father had been extremely strict with the children, and Shirley remembers being scared of him while growing up. She used to hide when he came home, because he was so mean to them. He would insist that the children do their chores and would punish them if they didn't do things exactly right. In a way, the strict and punishing attitude of her father mirrored Shirley's subconscious belief in a strict and punishing God, the Father. It was not evident, however, how Shirley's pattern developed, based *only* on this lifetime of experience.

THERESA'S BELIEF IN A PUNISHING GOD

Theresa was raised Irish Catholic and was continually threatened by her mother that if she ever did anything wrong, God would punish her. Unhappily, it seemed to Theresa, everything she did was wrong. "No matter what I did," Theresa moaned, "it seemed like it was inevitable that I would go to hell."

Throughout her entire life, from childhood through adulthood, Theresa was told that it was good to suffer, because that helped to release the souls in Purgatory from God's wrath. Theresa was afraid that if she wasn't good all the time, God would send her to Purgatory, where she would have to sit in flames until she paid her dues. "And no telling how long you were in the flames," Theresa exclaimed, dismayed at the prospect.

According to Theresa, there seemed to be no way ever to please God—who was always made out to be absurdly whimsical in his punishment. Moreover, if you didn't lead a perfect life, God would surely abandon you. One way that you could get saved, Theresa learned, is if you went out and took care of everyone else and sacrificed yourself for others—just like Jesus (and her mother) did. And of course, sex was out. Anything related to sex was too impure, too unchaste even to be considered. Since you were supposed to suffer, how could you possibly enjoy sex?!

As Theresa got older, she did date men but couldn't let herself enjoy the relationships; somehow it just wasn't right. She would always get involved with people who weren't compatible, or whose interests were totally different, or whose perspectives on life were diametrically opposed to hers, and this total lack of harmony and understanding would cause her to suffer in the relationship. Once, when a kind and loving man—who was actually a good match for Theresa—asked her to marry him, she turned him down. He just "didn't seem right." In truth, it would have been too good for her to accept, given her programmed need to suffer.

Her first marriage lasted four years. She was never really in love with the man but married him because he was a hard-working person. Somehow, that was important to her. They hardly had much of a sexual relationship, though, and eventually she discovered that he was playing around and had, indeed, found someone else he preferred as a partner.

But, Theresa was taught that once you're married, you're married for life—no matter what happens. Divorce simply wasn't an option. She stayed, terribly unhappy, for another five years, until the relationship became too unbearable and divorce imperative. Dating sporadically after that, she remained single for a number of years until she met Richard.

Richard had many wonderful qualities. He was affectionate, warm, caring. The relationship was fantastic in the beginning—and then it began to deteriorate. Soon his affection turned into lust, at least that's what Theresa perceived.

Then, Theresa started getting sick a lot and never seemed to have the time or inclination for sex. In fact, she shut down her sexual feelings completely, even creating a sexual illness, cervical stenosis, which ensured that she wouldn't be able to function sexually. (Needless to say, she also had **Pattern 16—Fear of Sex**.) Unconsciously, she had decided to live without sex. She explained that just looking at her husband made her feel separate and isolated, never affectionate or sexual.

HEALING YOUR "FEAR OF GOD/ FEELING ABANDONED BY GOD/BELIEF IN A PUNISHING GOD" PATTERN

Because you create your reality with your thoughts and beliefs, you can choose to create *ongoing* life as a possibility, rather than the inevitability of death.[1] Since God is the Infinite Life Force that flows through us, why would God want to kill that Life Force (i.e., "Himself") anyway? We do this to ourselves by our conscious and subconscious beliefs. Writings are available of people who have mastered life and have completely cleared the beliefs from their subconscious mind that they need to die.[2] These people do not experience the "death" that we have come to believe is inevitable.

---

1. Several pieces of literature contain true stories of "Masters" who have demonstrated an indestructibility of the physical body and the possibility for "physical immortality," as opposed to death of the body. Among these are: *Autobiography of a Yogi,* Paramahansa Yogananda; *Life and Teaching of the Masters of the Far East,* Vol.1, Chapter 15, Baird T. Spalding; and *Rebirthing in the New Age,* Chapter 6, Leonard Orr & Sondra Ray.
2. Ibid.

The bottom line is: since your thoughts create your reality, it feels better to believe that "God wants me to live and be fully alive" than to believe that "God (at some point anyway) wants me dead." Remember, ALL thoughts, even the subconscious ones, have an effect on your mind, body, and emotions! Believing that God wants you dead or that God will kill you (at some point) always creates a degree of fear within you that keeps you from feeling fully alive and safe in every moment. Trust that God supports you in staying alive as long as you want. Such trust always enhances your sense of safety, aliveness, and well-being!

Common Limiting Thought Pattern	New Thought Pattern to Integrate
I am unworthy in God's eyes I am undeserving in God's eyes. God wants me to suffer. God doesn't want me to be happy.	I am worthy in God's eyes. I am deserving in God's eyes. I now accept that God wants me to enjoy my life. God supports my happiness and allows me to create the life I want for myself.
I don't deserve love. I am a bad person.	I deserve love. I am a good person. I am innocent for being who I am.
I deserve to be punished. God hates me.	I have punished myself enough in God's name. I now deserve good things in life. God loves me.
God is angry with me.	God is pleased with me and supports me in having a good life. God supports me completely in being happy and successful in my life.

Common Limiting Thought Pattern	New Thought Pattern to Integrate
I'm afraid that God wants to hurt/kill me. God wants me to die (eventually).	I am safe in the presence of God. I can now relax and trust that God supports me in being fully alive and well. God wants me to live forever... or as long as I want to be alive.
God will kill me if I'm too happy. (I fear that I will die for choosing to be more alive.)	God supports me in being as happy as possible. It's always safe to choose greater aliveness and joy.
I am a sinner who doesn't deserve to be happy.	I forgive myself for thinking I have done something wrong, for which I deserve to be punished. I am now willing to learn from my mistakes and forgive myself completely for any past wrongdoings. God forgives me completely and supports me in creating happiness for myself. I am innocent and deserve to be happy.
God takes away the men/women I love. The men/women I love, die. I can't have love here.	God supports the men/women I love in staying with me as long as they want. I am now free to create a life in which the men/women I love choose to stay with me. I can have love here. Love is always here for me.

Common Limiting Thought Pattern	**New Thought Pattern to Integrate**
God has abandoned me. God isn't there for me. I am separate from God.	God loves me and stays with me always. I now feel God's loving presence with me at all times. I now remain connected and at one with God throughout my life.
Since God isn't there for me, I can't find love with a man/woman.	Since I now experience that God is there for me, I can now find love with a man/woman.
Life holds no meaning for me.	I move in the presence of God and create beauty, joy, and harmony in my life. Life is meaningful and rewarding for me.

See also Pattern 1—Fear of Rejection, Pattern 4—Fear of Abandonment, Pattern 8—Being Your Own Person, Pattern 11—Fear of Disapproval, Pattern 17—Fear of Displeasing Others, and Pattern 19—Belief in Separation from Love.

FEAR OF LOSING CONTROL

*"The most important thing between a man and a woman
is that one of them be good at taking orders."*
Linda Festa

COMMON EXPERIENCES IN RELATIONSHIPS

· Having inflexible partners (partners who don't support you in changing, growing, being spontaneous)

· Having authoritarian/domineering partners

· Attracting partners who look to you as the authority (or vice versa)

· Lacking spontaneity/trust in relationships

· Needing to dominate others/always taking control (whether it is appropriate or not)

· Having an overcautious attitude in life (either you or your partner)

· Being disproportionately unhappy when things don't go your way

· Holding on tightly to others, possessions, places, money, experiences

· Experiencing a continual tightness/tension in your body

Many people who have a **fear of losing control** don't trust life to work for them, and as a result, it doesn't—at least not without a lot of hard work and struggle! They think they must control things (and usually do so to excess) in order to get what they want.

People who have a strong need to be in control do not allow themselves to flow and be flexible as each new moment brings changes. Instead, they overlay a strong picture onto each moment of how things should be, then work hard to make them that way. Here's the problem:

when you are that focused on how things should be, you never allow yourself to enjoy how things are. As a result, you miss a lot of pleasure in life. You also expend an unnecessary amount of energy in the process of trying to control everything. Life lived in this way becomes stressful and tiring.

This pattern often develops when your parents are domineering, inflexible, or authoritarian with you (they may, indeed, have the same subconscious pattern themselves!). As a child, you unconsciously copy their behaviors and attitudes. Then, as an adult, you re-enact their fear of losing control in your own life. Also, since you experienced your parents as dominating, over-controlling, or authoritarian, you will tend to attract similar characteristics in a partner—until you are able to forgive your parents and release the pattern. It is also possible to attract a partner with the complete opposite characteristics, so that *you* can act out the dominating, authoritarian role in the relationship. Either way, the pattern must be healed within *you!*

MAX'S FEAR OF LOSING CONTROL

Max is thirty-four years old and has always wanted to be in a relationship for as long as he can remember. But, he hasn't dated that much because he has always felt extremely fearful being around women. Terribly insecure, he would feel as if he couldn't be himself, and most important, he would feel totally out of control. He never knew how he *should* behave.

In spite of this, however, Max has managed to have had five significant relationships since his college days. Most of his partners have been domineering, to some degree, and Max has always simply accepted their authority. "I give in a lot," he explained, matter-of-factly. "I always try hard to please people." (Max also had **Pattern 17—Fear of Displeasing Others.**) In addition, most of his partners left him to be with someone else before ever telling him that they wanted to terminate the relationship. This caused Max to feel extremely out of control, as well as to lose trust in future relationship partners.

Max complained of constant tension in his body and continual worry in his mind. "I'm always looking for how things *should* be," he grumbled.

"I can never seem to let things be as they are." Max was raised with a strong work ethic by a father who insisted that everything be done his way. There was no freedom for Max to be and do as he wanted. He was obligated to do everything his father's way, and thus he grew up following a set of rules—"shoulds"—and never really learned to be spontaneous and enjoy himself.

Max's father was a strict disciplinarian and wouldn't let him play or socialize with other children while growing up. He insisted, instead, that Max stay home and do his homework and chores. When he was allowed out, Max had to be home early—by the time the street lights came on. Max's father would whip Max frequently with a belt when he didn't obey his father's rules to the letter. One time, Max had to stand in the corner and say "thank you" a hundred times, because he didn't say "thank you" at the dinner table when he *should* have done so.

Max's mother was also prey to her husband's all-controlling ways. One time she came home from the department store wearing a new bra that she had just purchased. Max's father actually physically ripped it off of her, shouting that she shouldn't have bought it, that they didn't have enough money to pay for it, and that she should take it back immediately. Max was sure that the only reason his mother stayed around was for the sake of the kids. Indeed, his parents did divorce after all the children had grown up and left for college.

Max's most recent partner has a son, and interestingly enough, one of her biggest complaints about their relationship is that he is too strict and controlling toward the child. Max is apparently (unconsciously) acting out his father's behavior toward children. Max's response to her complaining was this: "It drives me crazy when she says that she doesn't like the way I treat her son, or when she says that she needs more from me than she is getting. I can't control that, and besides, I'm giving all that I can give." Again, Max feels out of control when his girlfriend wants him to be different, because he thinks that he *should* do what she wants in order to please her; he just can't.

PAUL'S FEAR OF LOSING CONTROL

Paul was thirty-nine years old. He became actively involved with women as a teenager and has always had a woman by his side ever since. However, all of his relationships were short-lived and ended as dismal failures. Paul always attracted women who were inflexible, domineering, and disapproving—just like his mother—and battled with them for control of the relationship.

Paul had been so controlled and dominated by his mother that he was (unconsciously) bound and determined never to have a woman do that to him again. (He actually had both a **fear of losing control** and a **fear of being dominated—Pattern 12**.) As a result, Paul would always tell his partner what she should do, where she should go, how she should dress, how she should eat, when she should exercise—in short, he would try to control her completely. Then, he would expect her to comply willingly with his wishes.

Whenever his partner would balk or rebel (which happened most of the time), he would fly off the handle and scream at her, or go into a deep depression, often to the point of feeling suicidal. He couldn't stand feeling that out of control and that rejected (**Pattern 1**) when his partner wouldn't do what he wanted.

His need to be in control often caused him to act haughty and superior, and this continually alienated those around him. He would go from one relationship to another but could never understand why things didn't work out for him. After years of unsuccessful attempts to control and dominate women, including three failed marriages, Paul's life turned to total chaos. He went bankrupt, lost his only daughter through a bitter divorce, and developed chronic fatigue syndrome. All of these events occurring simul-taneously created an overwhelming feeling of being out of control—the very thing that Paul feared happening and was trying so hard to avoid.

In Paul's case, he had to hit rock bottom and lose everything in order to get the lessons that life—and his Higher Self—were trying to teach him. As a result of all that happened, Paul finally became willing to acknowledge the part that he had played in causing his relationships to fail, and this enabled him to begin working on himself to clear his sub-conscious patterns. Today, Paul has a successful, nurturing relationship with a woman who is loving, flexible, and unlike any of the other women of his past.

HEALING YOUR "FEAR OF LOSING CONTROL" PATTERN

Trust that life can work for you—easily, effortlessly! Work on changing your deep programming about life, so that you can believe this! The key to success in life is in *letting go,* that is, in being flexible and trusting the process of life as it unfolds for you. Letting go implies a willingness to "live in the moment," to stay focused on the present, rather than worrying about the past or future. Living in the present heightens your intuitive faculties and gives you the awareness of which action needs to be taken in each moment. Your experience of life then becomes one of being "in the right place, at the right time" and having life work out for you along the way.

Here's the good news: you can be "in charge" of your life without having to be "in control." The word "control" itself implies the effort or struggle to make people and circumstances be a certain way. By being "in charge" of your life, you can be attentive to your needs and wants without having to struggle to shape life's events. Success at shaping your life comes from your *intention* to have what you want. It also comes from your *willingness* for life to support you and help you prosper on all levels.

Being "in charge" of your life allows you to relax and enjoy yourself. Conversely, being "in control" implies tensing yourself, as you prepare to wrestle with unwanted changes when they appear. Being "in charge" of your life allows you to take responsibility for your experiences, without blaming others or feeling victimized by circumstances. As a result, you can deal with your feelings in a *positive* manner—even if you have feelings of being "out of control."

Common Limiting Thought Pattern	New Thought Pattern to Integrate
I am not in control of my life. Men/women control me.	I now feel content and in charge of my life, whether I feel in control or not. I no longer need to give my power away to men/women. I take charge of my life in the presence of men/women. I now attract flexible, understanding men/ women, who support me in being in charge of my life.
Life is against me. Life does whatever it wants to me.	Life supports me. Life is on my side. Life works for me. I am responsible for my life. I can now create whatever I want for myself.
Life isn't safe.	Life is safe. I can now relax and trust that I am safe being alive.
Men/women are against me.	Men/women support me. Men/women are on my side. I now attract loving, understanding men/women, who support me in winning in life. I can now relax in the presence of men/women.
Men/women think I'm not okay when I'm not in control. Men/women like me only when I'm in control.	Men/women accept me and approve of me just for being who I am. Men/women naturally like me, whether I'm in control or not.

Common Limiting Thought Pattern	**New Thought Pattern to Integrate**
I'm bad when I'm not in control.	I'm innocent and good for being who I am, whether I'm in control or not.
Men/women don't give me what I want when I'm not in control.	Men/women support me and give me what I want, whether I'm in control or not. I can now relax and trust that my needs and desires are always met, according to my "Highest Good."
I'm not happy when I'm not in control. I hate being out of control.	I'm happy whether I'm in control or not. Since I always feel in charge of my life, I now allow myself to feel happy. I choose to love myself and my life, whether I feel in control or not. I now let go of my desire to be in control in order to experience the joy of being spontaneous and alive.
I'm out of control. I'm not able to be in control.	I am now able to be in charge of my life. It's safe to let go and trust that life always supports my "Highest Good."

See also Pattern 1—Fear of Rejection, Pattern 7—Fear of Love, Pattern 12—Fear of Being Dominated, Pattern 22—Fear of Being Manipulated, Pattern 23—Fear of False Love, Pattern 25—Feeling Out of Control in Love, and Pattern 26—Fear of Dying from Love.

FEAR OF BEING MANIPULATED/ TAKEN ADVANTAGE OF/ CONNED

"I trust only one thing in a woman;
that she will not come to life again after she is dead.
In all other things I distrust her."
Antiphanes, Greek dramatist

COMMON EXPERIENCES IN RELATIONSHIPS

- Feeling helpless/powerless in relationships
- Feeling manipulated/taken advantage of/conned
- Manipulating/taking advantage of/conning others (before they can do it to you)
- Distrusting the motives of the men/women you meet
- Attracting partners who have affairs
- Allowing yourself to be seduced (and then feeling taken advantage of)
- Joining cults in which you give your authority over to a leader/ guru (who turns out to be a fraud)
- Marrying someone because your leader, guru, or another authority advised it
- Marrying someone who later sues you for "all you are worth" at the time of the divorce
- Dominating your partner/others in relationships
- Feeling abused/attracting abusive partners
- Attracting partners who don't keep their agreements

This is a common pattern in our culture today, because most people have not yet awakened to the fact that they are responsible for their lives. They still live life in "victim consciousness," a state of mind in which they view themselves as the innocent and helpless victims of a cruel and unfair world that is ultimately out to get them. You might have had experiences early in life that made you think people couldn't be trusted. However, if you *continue* to believe that people can't be trusted, your beliefs will be proven right, and your fears will continue to be justified. Your universe always reflects back to you your own beliefs. There are no accidents.

Sometimes, with this pattern, you unconsciously set yourself up to be manipulated, taken advantage of, or conned, but then blame other people for doing it to you. For example, if you have a **fear of rejection** (**Pattern 1**) and are convinced that people don't like you the way you are, you might go out of your way to be helpful and giving to them, to ensure that they like you and want you around. However, because of your feelings of unworthiness, you don't believe that you deserve to receive what you want, so you continue to give and give. Then, not surprisingly, you feel as if those people are taking advantage of you and using you for what you can do for them, when, in fact, it is your inability to receive that prevents them from giving to you in return.

NANCY'S FEAR OF BEING TAKEN ADVANTAGE OF

Nancy is thirty-seven years old and has been divorced for twenty years. She is living with a man and really wants to marry him, but he keeps putting her off, acting as if he will probably agree one day—just not yet. While Nancy was growing up, her family always took advantage of her. They would borrow money and never pay her back, charge calls to her phone, borrow her car and bring it back with the gas gauge on "empty," and borrow her credit cards and run up her bills—even to the point of ruining her credit. Somehow, unlikely as it may seem, Nancy accepted such behavior as normal, and even necessary, in order to get them to love her. Her father, divorced from her mother when Nancy was twelve, was a disapproving, critical, grumpy man. Although he treated her rudely and disrespectfully, Nancy supported him for years after he lost his job due to alcoholism.

Nancy had gotten pregnant and then married in her late teens. One evening, when she and her husband were at a bar, Nancy sat there helplessly and watched while her husband blatantly propositioned other women. The marriage lasted another year, then ended in divorce. In her current relationship, Nancy discovered that the man had been having affairs on the side. They broke up for six months, as a result, but are now back living together. He is financially well off and takes good care of himself, buying himself whatever he needs and wants. When it comes to Nancy, however, he always skimps on her, buying her only cheap gifts, if any at all.

With this pattern of being taken advantage of, Nancy always gets into relationships that do damage to her, where her partner deceives her, feigning love, then uses her as much as he can. Once she actually got into a relationship with a decent, kind man whom she decided to leave, in order to be with her current partner, who treats her a lot worse. Nancy will have a hard time attracting kindness and respect from any relationship partner until she frees herself from this pattern.

ROBERTA'S FEAR OF BEING TAKEN ADVANTAGE OF

Roberta was raised on a dairy farm and made to work, starting at age six. She had to feed thirty calves in the morning before she went to school and had to wake up at five o'clock every morning in order to do so. At first, Roberta was excited to help her father, a very hard, intimidating man. In fact, Roberta was eager to do whatever she could to get his love and approval, which he never seemed willing to give. Roberta kept giving and giving, until she realized that nothing was being given to her in return. The chores kept mounting; the work grew harder and more demanding. Her father even began taking the belt to Roberta in order to make sure that she behaved.

At age fifteen, Roberta got heavily involved with drugs as a way to escape her unhappy existence. She felt that her family was taking terrible advantage of her, yet there was nothing she could do to change her circumstances. Her older brother, Marty, received the same treatment as Roberta did, except that he was so damaged by being abused and overworked as a child that he committed suicide when he was twenty. He had never felt any love whatsoever from his parents. Roberta explained to me that at age sixteen, she had finally put her foot down and said "enough" to her father. Her brother, unfortunately, had kept taking it and taking it, until he couldn't take it anymore.

Roberta got married at age twenty to Mike, a young man who appeared to be responsible and loving, and they had two daughters. Throughout the seven years they were together, Mike continually yelled at her and accused her of being incompetent, irresponsible, and an unfit parent. This turned out to be how Mike viewed himself but was unwilling to admit it. Thus, he projected all these judgments onto Roberta and blamed her constantly for not being good enough. Roberta began to feel as if she must really be a bad person, and this reinforced another pattern she had from childhood, the **fear of disapproval (Pattern 11)**. She kept trying to be the way Mike wanted her to be, but she was tired of all the accusations and blame continually directed toward her. When Mike finally threatened that he was going to leave if she didn't shape up, she said, "Fine, leave."

They got divorced shortly thereafter, and Roberta raised the two daughters entirely on her own. Seven years later, Roberta remarried. Her new husband, Dick, seemed very loving and supportive at first—until Roberta's pattern, the **fear of being taken advantage of**, surfaced. From that point on, Roberta experienced that Dick simply wasn't there for her. He wanted her around for all she could give him, but he was totally unwilling to give of himself in any way.

"He never offers me any help—" Roberta moaned, "financial or otherwise." Roberta always had to ask for everything she wanted; her husband never volunteered a thing. Even when she asked for something, Dick would always give her flak. Roberta felt as if she gave all she could to Dick, and all he did was use her for what he could get from her, without giving anything in return. Roberta continually tells Dick that their relationship isn't working for her in this regard. Nonetheless, until she is able to release this pattern and let go of the (unconscious) need to be taken advantage of, it will be probably be difficult for her to experience a change in the dynamics of the relationship.

HEALING YOUR "FEAR OF BEING MANIPULATED/ TAKEN ADVANTAGE OF/ OR CONNED" PATTERN

You must be willing to take responsibility for how your life is. Only by doing this can you empower yourself to make the changes you want to make. Your tendency, with this pattern, is to think: "I'll believe people are trustworthy when I see it." However, you have to start believing it *first*, and only then will you see it. Begin to trust people, and your trust will be rewarded. Act in a trustworthy manner, and you will attract trustworthy people to you. If you treat people with deceit, you will attract deceitful people. You always get back what you give out.

You can get conned only if you con others or believe that people are out to con you. You are not a helpless victim! No one is. Now that you know this, you are free to create a reality in which people treat you with respect and fairness. By releasing your beliefs of suspicion and distrust in humankind, you are not only helping yourself in your own individual life, you are helping to create a world of peace and harmony in which everyone can win!

Common Limiting Thought Pattern	New Thought Pattern to Integrate
Men/women deceive me. Men/women lie to me. Men/women are dishonest. Men/women can't be trusted. I can't trust men/women. I don't believe what men/women tell me. I have to be careful around men/women. I don't trust men/women. They never tell me what they really think.	Men/women are honest with me. I now attract trustworthy men/women to me who sincerely care about my satisfaction and well-being. Men/women support me by telling me the truth. It's safe to trust men/women. I can relax around men/women and trust that they have my best interests at heart. It's now safe to believe what men/women tell me.
Men/women cheat me. Men/women are selfish. Men/women take advantage of me.	Men/women treat me fairly. Men/women sincerely care about me and make sure I receive fair treatment. Men/women respect me and support me in getting my needs met.

Common Limiting Thought Pattern	New Thought Pattern to Integrate
I allow myself to be taken advantage of by seductive men/ women.	I can appreciate and enjoy being sexually attracted to men/women without feeling a need to involve myself further. I get all my needs for loving and nurturing met without having to compromise myself sexually. I now take responsibility for my sexual desires and choices, and choose to do what feels best for me. I now create healthy, loving relationships that satisfy all my sexual needs and desires.
I can't trust men/women in sex. Men/women take advantage of me.	I am in charge of all aspects of my life. I now create mutually supportive relationships with men/women based on love, caring, and respect. It's now safe to trust men/women in sex. I trust that I am able to take care of myself in all situations.
Men/women don't trust me. I am deceitful with them.	I am trustworthy. It's safe to be honest with men/ women.

See also Pattern 3—Fear of Hurting or Being Hurt, Pattern 6—Fear of Being Intimidated, Pattern 7—Fear of Love, Pattern 12—Fear of Being Dominated, Pattern 16—Fear of Sex, Pattern 21—Fear of Losing Control, and Pattern 23—Fear of False Love.

FEAR OF FALSE LOVE

"Swear not by the moon, the inconstant moon,
That daily changes in her circled orb,
Lest that thy love prove likewise variable."

Shakespeare, *Romeo and Juliet*

COMMON EXPERIENCES IN RELATIONSHIPS

- Avoiding relationships
- Having relationships where the love just seems to dwindle over time
- Having relationships where the physical attraction dwindles over time
- Attracting "gigolo" types (partners who act sincere but prove to be otherwise)
- Attracting partners who have affairs
- Attracting partners who leave you for someone else
- Attracting partners who don't keep their agreements
- Attracting partners who are blocked in their ability to give or express love
- Being unable to receive love from a partner (even when he/she is able to give it to you)
- Innately distrusting anyone who tells you that he/she loves you or cares for you
- Leaving or breaking up with a partner when things start getting good (when the level of love starts getting too high for you to tolerate)
- Feeling disappointed in love

With this pattern, there is a denial of the need for love. Such denial often stems from an experience where you felt terribly hurt by someone who said they loved you, when, in reality, they didn't. You believed the person at first and loved him (or her) in return, only to discover that there was no truth to the person's words. Perhaps you found out that he (or she) was secretly involved with someone else. Perhaps he (or she) was simply negative or abusive to you in some way that showed his (or her) love for you was minimal or nonexistent. In any case, you decided that love just isn't for you. You don't want to go through the pain of being deceived again by a false declaration of love, so you simply choose to do without love.

Often with this pattern, being in love has resulted in so much pain that it has felt like death to you—or at least you feel as if you would die if it ever happened again. Since love is equated with death here, it becomes almost imperative that you choose to live life without love as a way to ensure your survival. (See also **Pattern 26—Fear of Dying from Love.**) However, since love is the essence of life, choosing to do without love creates a state of tremendous inner imbalance. In such a state, you force yourself to become numb in the presence of love or whenever the desire for love emerges. To resist love in such a manner can create only unhappiness and suffering within you.

GARY'S FEAR OF FALSE LOVE

Gary is a sergeant in the Marines. Cocky, arrogant, and full of confidence, Gary has always been able to attract women easily. However, under his prideful exterior, Gary is often racked with doubt as to whether his relationships will be successful or not. Gary's false front makes him suspicious that others are being false with him, particularly in matters of love.

Once he dated a lady with whom he felt very much in love. They grew close during the time they spent together, and everything seemed wonderful between them. Then, after almost two years of being in the relationship, they suddenly started hating the differences they saw in each other. They seemed to have totally different points of view on everything and began to argue much of the time. Gary didn't understand what had happened to the love. They just didn't seem to mesh at all anymore and eventually decided to end the relationship.

Then, some time later, Gary got engaged to Betty. After a year, he shipped off to fight in Desert Storm. Betty wrote to him all the time, telling him how much she loved him and wanted to be with him. Gary happily imagined them getting married after the war was over. He looked forward to settling down and having a family. Finally, when the time came for his return, she met him at the airport and acted as if everything was fine and going along according to his plans.

Shortly thereafter, Gary received a surprise phone call from a concerned friend who told him that Betty had been having an affair with another man the whole time Gary had been gone. The news broke his heart. His hopes and dreams had been totally crushed. Obviously, the relationship was over.

Gary kept to himself for a long time after that, apprehensive about ever getting involved in a loving relationship again. He remained aloof, unavailable, and unable to emotionally commit for quite some time, before he could make peace with what had happened to him. (Needless to say, Gary also had **Pattern 3—Fear of Being Hurt**, **Pattern 10—Being Victimized by Love**, and **Pattern 22—Fear of Being Taken Advantage of/Conned**.)

Gary first came to be suspicious that love might not be all that it seemed based on his observations of his parents' behavior while growing up. Gary's mother was always cold and humorless in her interactions with her husband. Gary never really saw or felt any love coming from his mother toward his father—unless she wanted him to do something that he really didn't want to do. Gary sensed that his mother was trying to manipulate his father and displayed love only in order to do so. Thus, her love appeared false to the boy, who began to develop an unconscious wariness of false love.

ED'S FEAR OF FALSE LOVE

When Ed was a small boy, his parents shared a house with a woman and her five-year-old daughter. They lived in separate quarters on the upstairs floor. While Ed's mother was out working, Ed's father would go upstairs to be with the other woman. Ed remembers one time when his mother took him upstairs, he saw his father sitting on the woman's sofa in her living room. The moment felt extremely awkward, and Ed knew that something wasn't quite right. Shortly thereafter, his mother went upstairs again, found her husband in bed with the woman, and filed for divorce.

Ed's father then ran off with the woman upstairs and they left the state. Ed was four years old. Until that point, Ed's parents had fought a lot. Ed used to cover his ears regularly, so that he couldn't hear them; he hated to hear such quarreling. Ed's mother didn't like men; she didn't trust them. Ed's father had married her in order to avoid having to go to World War II.

A few years after his father left, Ed's older brother ran away to go live with him. Ed didn't see his father again until he was eighteen years old. His father had tried to see him once, but his mother wouldn't allow it because his father refused to pay the $5/week for child support that he was obligated to pay. Ed felt betrayed by his father and also felt as if he couldn't trust him. He felt hurt (**Pattern 3**) about him disappearing, and also, understandably, developed a fear of being abandoned by those he loved (**Pattern 4**).

Ed married twice. He is currently with his second wife. His first marriage, to Sally, took place when he was twenty-one years old. He broke out in hives all over his body on their wedding day because he was so anxious that both his mother and father were coming to the church. Ed and Sally were highly compatible physically when they first got married, but after about a year the physical intimacy started declining, until it was almost nil by the time Sally left five years later.

Ed confessed to feeling as if he had, somehow, over the years, done all he could to force her to leave. He admitted to flirting with other women in her presence. He also worked long hours during the day and played in a band on nights and weekends, making it extremely difficult for them to find time to be together.

"Sally would say she loved me, but she certainly didn't act like it," Ed explained, shaking his head, puzzled. "Sometimes she'd scream and yell at me. Sometimes she'd just look at me in a scornful manner, with disgust written all over her face." Sally finally packed up and left one day while Ed was at work. Because of Ed's **fear of false love**, he was unable to trust that Sally really loved him, and unconsciously he created obstacles to their relationship working out.

Ed's second marriage has taken a similar turn, particularly in the area of sex and physical intimacy. Ed and Marlene, his second wife, were extremely attracted to each other physically when they first got together. They have been married for nine years now, and their sexual relationship has continually dwindled over time, until it has disappeared altogether. His wife, who has **Pattern 16—Fear of Sex**, even created a physical illness that has made sexual contact both painful and impossible. Although frustrated in this area, Ed and Marlene are still together and are attempting to work through their difficulties in therapy.

HEALING YOUR "FEAR OF FALSE LOVE" PATTERN

Because of your earlier experiences with love, you certainly feel justified to continue fearing love. Trusting that love is real will feel risky indeed. However, to be free of this pattern, you need to integrate new beliefs about love and learn to trust love again.

As you learn to relax and feel safe in the presence of love, you will regain the parts of yourself that were afraid to feel alive. You will no longer need to feel numb or deadened by life. Allowing yourself to be enlivened by life and by love, you will notice great improvements in your health, well-being, and ability to enjoy all that you do. Relationships will improve dramatically, because you are now ready to experience that love is real for you.

Common Limiting Thought Pattern	**New Thought Pattern to Integrate**
I am unhappy when I am in love.	I am happy when I am in love. Love always works for me.
I do not want love in my life anymore. It hurts too much to be in love.	I welcome love into my life. Love uplifts me and brings me ever-increasing pleasure and joy.
I hate love. I want to die from being in love. Love kills me. I don't want anyone to love me anymore.	I cherish love. I am nourished by love. Love always supports me in feeling alive and joyful. It's safe to let others love me.
Love is bad. Love makes me feel unhappy.	Love is good. Love supports me in being happy.
No one loves me the way I want them to. Love disappoints me.	I am loved by others in a way that feels good to me. I am always satisfied in love.
I want to die. No one loves me here.	I am loved here. I now choose to live a joyful life, full of love.
I am hated by the ones I love.	I now attract sincere men/women into my life, who love me as much as I love them. I am loved by the ones I love.
Life is impossible with love.	Life is wonderful with love. It's safe to let love in and experience ease, comfort, and joy in my life.

See also Pattern 1—Fear of Rejection, Pattern 3—Fear of Hurting or Being Hurt, Pattern 7—Fear of Love, Pattern 10—Being Victimized By Love, Pattern 19—Belief in Separation from Love, Pattern 24—Not Getting Your Needs Met/Unwillingness to Care, and Pattern 26—Fear of Dying from Love.

PATTERN 24

NOT GETTING YOUR NEEDS MET/ UNWILLINGNESS TO CARE

"Frankly, my dear, I don't give a damn."

Rhett Butler, *Gone With The Wind*

COMMON EXPERIENCES IN RELATIONSHIPS

- Avoiding love/committed relationships since you know you won't get your needs met
- Dating numerous partners but unwilling to commit to one person
- Having affairs while in a committed relationship
- Having partners who withhold love/caring/sharing
- Being unwilling to help or support others (in either you or your partner)
- Having partners who are apathetic or don't seem to care about others' needs and feelings
- Having a desire or tendency to "step on" others in order to get what you want (because of your suppressed anger and desire to get even)
- Attracting partners who can't fulfill your needs sexually (you want more from them than they are able to give)

With this pattern, the "**unwillingness to care**" usually stems from your initial feeling that no one cares about you. This feeling generally comes from your early experience of life, when your basic needs for love and nurturing were not adequately met. As a result, you are angry, resentful, and withdraw your desire and willingness to care about others.

You are getting back at the world for the "raw deal" you felt you were given. This pattern can be *very* suppressed—not in your conscious awareness at all—and might reveal itself as an apathetic attitude or a lack of desire to support others. As a result of this suppression, you often feel unable to care about anything, that somehow it's "just not in you" to care.

The truth is, you have suppressed your rage and hurt about no one caring for you, along with an intense desire for revenge. This has caused you to feel numb, unaware of, and out of touch with your true feelings. You have become bored, apathetic, uncaring—better *that* than feel all of the intense feelings you have inside.

When you have this pattern, your fears often surface in the area of long-term, committed relationships. Because your first "long-term" relationship (with your parents) proved so unpleasant and unfulfilling, you are afraid of re-experiencing the same situation. You want to avoid the trauma of being in *another* relationship in which your needs aren't met. This might result in your wanting to "play the field" in dating. The underlying thinking here is: "If I date several people, surely I'll get my needs met. If I have to date just one person, I probably won't."

With this pattern, you often learn to be independent, to not *need* others. You learn how to take care of yourself and be on your own. When you attract a partner into your life, old childhood behaviors tend to surface, and you may begin to view the other person as "Mommy" or "Daddy." As a result, you begin wanting the person to meet the needs that your parents were never able to meet, and then you begin to project unrealistic expectations onto the person of what you want him or her to do for you. In short, you try to get your needs met by your partner but are usually thwarted in the attempt because of your subconscious pattern. If this happens enough, you'll tend to avoid relationships altogether, to avoid the negative feelings they *seem* to cause.

Sometimes, when your needs for love and nurturing weren't met as a child, you develop a *fear* of **not getting your needs met**. This fear may affect you in one of two ways. First, you may simply push love away, due to the fear and the negative thoughts accompanying it. You fear that another person will not be able to meet your needs, and sure enough, they are never there for you in the way that you need. (Remember, your fears always attract that which you fear!)

Second, your fear may manifest as a voracious appetite on your part—for love, sex, food, or whatever you think you need in order to feel love. However, because of your inherent distrust in your ability to get your needs met, none of the above avenues will ever fill you to where you feel as though you have received enough. You may, in fact, push your partner away because you are demanding that they fill you in ways that are impossible. In other words, no matter how this fear manifests for you, whether it is in people keeping their distance from you from the outset, or in you demanding more from people than they can give you, you are doomed to feel dissatisfied and frustrated—until you heal the pattern.

DAN'S UNWILLINGNESS TO CARE

Dan's father made his career as a military officer. As a result, his family moved around a great deal, living for a number of years in different places overseas and in the U.S. Dan was never able to establish good and lasting friendships with other children because his family was always moving. So, Dan missed the bonding that generally forms between children of similar ages and interests.

Dan's father was gone from home most of the time and didn't spend much time with his son. Even when he was home, his father ignored Dan. He was preoccupied with telling stories and being the center of attention and had no use for anyone who wasn't fully absorbed in his performances. His constant talking pushed people away, including Dan, who never felt that his father loved or cared for him. Although Dan's mother was a loving, caring woman, she had very little time for him either, because she was preoccupied with his younger sister, who had Down syndrome.

No one seemed to care about Dan. As a result, Dan started to withdraw more and more. He began deciding (unconsciously, of course) that if no one was going to care about him, he wasn't going to care about anyone else. Furthermore, none of Dan's family were ever demonstrative of affection, so Dan learned to be physically aloof from others and remained that way throughout all of his adult relationships.

Dan never dated much and had only two sexual experiences before he met the nineteen-year-old girl whom he decided to marry. He stayed married for eleven years but always kept his feelings, particularly his anger, suppressed. They would, instead, come out in insidious ways and create huge arguments with his wife. He would make subtle innuendos, little sarcastic remarks undermining and belittling her. Then, he would continue fueling the fire until she would finally explode in anger. Once that happened, Dan would play the innocent one and say that he couldn't understand why on earth she was so mad.

In addition, Dan was extremely apathetic and never took the initiative in the relationship. He never wanted to go anywhere or do anything, and his wife had to make all the arrangements if she wanted to do anything to have fun. Then, she would have to drag him along. He enjoyed himself once he went, but his extreme apathy kept him from participating in the planning process to any degree, and this continually irritated and frustrated his wife.

Another repercussion of this pattern happened at Dan's work. Dan owned his own business and exhibited little regard for his employees. He continually stepped all over them, not treating them with much respect. Apparently, this was quite unintentional on his part. Some employees would simply quit, rather than put up with the disrespectful treatment, but some did complain about how badly he behaved toward them.

This always took Dan by surprise. He had no clue that he was displaying such a lack of caring about others' needs and feelings, yet this behavior continues to surface at work, and the turnover of his employees remains unusually high. Until Dan works through this pattern, his subconscious programming will continue to control his actions.

MARTY'S LACK OF GETTING HIS NEEDS MET

Marty's mother and father had four children and then divorced each other when Marty was three years old. Marty's aunt and uncle adopted him and proceeded to hide his real parents from him. He didn't see them again until he was twenty-six. Marty felt terribly hurt by his parents' leaving him behind like that and didn't understand what had happened.

The hurt and anger he felt about being abandoned by the people who supposedly loved him stayed with Marty and influenced the outcome of all of his adult relationships. (Oddly enough, both his parents remarried and had more children—six in his father's new marriage and four in his mother's.)

Marty married at age twenty-eight and was very much in love with his first wife. However, only eleven months after they got married, Marty was caught dealing drugs and put in jail for a year. Married when he went to jail, Marty found himself divorced when he got out. His wife simply didn't want to wait for him. He really wanted her to stay (he also had **Pattern 5—Fear of Being Alone**) but couldn't convince her to do so. Besides, she had already known that he had been having affairs on the side. He had told her that up front when they first started dating. (P.S. She remarried shortly after their divorce and got murdered by her husband almost a year later. She had an intense version of **Pattern 10— Being Victimized by Love**, along with **Pattern 25—Feeling Out of Control in Love**.)

For the next ten years, Marty had dozens of relationships, many of which were one-night stands. Marty didn't want to get serious about anyone; he didn't dare pursue any relationship that had the potential to last. Finally, ten years later, Marty re-married. They were happy for a while. They had lots of friends and lots of fun. (Of course, Marty was still sleeping around on the side, but he had told her he would be doing that right up front.)

The problem seemed to come when they returned to her hometown to live. Suddenly, she didn't have time for Marty anymore, she was so busy spending time with all of her old friends. "The longer we were there," Marty recalls, "the more the relationship went downhill."

Marty never had any friends there. His wife began to fall into old ways of relating to people—ways that she had been so proud of leaving behind her when she had first moved away—and she started estranging herself from Marty. Marty began to retreat into a shell, angry that love never seemed to work out for him. However, Marty has learned to suppress much of his anger and hurt over the years, and continues to bury many of those feelings beneath cigarettes, alcohol, and drugs.

HEALING YOUR "NOT GETTING YOUR NEEDS MET/ UNWILLINGNESS TO CARE" PATTERN

To release this pattern, you must first change your beliefs about what others think and feel about you. Know that people do care and support you in being happy. Trust that you *can* get your needs for love and nurturing met in life. Life can be different for you!

As you work on integrating new beliefs, many of those old feelings of anger, resentment, or rage that you had suppressed may arise. It's okay to feel them now. These feelings are coming *out* of suppression. This is a good sign! Don't judge yourself for having them. Allow yourself to experience these feelings, without judgment, until they subside.

You can also express whatever you're feeling in order to release the suppressed energy from your body. Yell, scream, or shout (e.g., in your car with the windows rolled up, in the woods, into a pillow, anywhere it's safe to let go). Or, get support from an understanding friend or therapist who is willing to be with you through this process.[1]

You *can* heal these feelings. They will not last forever, as you once feared (which is why you suppressed them in the first place). As you change your basic beliefs and release all the pent-up energy in constructive ways (i.e., not "dumping" on another person), you will start to feel happier and more alive. A natural sense of loving and caring for others— as well as for yourself—will begin to grow.

To clear the pattern, you must finally forgive your parents completely and make peace with the past. Your parents did the best they could. Remember, they were dealing with their own subconscious issues, too. Take responsibility for your feelings, and choose to let love into your life again!

---

1. The Communications Breakthrough System is an excellent tool to assist you in getting in touch with and releasing old, suppressed, negative feelings (see Chapter 10, "More Powerful Healing Techniques," in *Prince Charming Lives!*)

Common Limiting Thought Pattern	New Thought Pattern to Integrate
I'm not able to do what I want; men/women get in my way.	I now experience men/women as an asset to my life. I now have kind, loving men/women in my life who support me in doing what I want.
No one cares about me. No ones cares whether I live or die.	I now experience men/women loving me, caring about me, and supporting me in getting my needs met.
Men/women don't care whether I'm here or not.	Men/women sincerely care about me and enjoy my presence.
I hate men/women for not caring about me. I hate men/women for hurting me.	Since I now experience that men/women love me and care about me, I can forgive them and let go of hating them for their past actions. I now let go of all need to get even.
I don't care about other men/women. I don't want to love anyone.	It's safe to experience how much I care for men/women. It's now safe for me to love men/women. My needs always get met when I open myself to love.
I can't love men/women. I hate being with men/women.	I can now love men/women. It's safe to care about men/women and enjoy being with them.

Common Limiting Thought Pattern	New Thought Pattern to Integrate
Men/women don't care about my needs, feelings, or desires.	Men/women respond lovingly as I communicate my true needs, feelings, and desires. I now have men/women in my life who care about my feelings and support me in having my needs and desires fulfilled.
I never get enough love. I never get my needs for love and nurturing met.	I always get enough love. It's now easy for me to get my needs for love and nurturing met.

See also Pattern 2—Fear of Commitment, Pattern 3—Fear of Hurting or Being Hurt, Pattern 7—Fear of Love, Pattern 9—Fear of Being Unimportant, and Pattern 19—Belief in Separation from Love.

FEELING
OUT OF CONTROL IN LOVE

"I hate and love. You may ask why I do so.
I do not know, but I feel it and am in torment."

Caius Valerius Catullus, Roman poet

COMMON EXPERIENCES IN RELATIONSHIPS

· Feeling as though you're on an emotional roller coaster in relationships

· Having relationships with unavailable men/women

· Pushing your partner away or him/her pushing you away

· Having affairs or attracting partners who have affairs

· Avoiding relationships or being unable to find someone you want to be with

· Feeling as if your partner pulls on or drains your energy in some way (or your partner feels this way about you)

· Being constantly "on the go" or committed to activities outside the relationship and never spending quality time with your partner (or having a partner who does this)

· Having long-distance relationships

· Feeling isolated and separate/feeling lonely both in and out of a relationship

· Creating conflict with a partner for no apparent reason

· Feeling an unexplainable need to leave a relationship or having partners that leave you for no apparent reason

· Having relationships that don't work out over time

· Not being attracted to the men/women who are attracted to you

· Sacrificing yourself in relationships

- Not finding what you want in relationships
- Either you or your partner being unemotional, detached, or uncommunicative
- Acting reclusive or anti-social

With this pattern, you are so sure that love isn't there for you, you will do *anything* for love. Because of this, you always feel that love, or the people you love, have the "upper hand," that *they* are in control of your life. Their decisions to be with you or not to be with you are what cause you to feel as though you're on an emotional roller coaster. You feel out of control because you've made their love more important than anything else.

The truth is, you are not in touch with loving yourself. As a result, you'll endure almost anything from your lovers or partners in order to have some amount of love in your life. It is so important to have love that you become desperate when it isn't there and feel out of control when relationships don't work out the way you had expected. With this pattern, you often feel as if you are on a treadmill, running as hard as you can, yet never reaching that elusive goal: love.

The problem is, because of your fundamental belief in the *lack* of love in your life, that is precisely what you create and experience: A LACK OF LOVE! Subconsciously you push people away or attract people who run from you when you get too close, thereby proving your beliefs right—that you are without love! Sometimes, because you are so desperate for love and so convinced that no one will give you any, you may develop a pattern of unconsciously "sucking" the energy of the person you're with, in an attempt to get that love. Of course, this unconscious way of "getting love" doesn't work and only serves to alienate the people around you further, since no one wants to feel pulled on or drained in such a manner.

This pattern can stem from early experiences of being unloved. If your parents (or caregivers) weren't there for you or treated you with cruelty or indifference, you experienced no love coming to you from others. Having difficulty creating a sense of love within you because of the harshness of your environment, you grew up maintaining the idea that love doesn't exist for you. Thus, in your adult life, you continue the pattern of being willing to do anything for love, but never really feeling it from others.

SAM'S FEELING OUT OF CONTROL IN LOVE

Sam's parents had a stormy relationship while he was growing up, and he never felt that love was there for him. His father, a real workaholic, was a local politician and spent very little time at home. His mother, who was affectionate with him at first, abandoned him emotionally when his sister was born eighteen months later. "She even abandoned me physically," Sam reported, annoyed. "She would take me places and come to pick me up thirty, forty minutes, even an hour late. Sometimes she'd even forget to come get me altogether. It made me feel awful." (As a result, he also developed **Pattern 4—Fear of Abandonment**.)

Sam felt that he could never get what he wanted from his parents, that they were never available to him. His mother was highly critical of everything Sam did, and Sam grew up with a tremendous amount of sadness bottled up inside at how unloved he felt. To compensate, Sam developed a tough exterior and became the neighborhood bully, beating up the kids who lived nearby.

As an adult, Sam has continued to feel unloved and unable to find love with another. Sam would attract partners who weren't available to him, either emotionally or physically. Some were married or living with other men and couldn't see Sam when he wanted to see them. Some lived out of town, which made the relationship quite difficult to pursue. So, Sam began drinking to escape his unhappy feelings.

He did get married at age twenty-six to a woman who was a "doormat" type and let Sam walk all over her. (She had **Pattern 5—Fear of Being Alone** and **Pattern 9—Fear of Being Unimportant**.) He not only bullied her but would go off and leave her frequently to have affairs with other women. She became angry with him and began refusing his sexual overtures. Sam felt more and more unloved and unlovable.

Finally, Sam divorced her, then remarried two more times. Each relationship was characterized by terrible fighting and a lack of sexual intimacy. Each time, Sam felt as if he had to spend all his money on his wife in order to get her to have sex with him. He felt totally out of control in each relationship, because he always felt as if his partner had the upper hand, that she was "pulling the strings."

Sam was so desperate for love—he had never learned to feel any for himself—that he would do just about anything to try and have some love in his life. Ultimately, Sam found himself in a total quandary: he couldn't live *with* women, yet he couldn't live without them.

MANDY'S FEELING OUT OF CONTROL IN LOVE

Mandy was always having trouble with men—the men she dated, the men who lived with her. There was always some problem with men that occupied the forefront of Mandy's attention. Mandy indeed felt as if she were on an emotional roller coaster, as far as her relationships were concerned. She never seemed to be able to find the love she sought, and even when it appeared that she had, something always happened to spoil everything. Mandy always felt as if she couldn't get close enough to the man she liked; he always seemed to reject her in the end.

Mandy was extremely attractive and had a very good figure. As a result, she attracted many men who were interested in her physically, but nothing more. In fact, Mandy had always used her sexual beauty to get love and attention. Unfortunately, however, her ploy always back-fired on her, and she would attract men who were only interested in that.

Mandy had so little love in her life, she would do anything for love. Often she attracted men who were clearly unavailable; yet, she got involved with them anyway. In several of her relationships, she got involved with men who were still living with previous girlfriends. In each case, Mandy would drive by their house and if the girlfriend's car was there, she would just keep driving. If the girlfriend's car wasn't there, Mandy would stop and go in. She would also make herself crazy each time she would pass by and see the girlfriend's car parked there. These were not healthy relationships, providing anything but peace of mind and high self-esteem!

Her most recent relationship was totally different. Or, at least, that's what Mandy proclaimed to her friends. Well, yes, he was married—but he didn't just want her for sex, as other men did. They had actually become friends first. Mandy felt that she could handle him being married, that it wouldn't be a barrier to their relationship.

Now the man is going through great confusion as to what to do. He tells all of his friends that he's crazy about Mandy and feels so much better with her than with his wife. However, he and his wife have three children, with whom he is very close, and he doesn't want to disturb his relationship with them. The man has decided to file for divorce from his wife, but in the meantime, he has also told Mandy that he cannot talk to her or see her because of the inner turmoil he is experiencing. Mandy feels totally rejected and abandoned and is angry with him for the way he is handling the situation. Mandy is also dealing with **Pattern 3—Fear of Being Hurt, Pattern 4—Fear of Abandonment, Pattern 7—Fear of Love**, and **Pattern 19—Belief in Separation from Love**.

Mandy had always felt left out of her parents' life. It never seemed as if they really cared about her, and Mandy always felt that, somehow, she was just in their way all the time. Ever since she could remember, they were sending her abroad to private boarding schools—to get rid of her, she was sure.

Shortly after Mandy was born, her mother actually became a nun and began following some unusual religious order. All of her energy became focused on God and religion, and she began to give away her worldly possessions. She never wanted to be around people after that, but just wanted to meditate, go on retreats, and practice her religion all the time. She and Mandy's father actually stayed married but stopped having sex when her mother became a nun. Mandy experienced an obvious lack of love in her early life, which then set the stage for the relationship problems that she later experienced.

HEALING YOUR "FEELING OUT OF CONTROL IN LOVE" PATTERN

To heal this pattern, you must learn to give yourself the love that you never had as a child. Begin to fill the emptiness you feel inside with your own loving thoughts and energies. When you are convinced you need that love from someone else, you will do anything to get it, which then keeps you stuck in this pattern.

As you learn to develop the love you want from within, you free yourself to create a different kind of relationship—one based on sharing the fullness of your love with one another, rather than trying to fill your own emptiness with the love you get from the other person. Love from the outside, when you don't have it within, is only temporary at best.

You can turn the pattern around by changing the way *you* treat yourself. As you treat yourself with greater love and respect, you will find yourself receiving the same treatment from others. Then, you will truly experience having the love you want, on an ongoing basis. Furthermore, you will no longer allow your external circumstances—that is, whether someone is there to love you or not—wreak havoc on your emotional state or on your ability to feel in charge of your life!

Common Limiting Thought Pattern	New Thought Pattern to Integrate
Men/women don't want to be with me. No one loves me. No one wants to be with me.	Men/women love me and want to be with me. I can now relax and trust that I am loved.
Love isn't here for me. I am desperate for love.	Love *is* here for me. I am now in touch with the love I have within me at all times. I now easily attract men/women who love me and want to be with me.

Common Limiting Thought Pattern	New Thought Pattern to Integrate
I can't stand it anymore; I don't want to be without love. I don't want to live without love in my life.	I now choose to live life to the fullest, knowing that love is always with me. Since I am able to have the love I want in my life, I now love being alive and enjoy my life fully.
No matter how hard I try, I can't make men/women love me.	Men/women love me easily, without any effort on my part.
I am out of control in love.	I now feel in charge of my life at all times, whether I'm in a relationship or not. Love supports me in feeling strong, capable, and in charge of my life.

See also Pattern 4—Fear of Abandonment, Pattern 5—Fear of Being Alone or Lonely, Pattern 7—Fear of Love, Pattern 8—Fear of Being Your Own Person, Pattern 10—Being Victimized by Love, and Pattern 19—Belief in Separation from Love.

PATTERN 26

FEAR OF DYING FROM LOVE

*"Love unbridled is a volcano that burns down and
lays waste all ground around it; it is an abyss
that devours all—honor, substance, and health."*

Baron Richard Von Krafft-Ebing
Professor of Psychiatry, 1866

COMMON EXPERIENCES IN RELATIONSHIPS

• Having difficulty getting close to others

• Having destructive relationships

• Attracting overpowering partners

• Being overpowered by your emotions in relationships

• Attracting "caretaker partners" who do everything for you

• Avoiding relationships altogether

• Finding ways (both conscious and subconscious) to push your
partner away when you feel as if you're getting too close (e.g.,
finding fault with him/her, looking elsewhere, having affairs, etc.)

• Having difficulties in relationships that impede your success in all
other areas of your life (i.e., all-consuming relationships)

• Feeling as if you can't win in relationships

With this pattern, you feel that you have had to sacrifice yourself to
such an extent (usually beginning early in life) for those who "loved"
you, that you feel "dead" as a result. You have given up your spirit, your
joy of self-expression, in the name of "love." You were never allowed to
express yourself as a youngster—at least not how you wanted to express
yourself. You were always told what to do and how to be.

Parents often teach "self-sacrifice" in the name of love. "Do this for
me and I'll love you." "Come here and show everyone your pretty new

dress..." ("and then we'll love you.") "Play the piano for grandma..." ("and we'll be pleased with you.") You feel that you have no choice but to do what they want you to do. You learn to give up your free will to please other people.

Sometimes, with this pattern, your connection with one (or both) of your parents was so intense that you lost your sense of individuality. You felt so overpowered as a child that to let someone get that close to you again (as in a loving relationship) feels threatening to your very existence. If parents are extremely dominating or overpowering, your life force can feel so suppressed that love seems to be killing you. If you feel as if love kills you (whether consciously or subconsciously), you will either attract destructive experiences in love or avoid love like the plague. In all likelihood, you will swing back and forth between these two polarities, creating either intense, destructive relationships or periods of deliberate isolation.

Another variation of this pattern can occur when your parent(s) did everything for you while you were growing up and made you feel incapable of doing anything for yourself. The problem here is that until you break the pattern, you will unconsciously continue to attract partners who will do everything for you and "rob you of your identity" in the process. In any case, because the relationship with your parent(s) was so intense, you will no doubt re-experience that level of intensity in your loving relationships and often feel overpowered by your emotions. Sometimes the emotions are so intense that they seem to impede your normal functioning in other areas of your life, which then reinforces your desire to get as far away as possible from anything resembling love.

LESLIE'S FEAR OF DYING FROM LOVE

Leslie didn't date much, or at least her dating was very sporadic. All the relationships she had been in were, for the most part, short-lived. Leslie never seemed to find men who interested her very much, so she kept to herself most of the time. Once, however, she met a man whom she felt sure was "the one." She was extremely attracted to him from the moment she saw him and was quite upset to find out that he had just moved to town to be with his girlfriend. Nevertheless, she and Jerry became friends. They seemed to have a lot in common and enjoyed long conversations together over lunch. Leslie was sure that it wouldn't work out though—even if the girlfriend wasn't in the picture. "I'm probably not good enough for him. He's so handsome, he could probably have any woman he wants," she sighed wistfully.

Then, Jerry started flirting with her. He would rub her hand once in a while; he would even kiss her after their luncheon dates. Leslie felt so thrilled but didn't dare let him know how she felt. She was sure that he would wind up rejecting her. (Yes, she also had **Pattern 1—Fear of Rejection**.) Finally, Jerry did break up with his girlfriend and began spending more time with Leslie. The passion between them increased dramatically, and they soon became lovers. Leslie felt deeply in love with Jerry.

A few months later, Jerry met a woman from Venezuela and fell head over heels in love with her. Several weeks later, he proposed to her, and they were married shortly thereafter. Leslie suffered tremendously when this happened and actually continued to sleep with Jerry, on occasion, when his wife was out of the country. She hadn't felt deserving of the relationship in the first place and was willing to take whatever she could get. Leslie finally decided to end their affair several months later. However, she continued to experience intense pain and suffering for a number of years, as a result of her relationship with Jerry.

A few words about Leslie's background will give further insight and understanding as to how this pattern developed. Leslie's mother was an extremely dominating woman who continually forced Leslie to engage in activities against her will, throughout Leslie's childhood. Leslie always had to do things according to her mother's agenda; there was no room to be herself or do what she really wanted to do.

Her mother would force Leslie to entertain certain people at her home with whom she had no desire to spend time. When Leslie wanted to spend time alone in her room and read or write poetry, her mother would insist that Leslie join her in the living room to watch television. Leslie learned to suppress herself completely and do whatever her mother wanted. As a result, the "love" she got from her mother felt deadly and destructive. But, since this was the only love Leslie ever knew, she decided (unconsciously, of course) that she must avoid love at all costs. This turned out to be a major factor in shaping her relationship experiences in life.

GLORIA'S FEAR OF DYING FROM LOVE

Gloria's mother always told her what to do, when to do it, and how she should be. She was so domineering and demanding that Gloria felt as if she had no choice but to comply with her mother's wishes. If she ever spoke out and expressed herself, Gloria was punished. In fact, her mother was always doling out punishment, at her whim. Understandably, Gloria did everything her mother told her. She learned to be the perfect little girl, hoping desperately to avoid punishment.

Often, her mother would deny Gloria permission to join her friends in fun activities. Instead, she would insist that Gloria do chores, such as fixing dinner, taking the clothes off the line, and cleaning the house—even though her mother stayed at home all day. She told her when to do her homework, what to eat, what to wear; Gloria had no opportunity to be herself or to do what she wanted.

The day Gloria graduated high school, her mother went into total shock when Gloria announced that she wasn't going to take any more crap from her mother (Gloria's expletives were much stronger, actually), and that she had better stay out of Gloria's life once and for all. Gloria had been such a perfect child that her mother couldn't believe the "Dr. Jekyll" and "Mr. Hyde" behavior she was witnessing in Gloria.

Because of the intense negativity with which she experienced her mother's "love," Gloria was afraid to get close to anyone. She would leave relationships at the drop of a hat—before there was any real possibility of experiencing love. She found the smallest excuses to leave; for example, she broke up with her first boyfriend because he didn't give her a birthday card.

Most of her relationships were extremely destructive and even life-threatening at times. Married four times, Gloria's relationships have all been hellacious. Her first husband would beat her regularly and threaten her with guns. She decided that killing herself was the only way out;

however, she was rushed to the emergency room in time to have her stomach pumped from the overdose of sleeping pills she took. After she divorced the man, he continued to stalk her and threaten her life, and she remembers sleeping on the floor of the closet in her new apartment, huddled in fear.

Her next husband, nice at first, became an alcoholic soon after they married and would beat her as well, smashing her head into the console of her car during his drunken binges. When she left him, she immediately married a large, burly, ex-professional boxer—to protect her from her second husband, who also continued to threaten her after the divorce.

In all of her relationships, Gloria felt that she couldn't be herself. If she spoke out and expressed herself, her partners would get mad at her. She would then simply shut down—just as she did as a child—and be the "good little girl," perfectly well-behaved, never saying anything to upset or anger anyone.

Inside, however, Gloria seethed with rage. Inevitably, that rage would cause major blow-ups in each of her relationships. Her relationship with her mother set the stage for tremendous unhappiness and self-sacrifice in her adult relationships, and Gloria needs to heal that hurt child within, in order to experience and enjoy intimacy in a loving relationship with a man.

HEALING YOUR "FEAR OF DYING FROM LOVE" PATTERN

Don't judge yourself for the feelings you have, no matter how intense they may be. Be willing to feel them deeply rather than deny them! This is an important part of the healing process. Most important, forgive yourself for believing that love destroys you. Then, work on integrating new beliefs about love that will allow you to experience the positive, uplifting, liberating aspects of love and to create success for yourself in loving relationships.

The belief that love is destructive is contradictory to the essential nature and truth of life and therefore will always produce an intense experience of inner conflict for you. This conflict will then be reflected in your outer reality—in the form of destructive relationships in which you can't win. Belief in the positive, healing qualities of love is vital in order to restore inner balance and harmony, and to give you the welcomed opportunity to create peace and satisfaction in all of your loving relationships.

Common Limiting Thought Pattern	New Thought Pattern to Integrate
Love destroys me. I am destroyed by love.	Love enlivens and uplifts me. Love supports me in feeling fully alive and well.
When I am loved, I am dead.	When I am loved, I am fully alive and vibrant with joy.
Love kills me.	Love uplifts me and supports my natural life force. Love leads to an ever-increasing aliveness and vitality in me.
The men/women I love, want me dead.	The men/women I love support me in feeling fully alive and joyful.
Love is deadly.	Love is safe. Love is healing.
Love brings destruction. Love causes my downfall.	Love always improves my life. Love always uplifts me and brings me greater success in my life.
The people I love run my life. I need others to survive. I can't do anything on my own.	The people I love allow me to be in charge of my own life. I can survive on my own. I can easily make it in life on my own.

See also Pattern 3—Fear of Hurting or Being Hurt, Pattern 7—Fear of Love, Pattern 12—Fear of Being Dominated, and Pattern 19—Belief in Separation from Love.

6

Healing the Relationship with Your Parents

You have learned, as you read through the various subconscious patterns, that most relationship difficulties originate in early childhood. Your experience with your parents (or caregivers) when you were young determines much of your behavior in relationships as an adult. Consequently, it is a good idea to focus specifically on healing your relationship with your parents.

Any feelings of anger or resentment against your parents that are not cleared from your mind and body will continue to haunt you in your relationships. You will attract partners who tend to exhibit attitudes or behaviors similar to those of your parents—particularly the ones that caused you the most difficulty as a child. In other words, at some point, your current relationships will activate your negative subconscious programming that stems from your early relationship with your parents. In this way, you have an opportunity to heal yourself of your old subconscious "baggage." By re-creating the old scenario in your present situation, you are giving yourself another chance to deal with issues that remain incomplete, in terms of the learning and development that you require in your life.

You are here to learn, grow, and experience the loving Being that you are. Ultimately, you must learn that harboring negativity for *anything* from the past doesn't work. Holding onto old anger and resentment only blocks your own mental, emotional, and physical capabilities and prevents you from moving forward in life with maximum ease and comfort. Clearing the negativity from your past is essential to being able to enjoy your life fully—here and now.

Therefore, it is important to heal your subconscious negativity at its source—with your parents. Work on forgiving your parents for any "wrongdoing" you may have perceived on their behalf. Let go of believing that your present partner or circumstances are to blame for your negative feelings.

No one is actually to blame. Acknowledge that *your subconscious programming* causes you to experience life in the way you do. Then, be willing to forgive your parents for the role they played in creating that programming. They did the best they could with what they knew at the time. If they could have done it better or differently, they would have. The past is over. Now it's time to choose how *you* want to experience life—regardless of your past!

In this section, the specific intention is to forgive your parents for anything they might have done which now causes you to respond to life in negative ways. It is designed to help release feelings that you might have suppressed when you were young, which have not yet been cleared from your mind and body. Many new, positive thought patterns—affirmations—are presented here that you can work with to help you in this endeavor.

Of course, you will want to use the new affirmations technology (the "A.S.C." Technique) to facilitate the deepest level of healing and clearing possible. However, you may also want to spend additional time with each affirmation—reading, writing, and speaking it aloud, allowing yourself to really *feel* your response to it. This will help you bring many old emotions up and out of suppression and ultimately free you to feel greater happiness and joy within.

This is truly an invaluable and life-altering process, so take as much time as you need.[1] Remember, your goal is to truly believe each new thought pattern with your entire being, and to know that it is true for

---

1. There is another method, "The Rapid Integration Technique" **Prince Charming Lives!**, Chap. 9 that you may want to use, to help you release suppressed emotions from your body. In fact, all of Chapter 9, "Healing Yourself" may be useful to you in this regard.

you. This can only happen as you spend time with each one and focus carefully during the process. Keep breathing as you work with the different positive beliefs. Breathing helps you to let go of any negative feelings that may surface as you integrate the new ideas more deeply.

Don't judge yourself for any negativity that you feel as you work with these affirmations. Many feelings will surface in order to be cleared. This is a natural part of the integration process. Allowing yourself to feel whatever emotions surface (anger, unhappiness, resentment, etc.) will ultimately transform the negativity into positive feelings of love and acceptance. Understand that it is sometimes necessary to move through and experience the negative in order to reach the positive.

Healing your relationship with your parents is an ongoing process that requires patience and persistence. It is seldom an "overnight" process (i.e., reading this section once and never thinking about it again will not suffice!). However, all work that you do in this area will be rewarded, and you will definitely experience your relationships improving with time.

How will you know when you are "complete" with this healing process? When you can think of your parents and experience feelings of love, warmth, appreciation, understanding, and acceptance. If reading through the positive beliefs in this section or thinking about your parents causes you to feel uncomfortable, angry, upset, sad, or apathetic in any way, you are still "in process." Don't fret, though. It will take a lot less time to *release* your negative programming than it took to create and reinforce it!

NEW THOUGHT PATTERNS TO INTEGRATE:[2]

These affirmations were designed to cover all possible variations of your issues with your parents. Some may be more relevant to your situation than others. Some may be harder to accept as true than others. Simply do the best you can and be diligent in your efforts to make peace with your parents.

---

2. Some of the "New Thought Patterns" may not be appropriate for men as written. These are marked with an asterisk (*), and a revised version is listed separately and designated: "Specifically for Men." In fact, any time the gender in a particular affirmation is not appropriate in your circumstance, feel free to change it.

The first step in the healing process is to forgive the past. Forgiveness releases the hurt and negativity stored within you, and opens your heart to more love. It is important to understand this. You are not condoning your parents' actions; nor, are you inviting them to do whatever they did to you again. You are simply willing to open your heart, experience greater compassion for them, and let go of the negativity you've been harboring. This allows *you* to feel better and experience more love and compassion in all of your relationships.

The problems you experience in your current relationships will generally reflect your relationship with the parent with whom you had the most difficulty. Although typically a woman will attract a man who resembles her father, and vice-versa for a man, other variations are possible. If you are a woman and had a critical mother, you may attract a man who criticizes you in the same fashion.

Therefore, feel free to modify the new thought patterns in any way you like, in order to best apply them to your particular situation. For example, in this section, the new thought patterns appears: *"I'm now able to get close to women, whether I was able to get close to my mother or not."* If you are a woman, this will help you to feel closer to other women. However, to best support your relationships with men, you may also want to change it to: *"I'm now able to get closer to men, whether I was able to get close to my mother or not."* Feel free to modify the new thought patterns in whatever way will best serve your needs.

MOTHER

I forgive my mother for not loving me.
I forgive myself for thinking that my mother didn't love me.
I forgive myself for thinking that I am unlovable because of my early
    experiences with my mother.
I forgive myself for not being able to perceive that my mother loved me
    in the best way she knew how.
I forgive my mother for not having been able to love me in a way that
    felt good to me.

> *"Nothing is as important as what goes on in your family, absolutely nothing... that's where the real search has to begin. My (recent knee) injury was the catalyst for my looking at my whole life and realizing that I could think I had all the answers in the world, but nothing (gave me answers like) working out my problems with my parents."*
>
> Shirley MacLaine, Oprah Winfrey Show, October, 1991

I am now willing to experience how lovable I really am, no matter what my mother thought of me.

I am now willing to love myself completely; I deserve to be loved.

I am now willing to give myself the love that I never felt from my mother.

The more I love myself, the more women love me.

I am now willing to love myself, whether my mother was able to love herself or not.

I forgive my mother for rejecting me.

I forgive myself for thinking that my mother rejected me.

I forgive my mother for disapproving of me when I was young.

I forgive my mother for being displeased with me.

I forgive myself for thinking that I am displeasing to women because of my experience with my mother when I was young.

I forgive myself for thinking that I am a bad person because of how my mother treated me when I was young.

I forgive my mother for making me think that I am a bad person.

> *"Children begin by loving their parents. After a time, they judge them. Rarely, if ever, do they forgive them."*
>
> Oscar Wilde, Anglo-Irish playwright, 1891

> *"When I was away from home and missing my children, I asked myself why I didn't show my approval and enjoyment of them more when I was with them, when it would do them—and me—a lot of good. But I don't think I was ever able to take my own advice. The psychological explanation for this is that we crabby perfectionists were started in that direction in our own childhood by the frequent criticism of our parents; it is very difficult to overcome the compulsion to repeat what was done to us."*
>
> Benjamin Spock, U.S. pediatrician and author, 1981

I now experience women loving me.

I'm now able to get close to women, whether I was able to get close to my mother or not.

I now experience being naturally pleasing to women the way I am.

I now love and accept myself, whether my mother does or not.

I now know that I am okay just the way I am, no matter what my mother thinks.

I am now willing to see the loving intention underlying my mother's thoughts and actions toward me.

I am my own authority, and I now choose to feel good about myself, regardless of my mother's attitude toward me.

I now experience that women love and accept me just the way I am.

I am innocent for being who I am.

I am lovable and acceptable to women the way I am.

I now create loving, harmonious relationships with women who love me, accept me, and support me in being who I am.

> *"One of the most highly valued functions of used parents these days is to be the villains of their children's lives, the people the child blames for any shortcomings or disappointments. But if your identity comes from your parents' failings, then you remain forever a member of the child generation, stuck and unable to move on to an adulthood in which you identify yourself in terms of what you do, not what has been done to you."*
>
> Frank Pittman, U.S. psychiatrist and family therapist, 1994

I forgive my mother for suffocating me.
I forgive my mother for dominating me.
I forgive my mother for intimidating me.
I forgive my mother for not understanding me.
I forgive my mother for not being there for me when I needed her.
I forgive my mother for hurting me with her love.

I forgive myself for feeling hurt in my relationships with women because of my early experience with my mother.

I forgive myself for thinking that I am obligated to please women because of my early experience with my mother.

"Never marry a man who hates his mother because he'll end up hating you."
Jill Bennett, English actress

I forgive my mother for making me do whatever she wanted.
I forgive myself for thinking that I have to sacrifice myself in order to please women because of my early experience with my mother.
I forgive myself for thinking that I can't be free in my relationships with women because of my early experience with my mother.

I'm now ready to create a new experience of my relationships with women.
I am now loved by a woman in a way that enhances my aliveness and well-being.
I now have love in my life that satisfies and uplifts me.
It's safe to let love into my life.
A woman's love always has a positive, uplifting influence on my life.
I no longer have to sacrifice myself to please women.
I now attract women who support me in having my needs met in relationships.
I now create loving relationships in which my partner and I both feel that we are winning and getting our needs met.

I now allow myself to experience the safety, joy, and intimacy of loving
   relationships, while allowing myself the freedom to be who I am.
Women love me in a way that feels good to me.
I now create mutually supportive relationships with women, in which I
   am free to be who I am.

> *"My mother had a great deal of trouble with me, but I think she enjoyed it."*
> Mark Twain (1835-1910)

I forgive myself for thinking that I was a bother to my mother.
I forgive myself for thinking that my love pushed my mother away.
I forgive myself for thinking that my love is bad.

I no longer push people away with my love.
My love is healing.
My love is welcomed.
Women are attracted to my love and enjoy my presence.

I forgive my mother for wanting me to be something I was not.
I forgive my mother for wanting me to live up to her expectations.
I forgive myself for thinking that I had to live up to my mother's
   expectations.
I forgive my mother for making me think that I am not good enough.
I forgive myself for thinking that I'm not good enough because of my
   early experience with my mother.

> *"Being a good parent is a tough job. I believe it is the hardest job any of
> us will ever do. My mom tells how painful it was for her to put us through
> schedule feeding, but she did it because the 'experts' recommended it. It
> was also painful for her when she went against the experts' advice and
> sneaked in to comfort me when I was crying."*
> John Bradshaw, *Homecoming*

It's safe to be who I am.
I now love and accept myself for who I am.
I am okay the way I am, whether I live up to my mother's expectations or not.
I now accept myself as good enough, no matter what my mother thinks.
I forgive my mother for not realizing how valuable I really am.
I now attract women who perceive my worth and enjoy my presence.
I am successful in my own way. My way is good enough.
Women now accept me and enjoy me the way I am.

I forgive my mother for hating me.
I forgive myself for thinking my mother hated me.
I now accept that I am lovable.
I now accept that women love me.
I forgive my mother for not perceiving how lovable I really am.

"The children despise their parents until the age of 40, when they suddenly become just like them—thus preserving the system."

Quentin Crewe, British author, 1962

I forgive my mother for making me think that my body is bad or dirty.
I forgive my mother for making me think that sex is bad or dirty.
I forgive my mother for making me feel guilty about my sexual desires.
I forgive myself for feeling guilty about sex because of what I learned from my mother when I was young.
I forgive myself for not allowing myself to enjoy my sexuality because of what my mother taught me when I was young.

It's now safe to be my own authority in the area of sexuality.
It's now safe for me to enjoy my body and experience sexual pleasure.
I am innocent for my sexual desires.
I am free to be who I am and express my sexuality, no matter what my mother thinks.
I deserve love and sexual pleasure in my life.

I am free to be who I am and express my sexuality, whether my mother was able to do this or not.

I forgive my mother for not showing me how to have successful, loving relationships with men.*
I can now have successful, loving relationships with men, whether my mother was able to do this or not.*

I forgive myself for blaming my mother for making me be alive.
I release all blame toward my mother for my being here.
I take responsibility for my own life.

> *Remember, children are unformed, emotionally unstable, ignorant creatures. To make them feel secure, you must continually remind them of the things which you are denying yourself on their account, especially when others are present. Fail to master this technique and you hasten the black day you discover your children can get along without you.*
>
> Dan Greenburg, *How to Be a Jewish Mother*

I accept that I am here.
I now choose to be here.
I now choose to be fully alive.
I am grateful for the opportunity to be alive.
I am grateful to my mother for all the ways in which she supported my growth and learning.
I appreciate my mother for taking care of me in the best way she could.
I thank my mother for giving me life.

I forgive my mother for everything she did, consciously or unconsciously, that hurt me or my family.

> *"Every word, facial expression, gesture, or action on the part of a parent gives the child some message about self-worth. It is sad that so many parents don't realize what messages they are sending."*
>
> Virginia Satir, U.S. family therapist and author, 1987

FATHER

I forgive my father for not loving me.
I forgive myself for thinking that my father didn't love me.
I forgive myself for thinking that I am unlovable because of my early experience with my father.
I forgive myself for not being able to perceive that my father loved me in the best way he knew how.
I forgive my father for not having been able to love me in a way that nurtured me.

I am now willing to experience how lovable I really am, no matter what my father thought of me.
I am now willing to love myself completely, because I deserve to be loved.
I am now willing to give myself the love that I never felt from my father.
The more I love myself, the more my relationships with men improve.*

I forgive my father for rejecting me.
I forgive myself for thinking that my father rejected me.
I forgive my father for disapproving of me when I was young.
I forgive my father for being displeased with me.
I forgive myself for thinking that I am displeasing to men because of my experience with my father when I was young.
I forgive myself for thinking that I am a bad person because of how my father treated me when I was young.

> *Most parents have not been able to fulfill their responsibilities as success-fully as they would have wished. In general, parents have been confused about their roles and responsibilities. They haven't had any clear models or guidelines... there are very few resources for educating oneself about how to be a parent... So (most parents have) made plenty of mistakes.*
> Shakti Gawain, *Living In the Light*

I forgive my father for making me think that I am a bad person.
I forgive my father for not loving me because I was a girl.*

I now experience men loving me.*
I now experience men approving of me.
I now experience being naturally pleasing to men the way I am.*
I now love and accept myself, whether my father does or not.
I am okay just the way I am, no matter what my father thinks.
I am willing to see the loving intention underlying my father's thoughts
    and actions toward me.
I am my own authority, and I now choose to feel good about myself,
    regardless of my father's attitude toward me.
I now experience that men love and accept me just the way I am.*
I am innocent for being who I am.
I am lovable and acceptable to men the way I am.*
I now create loving, harmonious relationships with men who love me,
    accept me, and support me in being who I am.*
I now forgive myself for not being able to get close to men because of
    my early experience with my father.

I forgive my father for dominating me.
I forgive my father for intimidating me.
I forgive myself for fearing my father's power.
I forgive my father for not understanding me.
I forgive my father for not being there for me when I needed him.
I forgive my father for hurting me with his love.
I forgive myself for feeling hurt or judged in my relationships with men
    because of my early experience with my father.
I forgive myself for thinking that men have to dominate me in
    relationships because of my early experience with my father.*
I forgive myself for thinking that men are smarter or better than I am
    because of the way my father treated me when I was young.*
I forgive myself for thinking that men are more powerful than I am
    because of my early experience with my father.*
I forgive myself for thinking that I am obligated to please men because
    of my early experience with my father.*
I forgive my father for making me do whatever he wanted.

I forgive myself for thinking that I have to sacrifice myself in order to please men because of my early experience with my father.

> *To make peace with your parents, you may have to give up alot. You may have to give up your resentments, your anger, your annoyance, your desire to punish and your need to blame. Be prepared even for times when it appears that they win and you lose. You may have to learn to admire and respect a parent for whom you may now feel a degree of contempt or hate. Indeed, you may need to learn to accept your parents exactly the way they are rather than the way you think they should be.*
>
> Harold H. Bloomfield, M.D., *Making Peace With Your Parents*

I forgive myself for thinking that I can't be free in my relationships with men because of my early experience with my father.
I forgive myself for thinking that I can't be myself in my relationships with men because of my early experience with my father.

I now create a new experience of my relationships with men.
I now feel loved by a man in a way that enhances my aliveness and well-being.*
It's now safe to let love into my life.
I now have love in my life that satisfies and uplifts me.
A man's love always has a positive, uplifting influence on my life.*
I now create balanced, harmonious relationships with men that support me in being powerful.*
Men respect me and support me in being powerful and capable.*
I no longer have to sacrifice myself to please men.*
I now attract men who support me in having my needs met in relationships.*
I now create loving relationships in which my partner and I both feel that we are winning and getting our needs met.
I now allow myself to experience the safety, joy, and intimacy of loving relationships, while allowing myself the freedom to be who I am.
Men love me in a way that feels good to me.*
I now create mutually supportive relationships with men, in which I am free to be who I am.

I forgive myself for thinking that I was a bother to my father.
I forgive myself for thinking that my love pushed my father away.
I forgive myself for thinking that my love is bad.

I no longer push people away with my love.
My love is healing.
My love is welcomed.
Men are attracted to my love and enjoy my presence. *

I forgive my father for wanting me to be something I was not.
I forgive my father for wanting me to live up to his expectations.
I forgive myself for thinking that I had to live up to my father's
   expectations.
I forgive my father for making me think I am not good enough.
I forgive myself for thinking that I'm not good enough because of my
   early experience with my father.

---

*"When I was kidnapped, my parents snapped into action. They rented out
my room."*

Woody Allen

It's safe to be who I am.
I now love and accept myself for who I am.
I am okay the way I am, whether I live up to my father's expectations or
   not.
I now accept myself as good enough, no matter what my father thinks.
I forgive my father for not realizing how valuable I really am.
I now attract men who perceive my worth and enjoy my presence. *
I am successful in my own way. My way is good enough.
Men now accept me and enjoy me the way I am. *

I forgive my father for hating me.
I forgive myself for thinking that my father hated me.
I now accept that I am lovable.
I now accept that men love me. *
I forgive my father for not perceiving how lovable I really am.

I release all blame toward my father for who I am.

I take responsibility for my own life.

I now choose to be who I am.

I accept who I am.

I am grateful to my father for all the ways in which he supported my growth and learning.

I appreciate my father for taking care of me in the best way he could.

I forgive my father for everything he did, consciously or unconsciously, that hurt me or my family.

*SPECIFICALLY FOR MEN:

I forgive myself for thinking that other men are smarter or better than I am because of the way my father treated me when I was young.

I forgive myself for thinking that other men are more powerful than I am because of my early experience with my father.

I forgive myself for thinking that I can't get close to men because of my early experience with my father.

I forgive myself for thinking that men don't understand me and don't care about my feelings because of what I learned in my relationship with my father.

I forgive myself for thinking that I am obligated to do what other men tell me because of my early experience with my father.

I forgive myself for thinking that I can't be myself around other men because of my early experience with my father.

"Personality characteristics and traits begin forming in utero. The fetus can see, hear, experience, taste, and, on a primitive level, even learn and feel. What the fetal child feels and perceives begins shaping his attitudes and expectations about himself. Deep persistent negative emotional patterns can leave a deep scar on an unborn child's personality. On the other hand, life-enhancing emotions, such as joy and elation, can contribute significantly to the emotional development of a healthy child. How a father feels about his wife and unborn child is also of primary importance."

Thomas Verny, M.D., *Secret Life of the Unborn Child*

I now experience men liking me, whether my father seemed to like me or not.

I now experience men approving of me the way I am, whether my father approved of me or not.

It's safe to experience a closeness and friendship with men, whether I had that with my father or not.

It's safe to experience men appreciating me, whether my father appreciated me or not.

I now experience other men accepting me just the way I am.

It's safe to create harmonious, supportive relationships with other men, whether I had that with my father or not.

Other men always have a positive, uplifting influence on me.

Other men support me in being who I am and enjoy my presence.

I forgive my father for not teaching me how to be a man.

I forgive my father for not teaching me how to protect myself.

I forgive my father for not teaching me how to love a woman.

I forgive my father for not living up to my expectations of him.

"I knew I was an unwanted baby when I saw that my bath toys were a toaster and a radio."

Joan Rivers

It's safe to be in touch with my feelings, whether my father was able to do that or not.

I can now share my feelings with others, whether my father was able to do that or not.

It's safe to be who I am, whether my father allowed himself to do that or not.

It's safe to be close to women, whether my father was able to do that or not.

I now create happy, successful, lasting, loving relationships with women, whether my father was able to do that or not.

I no longer need to fail in order to prove my father right.
I no longer need to fail in order to be like my father.
I no longer need to compete with my father.
I no longer need to stifle my success to prevent surpassing my father.

I'm okay whether I succeed or fail.
It's safe to love myself whether I create success or failure.
I now take responsibility for my life, and I'm willing to create success for
    myself.
I am now free to succeed in the way that is right for me.
It's safe for me to succeed in the field of my choice.
I can now be a success, whether my father was or not.

I can now succeed, with or without my father's approval.
I am the one who defines success or failure in my life.
I no longer need to measure up to my father's standard of success.
The more I am true to myself and do what I really want, the more
    successful I am.

HEALING YOUR PERSONAL ISSUES

In this section, you have an opportunity to heal the specific negative "programs" created as a result of your relationships with your mother and father. First, you need to list the specific characteristics, attitudes, or behaviors your parents exhibited that bothered you or for which you still feel angry, hurt, resentful, etc. These are the characteristics, attitudes, or behaviors, you will tend to experience in your present relationships— either in yourself or your partner—until you release the negative emotional energy surrounding the issues.

Then, for each item on your list, note, in the adjacent column, any similarities in your current or past relationships. Generally, the correlation is surprisingly high. This will help you see clearly how your early life experiences have influenced your adult relationships.

Finally, create your own affirmations of forgiveness, acceptance, and love, which will help you make peace with your past and clear any negativity that you still harbor. You may need additional paper for these exercises.

YOUR MOTHER

LIST:
Anything your mother said or did that bothered/bothers you or anything you didn't/don't like about her or her behavior

(Example: *My mother always criticized how I looked.*)

NOTE:
Any similarities to current or past partners

(Example: *My partners have always found fault with my physical appearance.*)

_____

_____

_____

_____

_____

_____

_____

_____

Create your own affirmations of forgiveness, acceptance, and love, related to your specific issues. For example:

I forgive my mother for *always criticizing how I looked.*

I love and accept my mother, even though she *made me feel bad about my physical appearance.*

Continue in this manner, on the next page, for each issue.

I forgive my mother for _____

_____ .

I love and accept my mother, even though she _____

_____ .

I forgive my mother for _____

_____ .

I love and accept my mother, even though she _____

_____ .

I forgive my mother for _____

_____ .

I love and accept my mother, even though she _____

_____ .

_____

_____

_____

_____

_____

_____

_____

YOUR FATHER

LIST:
Anything your father said or
did that bothered/bothers you
or anything you didn't/don't like
about him or his behavior

NOTE:
Any similarities to current or past
partners

(Example: *My father made me feel
stupid if I wanted to do something
any way other than the way he
suggested.*)

(Example: *My current partner
belittles me when I want to do
things my own way.*)

_____	_____
_____	_____
_____	_____
_____	_____
_____	_____
_____	_____
_____	_____

Create your own affirmations of forgiveness, acceptance, and love,
related to your specific issues. For example:

I forgive my father for *making me think I was stupid for wanting to do
things my own way.*

I love and accept my father, even though he *belittled me and made me
feel bad about myself.*

Continue in this manner, on the next page, for each issue.

I forgive my father for _____

_____ .

I love and accept my father, even though he _____

_____ .

I forgive my father for _____

_____ .

I love and accept my father, even though he _____

_____ .

I forgive my father for _____

_____ .

I love and accept my father, even though he _____

_____ .

_____

_____

_____

_____

_____

_____

HEALING YOUR PARTICULAR ISSUES WITH BOTH YOUR PARENTS

You tend to copy your parents' behavior toward each other (sometimes this happens unconsciously), and use them as role models for how you interact in your relationships. Here, it is good to look at and forgive them for what you didn't like or felt angry, upset, or hurt about in their relationship with each other. In making peace with what they created for themselves, you don't have to re-create their relationship in your life. You free yourself to create the relationship *you* want!

First, list specific ways in which they interacted with each other or specific attitudes or behaviors they exhibited toward each other that made you uncomfortable, unhappy, angry, etc. Second, note any similarities to ways in which your partners (current or past) have treated you or ways in which you have treated them. Then, create statements of forgiveness to help you release any negative feelings surrounding your particular issues. Finally, write positive affirmations stating what you wish to create for yourself.

LIST:
Any attitudes or behaviors your parents exhibited toward each other that bothered/bother you

(Example: *My father often treated my mother as if she were stupid and unimportant.*)

NOTE:
Any similarities to current or past partners

(Example: *Past partners often acted as if my opinions didn't matter and as if I didn't know what I was talking about.*)

_____

_____

_____

_____

_____

Create statements of forgiveness for each specific issue
(For example: *I forgive my father for not treating my mother with respect.*)

_____

_____

_____

_____

_____

_____

Here are some additional affirmations that may be relevant to your situation:

I forgive my mother for not loving my father (or vice-versa).

I forgive my father for hurting my mother (or vice-versa).

I forgive my mother for feeling victimized by my father (or vice-versa).

I forgive my father for not being there for my mother (or vice-versa).

I forgive my mother for belittling my father (or vice-versa).

I forgive myself for hating my parents for their unloving behaviors toward each other.

I forgive my parents for not showing me that they loved each other.

I forgive my parents for divorcing when I was young.

I forgive my parents for not being able to communicate effectively/honestly/lovingly with one another.

I forgive my parents for making me think that relationships had to be unhappy and full of struggle.

I forgive my parents for making me think that love is impossible.

_____

_____

_____

_____

_____

_____

_____

_____

_____

Then, write positive affirmations stating what you intend to create for yourself in *your* relationships. (Use verbs in the *present* tense in order to speak most effectively to the subconscious mind. For example: *I now create relationships in which my partner respects me for who I am.*

_____

_____

_____

_____

_____

_____

_____

_____

Here are some additional affirmations you may want to use:

I now create relationships in which love and harmony are always present.

I now experience clear and truthful communication with my partner.

I now create happy, loving relationships that are smooth and easy.

It's safe to maintain a lasting, loving relationship with my partner, whether my parents were able to do this or not.

_____

_____

_____

_____

_____

_____

_____

_____

_____

_____

_____

_____

_____

7

Additional Healing Techniques

Here are a few visualization techniques that will help you to transform your negative beliefs, attitudes, and feelings into positive ones. These can be used in conjunction with the "A.S.C." (Advanced Subconscious Clearing) Technique described in Chapter 4, to achieve a deep level of healing and transformation.

The A.S.C. Technique helps you to effectively clear your subconscious programming, the "old baggage" you carry that continually causes you to experience negativity in your life. The visualization techniques described in this chapter will help you to consciously create the new reality you want to experience. Using both techniques will greatly empower you to release the old unconscious roadblocks to healthy relationships and create new relationships based on mutual love, trust, respect, and support. In other words, you may want to practice the following exercises in order to accelerate the progress you make using the A.S.C. Technique.

The following exercises are designed to move a new positive energy through your mind, body, and chakra system in a way that will energize and support you in transforming your old negativity. Do them to the best of your ability and don't worry whether you are doing them "right" or not. These techniques will work for you, out of your intention to heal and transform your negative patterns. Simply trust the process, and you will get the most from each exercise as you do it.

Some people are better at "visualization" exercises than others. Some people merely "sense" or "feel" something happening, rather than perceive actual visual images. That's perfectly normal. Whatever takes place as you practice these techniques is right for you. Simply trust that whatever happens is the *most healing thing possible* for you to experience at the time. In other words, do the best you can with each exercise, and trust that you are getting the help and healing you need.

You may first want to read through each technique in its entirety. Then, once you understand the process, do the technique on your own, with your eyes closed. Or, for some of the techniques, you may want to have someone else read the steps to you slowly, talking you through it as you go. Another possibility is to make a recording in your own voice of a particular technique, talking yourself through each step slowly. Simply choose whichever option works best for you for each of the different techniques, and practice them in a way that is most comfortable for you.

First, you will read a description of what each technique entails. Then, the actual step-by-step process is presented, allowing someone to read it to you, or for you to record the steps for yourself. This second part may sound a little corny or repetitive at times when you read through it because the steps are designed to support you in an "eyes-closed" process. The brain operates in a different mode when you close your eyes and listen to instructions given to you, one step at a time.

Some of the techniques may seem easier for you than others. Some may seem to work better for you. Pick and choose the ones that are the most comfortable or seem to work the best. You can even experiment with combining them in any way that suits you.

You are the creator of your life and these are additional tools designed to help you accomplish your goal of re-thinking and re-creating your life. Use whichever ones support you the most to this end. And by all means, do your best to enjoy the process.

You may want to adopt a willingness to "suspend disbelief" as you work with the different techniques. Some of the concepts presented may seem a little foreign or even far-fetched to you. However, do your best to put aside any skepticism or doubt which could hamper your success here. There is a reason why each technique is designed the way it is, so although you may not be able to see or understand exactly how it works, it is important for you to trust the process as you go along.

Remember: *"By your faith ye are healed; and, by your skepticism ye are kept from being healed."* Do your best to trust the results you get as you do the different techniques. Know that the more you practice them, the easier it will be to overcome the old doubt and skepticism that may creep in along the way. You are the master of your life, and the more you say "yes" to faith and "no" to skepticism, the more you will experience your true power to manifest the life you want.

Practice each exercise in a relaxed sitting position. Lying down often sends a signal to the body that you are preparing to fall asleep, so sitting comfortably is preferable to lying down. Since the goal here is to become more powerful and more aware, the techniques work better if you stay awake while practicing them.

You may want to start each technique by closing your eyes and relaxing for a minute or two. Taking a few deep breaths helps. Breathing easily and continuously rather than "holding" or controlling your breath will allow you to settle into your body and relax your mind. Practicing the techniques from this place of greater relaxation and peace at the outset will enhance your success with them.

CREATE A POSITIVE INNER MOVIE

With this technique, you will be visualizing or imagining that your new positive belief (under "New Thought Pattern to Integrate"[1]) is true for you. You will be creating an inner "movie," a scenario in your mind's eye of what your life would be like if, indeed, your new affirmation were totally true for you.

For example, if your new thought pattern is: "Relationships now energize and enliven me," you will create a scene in your mind where you see and feel this to be true. You will be instructed to see yourself with a relationship partner. It can be a current or even past partner, or you can

---

1. You can also use any of the affirmations you created in the previous chapter, "Healing the Relationship with Your Parents," but you may have to modify the instructions slightly to fit your circumstances.

simply imagine someone new who represents a relationship partner to you.

The key is to be able to imagine a scene with only positive thoughts and feelings. You wouldn't want to put your current relationship partner in the scene if that would create any negativity or discomfort within you. What you're doing here is letting yourself know that you can have a relationship that energizes and enlivens you. You are imagining the possibilities that life holds in store for you, even though they are not yet realized.

This technique is valuable because it helps you begin believing a *new* reality where life is different from how it has always been for you. By first creating an inner experience of your new reality, you are paving the way for it to happen in real life—in the third-dimensional world. By imagining that the new life you want to create is *already* a part of your experience, you are building the beliefs necessary within yourself to then create such a reality in your outer circumstances.

First, you must believe it from within. Then you will perceive it in your outer world. The more you can see it and experience it within yourself, the more you will come to believe that it can happen for you, and the more you will attract it in your life. Persistence is the key.

The more you practice this technique, the easier it will become for you. Remember, you may encounter doubts or skepticism at first. This is natural. Refrain from criticizing yourself for not doing it better. Simply do your best, be persistent, and you will see your life begin to change in wondrous and magical ways.

STEP-BY-STEP PROCESS:

Pick the affirmation you want to work with. Close your eyes and imagine how your life would be if this new belief were true for you. Simply pretend or imagine that this new belief *is* true for you and see a scenario in your mind's eye which portrays you experiencing this.

Imagine whatever scenario would best portray your new thought pattern coming to pass. Create an "inner movie" of how you want life to be, how you want to feel, and how you want others to treat you. Imagine what your life would be like—how it would actually look and feel—if your new belief were absolutely true for you.

See your wonderful relationship partner there with you. See yourselves having a joyful time, loving being in each other's company. Imagine that the relationship is giving you all that you need and want. Visualize your life as you would like it to be, with your beautiful relationship partner.

Get in touch with the wondrous feelings that arise, as delightful images of your new life float through your mind. Use as many senses as you can—hearing, seeing, touching, tasting, feeling, smelling—as you create your "inner movie" of how you want your life to be. The more you engage your senses, the more concrete your vision will become.

What sounds do you hear as you experience your new reality? What is your partner saying to you? How does it feel to have your partner by your side? Imagine what wonderful smells there are as you continue to picture your experience of how you want your life to be. What colors do you see? What do you feel as you continue to experience your new positive world?

Continue imagining in this way for as long as you want. Continue to see yourself and your relationship partner enjoying yourselves immensely and having all that you want, being happy with yourselves and with each other. Imagine that you are filled with love and joy as you continue to picture what your life would be like if your new affirmation were totally true for you. Continue for as short or as long a time as you like.

When you feel comfortable, bring your awareness back to the room you are in. You may want to rub your hands or feet together and stretch a little, just to help you get back into your body and present time. Then, when you are ready, slowly open your eyes.

THE "GOLDEN LIGHT" TECHNIQUE

With this technique, you will be creating in your mind's eye a beautiful ball of golden light that represents a powerful healing force, and bringing this light through you, from head to toe, in order to transform old negative thoughts and feelings stored within you.

Although this is an inner imaginary experience, there will be a corresponding shift in your real world as well, and you may experience feeling lighter in your mind, body and emotions once you have completed the technique. Again, the more feeling you put into it, the more you will get out of it.

Trust that what you imagine is real. Put your skepticism aside and let yourself be open and aware as you follow the instructions.

STEP-BY-STEP PROCESS

Imagine a beautiful golden ball of light just above the top of your head. This beautiful golden light represents a powerful healing force that will help transform old negative thoughts and feelings in your mind, body, and heart. Soon you will be bringing this light in you, and through you, allowing it to wash away old hurts, sorrows, and fears—any old negative energies that may be lurking inside you.

Remind yourself of the new thought pattern, the new affirmation you want to integrate. Take your new belief, for instance, "I can easily accept love," and fill that golden ball of light with the energy of being able to easily accept love, or whatever your new positive belief is. Keep filling that golden ball of light with the positive and uplifting thoughts and feelings that your new belief stirs within you.

What would it feel like if that belief were totally true for you? Fill the golden ball with those feelings. Fill it with your new belief, more and more. See the golden light glow stronger and brighter. Keep filling it more and more with the thoughts and feelings of your new belief. Once that golden ball above your head is glowing brightly and powerfully radiating the energy of your new belief, start to move it downward, filling and surrounding your crown chakra, the spiritual center at the top of the head.

As it fills and surrounds the crown chakra, allow it to cleanse and release any negativity stored there, in any old parts of you that have doubted this new belief to be true. Allow this golden light to fill and surround your head, releasing any resistance you might have to this new belief being true for you. Allow this beautiful, radiant, glowing ball of golden light to stay in and around your head as long as you want, until you feel ready to move on to the rest of the body. You may want to keep it there for a minute or two, until it has cleansed and enlivened the whole area in and around your head.

Then, when you are ready, let this beautiful, radiant, glowing ball of golden light, filled with the positive energy of your new belief, continue to move down your body, filling and surrounding it with its healing energy, releasing all negativity and resistance to your new belief, until it settles in and around the chakra in your throat area. This is your will center. Allow this beautiful ball of golden light to transform your ability to live your new belief, to express it and make it a part of who you are.

Feel the positive feelings you have, as your new belief, stored within the ball of golden light, fills your throat area. "This is who I am," think to yourself. "I am this." Let the golden light stay there for a minute or two, or until you feel comfortable, healing and cleansing any old fears or negativity stored there.

Then, when you are ready, continue bringing that beautiful golden ball of light down through and around your body, having it cleanse and release any negative parts of you that are contrary to the positive energy the ball of light is holding. As the ball of light moves through you, feel it making you lighter, freer, more in touch with the real love and joy within you.

Next, allow the beautiful, glowing ball of golden light, filled with the positive energy of your new belief, to move into and around the heart chakra area, located in the center of the chest. How wonderful and expanded you feel having this golden ball of light fill and surround your chest and heart. "I feel good." "I love who I am," you may want to think to yourself and remind yourself of your new belief.

Feel the golden light within your chest radiating the powerful energy of your new belief through you. Life is good. How wonderful it feels to be alive. Allow whatever feelings, images, or thoughts you have to surface. Trust that whatever you experience is okay and an important part of the healing process.

Let the golden light rest within your chest area for a minute or two, or as long as you wish, and then let it continue to move through your body, releasing and cleansing all negative thoughts and feelings that are contrary to your new belief. Feel the power and the beauty of the golden light melting all negativity and doubt within you, allowing your new belief to take hold and flourish within you.

Now, allow the beautiful ball of golden light, so alive and brimming with the positive energy of your new belief, settle just below your breast bone area into the solar plexus, filling and surrounding that area with the positive, loving energy of your new belief. Feel negativity dissolving within you as more and more old parts of you surrender to your new belief, taking it in, making it a part of who you now are.

Remind yourself of your new belief. See and feel the ball of golden light radiating brightly with the energy of your new belief. Feel how good the golden light feels, filling and surrounding your solar plexus area, just below the breast bone. Allow the light to stay there, radiating peace, harmony, and joy, for a minute or two, or as long as you wish.

When you are ready, allow this beautiful, glowing ball of golden light, filled with the positive energy of your new belief, to continue moving through your body—healing, cleansing, and releasing negativity, as it travels through and around your torso, finally coming to rest within and around you, just below your navel in the second chakra. Continue seeing and feeling this glowing, radiant, beautiful golden light—filling you with its positive, healing energy, allowing you to feel calm, peaceful, yet energized and alive. Allow this beautiful, radiant ball of golden light to remain within you, just below your navel—within and around your second chakra—cleansing and releasing all negative parts of you that are not in harmony with your new belief, for at least a minute or two, or as long as you wish. You feel strong, powerful, and very alive. Feel how good you feel as the golden light fills you with the positive radiant energy of your new belief. When you are ready, continue allowing that beautiful, radiant, glowing ball of golden light, that contains the powerful energy of your new belief, to move down and through your body, cleansing and releasing all negativity that comes into contact with it, bringing a new sense of peace and well-being to every cell, every part of you.

Now allow that beautiful, powerfully glowing, radiant ball of golden light to move through and around your body, settling in the tail bone area where the first chakra is located. Feel the powerful energy of your new belief radiating from this beautiful golden light. Allow this new energy to fill you and fill the tailbone area, cleansing and releasing any old fears or doubts or negativity stored there that would keep you from truly owning and accepting your new belief into your life.

"It's okay to change," you may want to tell yourself. "It's safe to change." Continue to feel the powerful healing presence of that golden light within and around your tailbone, the first chakra area, for a minute or two, cleansing and releasing all old parts of you that have resisted or denied yourself love or happiness in any way. And when you feel complete, you will be moving that beautiful, radiant ball of golden light slowly through the rest of your body, at your own pace, healing and cleansing any old negativity it touches along the way. You may want to start with your hips and thighs.

Allow this beautiful ball of golden healing light to move slowly through and around your hips and thighs, slowly down and around your legs, through your knees, into your ankles, and finally your feet, cleansing and healing all old negative thoughts and feelings stored there that are contrary to your new positive belief.

Continue at whatever pace feels comfortable for you until that beautiful ball of golden light has passed through and around your entire body, healing and cleansing it as much as possible, making room for your new positive belief to take hold within you and to flourish in your life.

Once that radiant golden ball of healing light has finished passing through you completely, feel how your entire body—your entire Being—is alive and glowing with the positive energy of your new belief. Give thanks for the deep healing of your mind, body, and Spirit you have just received. And when you are ready, you can slowly open your eyes.

THE "GOING BACK IN TIME" TECHNIQUE

This process can be used to transform negative thought patterns in your subconscious to positive ones. You will tapping into the power of your mind and your creative abilities, in order to go back in time, *before* your negative patterns developed, and "re-wire" your subconscious, freeing you to believe something new and different about your life and relationships—here and now.

You will be going back in time, in your mind's eye, to the time when you first decided that the negative belief you wish to transform was true. It may be some time in this life, or it may be a very long time ago, in some distant past life. Based on my work with people, where I tap into their subconscious minds, the latter often seems to be true.

You will be going to this place by intention. That is, because it is your desire and your will to go there, you will simply go there. You need only trust the process and trust that you are capable of doing this.

Once you are there, at the moment you made the negative conclusion you did about yourself or relationships, you will be going back a little further in time, that is, turning the clock back a little further, as if you were rewinding the movie a few more frames, so that you will be in a time where this negative belief wasn't yet true for you. At that point, you will start reminding yourself of the new positive belief that you want to make a part of your reality.

You will tell yourself what you *do* want to believe, and fill yourself with the feelings and energy of this new belief. Then, you will visualize yourself being grounded to the Earth, and at the same time, connected to God (whatever your concept of God is), so that you will feel incredible power and support in experiencing the new positive thought pattern as true for you. This part of the technique adds energy to you and helps you to make your new belief as real as possible in your life.

In order to feel grounded or connected to the Earth, you will imagine three "cords," one coming from your tailbone and the other two coming from your ankle bones, going down deep into the Earth. Then you will imagine a "cord" coming out of your head, at the crown chakra, going heavenward, finding the "throne of God," however you envision this. Then, once you feel more powerfully connected to your new belief, you will move forward, through the time line, to the present, carrying the positive energy of your new belief with you.

Again, don't worry whether you are doing this "right" or not. Take whatever feelings or images come during this process and allow it to unfold in whatever way it does. This is an extremely powerful technique.

Simply follow the instructions and do it the best you can. Your best is good enough.

STEP-BY-STEP PROCESS

Pick the negative thought pattern you want to work on transforming. You will also need to remember what the opposite of that thought pattern is—the *positive* thought pattern you want to integrate, although this won't be used right away.

Close your eyes, and allow yourself to go back in time, way way back if necessary, to the time when you first started believing this negative pattern. Just go way back in time, to whenever it was, that you first made the decision to believe this negative thought pattern.

It doesn't matter where you are or how far back you have to go, but by intention, allow yourself to go to the first time when this negative belief became a part of your way of thinking. Be there now. And remember, you can do this just by your intention.

See, feel or sense where you are. You may get images; you may only get feelings or sensations. Or, you can simply trust that you are where you need to be, whether you have any particular experience or not.

Basically, allow yourself to feel the negative belief to be a part of your reality. This was the first time you decided that it was true for you. Experience, for a moment, how real that negative belief is for you. Again, whatever happens, whatever you see or feel while you do this is okay.

Now, run the scenario back a few frames, to a time shortly *before* this time, when you *didn't* believe that this negative thought was true for you. This can be a minute, an hour, a day, a week—any time you wish—but it will be a time *before* you decided that the negative belief was true for you. It is a moment of innocence, a time when life worked for you and you were open to things working out in your favor.

In this place of innocence and openness, begin to tell yourself what you WANT to believe. Remind yourself of your new positive thought pattern. Tell yourself of how you would like life to be. You are ready for life to be different for you. You are ready to experience life and relationships in a new way.

Here is where you make a *new* decision of how you want your life to be. Begin filling yourself with the positive feelings associated with your *new* belief—the opposite of your old negative thought pattern. See, feel, or sense, that you totally own, in every part of your being, this new positive belief, that it is truly a part of your world. Allow yourself to feel happy that this new positive belief is now a part of you. Keep reminding yourself of your new belief and what you want to create for yourself in your life.

Imagine a scenario of how your life could be, if this new positive belief were totally true for you. See or feel how good you feel, once you start believing that this new belief is true for you. Fill yourself with the positive energy of your new belief. Feel how good it feels to finally experience something different than you've been experiencing for so long.

Now that you are feeling full of the positive energy of your new belief, we will be adding to your power, to help make this new belief even more real for you. You will be grounding yourself fully to the Earth, to receive all of Earth's power and strength, and this will add to your own power and ability to make this new belief real in your life.

Imagine three cords, that is, three connector pieces, one going from your tail bone, and the other two going from your ankle bones, down through your feet. Imagine all three cords, leaving your body, from your tail bone and your ankle bones, twisting around each other to form one large solid cord, going down into the Earth, way way down, to the Earth's molten core, where you find an unusual thick and solid tree. Wrap your cords firmly around that tree. Take a deep breath and feel how solidly you are connected to the Earth and share Her power, strength, and stability.

Once you feel rooted to the Earth in this way, imagine a cord coming out of the top of your head, going way way up, into the heavens, as high as you possibly can go, until you reach the "throne of God." However you see or sense this is okay. Imagine this however you want. Let whatever images or sensations come into your mind as you do this. Whatever you see or experience is okay.

See the cord firmly attach itself to the throne of God, however you experience this, allowing the Love and Power of God to run through you, filling you with confidence and joy, and the knowing that your new belief is now a part of your reality. With the Love, Power, and Strength of both God and Mother Earth filling you and supporting you, you are now ready to transform yourself and experience positive changes in your life. You are ready to make your new positive belief real and a part of your life here and now.

Give thanks for your new power and connection to the Source of all Life. How expanded and positive you feel, as the Love, Power, and Wisdom of God fills you from head to toe, and how strong and secure you feel, with Mother Earth there for you totally, giving you strength, stability, and support.

Bathe in this powerful energy for a few more moments, this energy of knowing and feeling your new belief to be true for you, and then, continuing to keep your eyes closed, bring the positive energy of this experience back to the present time. Come back down the timeline, from wherever you are in the past, to the present moment, and bring with you this wonderful, powerful experience of fully owning and accepting your new belief as true for you.

Remind yourself again of your new positive belief and what you intend to create in your life. You are now free to experience your new belief as true in your life, here and now, on an ongoing basis. You are ready for life to be different for you. You are ready to love and accept yourself for who you are, in every moment of your life. You are ready to experience more love and harmony in your relationships than you have ever known before.

Continue to bathe in the warm and comforting feelings you have for as long as you want. And, whenever you feel ready, you can open your eyes.

8

The Journey Back Home, To Love

WHERE TO BEGIN

First, we must acknowledge that there is, indeed, a journey to be taken. We are not where we could be if we lived life according to our true spiritual potential, or even where we would like to be, as far as matters of the heart are concerned. Furthermore, there is a process that needs to take place within ourselves, in order for us to achieve our goals and experience the fulfillment we seek.

However, in undertaking this journey, be careful not to fall into the trap of making yourself wrong for being where you are. The truth is that you are innocent as you are. Refrain from judging yourself for not being more loving, caring, or somehow different from how you are. Forgive your past, for it is over. If you could have done it differently, you would have. You did whatever you thought was best at the time. Accept your past for what it was, and *now* choose new ways of participating in life and relationships.

Instead of judging yourself for past relationship experiences, simply acknowledge your need to improve how you relate to others, and be willing to do the work necessary to get yourself to where you want to be. The key is to love and accept yourself in the process.

To begin this journey, you must be willing to work on yourself. To work on yourself means to stay aware and notice what you think and feel. Notice how you respond to others. Be aware of how your energy flows when you communicate. Ask for feedback from others. Be open to learning about yourself, and welcome new ideas for doing things differently.

Notice if your ego wants to build walls of defense, in an attempt to prevent change. Remember, wanting to change does not mean that you are bad or wrong for being the way you are. It simply means that you have decided that there is a better, more loving way to do things than the way you've been doing them.

If your ego hollers at you to stay the way you are and makes you defensive about changing, make peace with that for now. Sometimes change needs to happen slowly, to help you feel more comfortable with the process. Remember, you are okay for being the way you are. However, you can continue to take steps toward making the deep changes within yourself that will allow you to experience more love, light, and joy in your everyday life. This is what the *real* you wants, at the deepest levels of your being.

In truth, every human on the planet needs to learn a better way of participating in life and relationships—if we truly want to make the world a safe and loving place in which to live. For those of you who have been bent on changing the world, be willing to change yourself first. All change must start from within. Only when each individual changes will we see change collectively, within society as a whole.

RELATIONSHIP AS MIRROR

Be willing to learn from what you see in those around you. What you see in others will always provide a big clue as to what you believe or feel about yourself. Relationships can be incredible teachers—if you're willing to learn from your experiences!

Notice where you judge others. Notice any negativity you experience in the presence of those around you. It is never an accident whom you attract to you at any given time. The people around you always reflect some part of you. That is why they are there in your life.

The people you attract will reflect parts of you that you love and adore, making those people lovable and adorable. Or, they will reflect parts of you with which you haven't yet made peace, making those people seem bothersome and irritating. The beauty is that you can always learn something about *yourself* by what you experience in your relationships with others, and, in doing so, come to a greater sense of self-love and self-acceptance.

You don't have to be perfect to have successful, loving relationships in your life. You must, however, be willing to learn and grow, as your relationships mirror back to you those aspects of yourself that need some work. And know that you are not bad for "needing work." The work is simply un-doing the years' (and even lifetimes') worth of erroneous programming, which blocks the flow of love and joy between people and keeps you from being who you are. In actuality, your true essence is perfect just the way it is and needs no work.

LOVE FROM WITHIN

To feel genuine love for another, you must truly love yourself first. If you are not in touch with your ability to generate love from within, you will fall into the trap of thinking that the other person is your only source of love. Once you do this, you will start to need him (or her) to be there, in order for you to feel good, happy, or loved.

At this point, your innocent outpouring of love often becomes tainted and overshadowed by your needs and expectations of what the other person will do for you. Your attachment to the person being there for you and loving you in a particular way colors your ability to give and receive love genuinely. When this happens, you leave the present moment and lose contact with the simple pleasure and enjoyment of being with the other person.

> *"In real love, you want the other person's good. In romantic love, you want the other person."*
>
> Margaret Anderson

When you genuinely love another person, you happily support them in being who they are; you want the best for them. You want for them

287

what they want for themselves. When you are attached to them being a certain way for you and meeting your expectations, as many do in "romantic" love, you want them to be "there for you," to meet your needs for love—no matter what they may want for themselves. You are more concerned with getting something (e.g., love, attention) from them, to alleviate your own fears and insecurities, rather than creating a mutually satisfying relationship based on honesty, support, and genuine heart-felt love.

As your negative programming surfaces, you lose touch with the love you have inside you and with your natural ability to outpour love from your heart. Often, you begin feeling anxious as to whether the other person really loves you or not. Part of you starts to feel dependent on them for love and deplores the thought of things not working out between you. You may become preoccupied with thoughts about the relationship's future and forget to enjoy the love and beauty that can only flow between hearts that are present and aware in each moment.

Love can't happen when you are living in the future. Love is a present-time, spontaneous experience that arises when two people allow themselves to relax and be open to the comfortable flow of energy between them. Love happens when you can trust your experience of being with another, without any hopes or expectations of what the relationship means, where it's going, or what it will do for you.

In living in the moment, you can fully enjoy the other person. And at some point, if one of you chooses to move on, you will both have made the most of the time you spent together. You can never lose when you choose to open yourself to the current of love that naturally flows between two people. And since that love comes from within you, it will always be available to you, no matter who comes into or goes out of your life.

THE REAL MEANING OF THOSE THREE LITTLE WORDS: "I LOVE YOU"

When I feel love for you, what is actually happening? In truth, what am I expressing when I tell you, "I love you"? It is simply this: "Being in your presence stimulates feelings of love within me. When I am with you, I am in touch with parts of myself that I love. You help me to be in touch with my loving essence (which is who I am all the time, whether you are in my life or not)."

So, when I say: "I love you," I am saying, "I am feeling love for you; love is flowing out from me to you. I am in the process of outpouring love to you, which allows me to feel it within myself. In a way, this love has nothing to do with you. Of course, you are stimulating something in me which allows this outpouring of love to take place, but the love is within *me*; it is *my* experience of love."

Because most people are convinced that love is something that comes from outside themselves, something that they can only *get* from someone else, they take it personally, whether or not the person they are with expresses love for them. When someone loves you, it is not about *you*. It is about *that* person's ability to feel and outpour love. By the same token, if the person you are with doesn't act as if he or she loves you, it is most certainly not about you. It is about that person's inability to feel and outpour love.

When you believe that love comes from outside yourself and someone doesn't love you, you take it personally and think that you are unlovable. When you realize that love comes from within, you can feel lovable and loved, whether or not the person you are with is able to feel and outpour love to you. His (or her) ability to love doesn't affect your sense of worth or self-esteem.

Of course, it's a lot more fun when both people are able to freely give and receive love. That is why it's ideal for both people in a relationship to be willing to work on themselves and clean up their inner negative programming. Having two hearts that are open and able to share love certainly feels more fulfilling and inspiring for both partners in the relationship.[1]

---

1. Be careful here of the tendency to blame your partner if you feel that his (or her) heart isn't open. You must take responsibility for attracting this person into your life, and you need to tell the truth about which negative program of yours, his (or her) behavior validates. Maybe there is a part of you that doesn't feel safe sharing love with another. Remember, whom we choose for a relationship partner is never an accident!

TELL THE TRUTH

Because relationships have become so complex and challenging, the most practical advice is to do your best to communicate from your heart and share whatever feels true for you. Again, this may be challenging at first, because it is foreign to the way that most of us have been programmed to relate to others. So, be willing to re-learn the process of relating to others, and be willing for your communications to be as loving and clear as possible.

Do your best to tell the truth about what you feel and experience. If you feel afraid, share that. If you feel upset, share that. But don't make the other person responsible for what you feel. Whatever you feel and experience is a direct by-product of *your* programming—*your* subconscious thoughts, attitudes, and beliefs about life. The other person is simply behaving in such a way as to activate your negative programming, and this is what causes you to feel unhappy, hurt, angry, or whatever.

Be willing to both communicate what you experience *and* find the programming within you that is making you feel the way you do. Blaming your partner for what you feel never works. It creates only separation and anger between you and never serves to bring you closer together— which is what you truly want.

Sharing your truth with another person will always lighten your load and ultimately bring the two of you closer together. But again, be sure that neither of you finds fault with the other person for whatever he or she shares. Sharing your truth with another helps bring mutual understanding and peace. There is no place for judgment, criticism, or defense in this process.

Also, sharing your truth with another is about clearing the air from *your* side—not about getting the other person to change. Do not try to make the other person feel that he or she is to blame for how you feel. The purpose of sharing your truth is to let the other person know what's going on inside of you. This builds intimacy and trust and strengthens the foundation of your relationship.

However, if you continue to feel the same way again and again in your relationship, and you have worked diligently to change your negative subconscious programming, then perhaps it is time to acknowledge that the relationship is not meeting your needs on certain levels. Perhaps it is time to change the form of the relationship, since it is not working for you in ways that are important to you.

You are not bad if you want to change the form of your relationship from lovers to friends, for example. This may be totally appropriate for you. The only way to have what you truly want in a relationship is by saying "no" to what you don't want. Saying "no" doesn't mean that the other person is bad, or that you're bad either. As you get clearer, you may simply realize that the relationship is no longer for your "Highest Good." And, that's okay. You are in touch with your heart's truth.

Trust that you can have what you want in relationships, and keep working on yourself to get free of the subconscious programming that has burdened you for so long. The more you free yourself of your negative programming, the more you will be able to experience the loving and endearing qualities that you seek in a partner, whomever you choose. You can't go wrong.

Do your best to stay optimistic and receptive. Keep your heart as open and loving as possible. Then you'll find that the experience of sharing love awaits you around every corner, in every face you see, and in every heart you encounter.

TWO KINDS OF LOVE

There are two different kinds of love—one which produces genuine satisfaction and joy between individuals, and the other which propagates the unhappiness and suffering that have plagued us, the members of the human race, for so long in our quest for true love. The first kind of love is the one that arises effortlessly and spontaneously between two hearts, in the absence of fear or other negative emotions.

The second kind of love is what we call "co-dependent," a love that is based on need and fear of loss, rather than a genuine love that flows between hearts. This kind is based on the mistaken understanding that loves come from outside of ourselves, and if we don't experience someone loving us, we will be empty, void, even dead.

> *Eric Fromm stated it well when he said: "Immature love says, 'I love you because I need you.' Mature love says, 'I need you because I love you.'"*

When you love someone because you need him, what Fromm calls "immature love," the love is not genuine, but based on fear. Your *unconscious* thought process here goes something like this: "I'm afraid to make it on my own, to be without someone to love me, so I need you to be with me, to be my source of love and happiness. Therefore, I love you. (And hopefully, if I let you know I love you, you will stay with me and continue to alleviate my fears of not having someone to give me the love I need.)"

Once you feel free to experience and express the love in your heart for another, as in Fromm's "mature" love, it's okay to "need" that person. We all need people in that sense. None of us lives in a vacuum. People are an important part of our lives, and it's vital to have others around with whom we can relate deeply and genuinely, and with whom we can share a healthy expression of love.

In co-dependent love, you often cling to someone, thinking that you need the person in order to feel love. In doing so, you diminish your value. You disempower yourself and set the other person up in a position to control you. After all, in your mind, you *need* him (or her) to be there for you. You become at the person's mercy, doing whatever he (or she) wants, in order to ensure that the person will love you and be there for you.

It doesn't feel good to be controlled or to sacrifice yourself for love. Yet, many of us think that this is our only choice—if we want love in our lives. And the problem is that love given in this fashion is conditional; it has strings attached.

When you feel as if you have to work to earn a person's love, you will do things that are not in alignment with your truth. You give up your will and do whatever pleases the other person. However, you are not doing this out of a true sense of love and desire to give to them. You are doing this in order to get that precious commodity, love, in return. Your love has strings.

This kind of love never feels good, because it lacks sincerity. It is given out of an underlying need, a hidden motivation to get something from the other person. Thus, it doesn't feel good to the recipient of such attention, nor to the giver who is disempowering himself in the process.

With the first kind of love—the kind that flows spontaneously between hearts in the absence of fear and negativity—you feel good about yourself and radiate a certain sense of pride, which is not egotistical or self-centered in nature. You simply radiate a feeling of self-acceptance and peace, from having made peace with being who you are. The positive energy emanating from you inspires and uplifts others, who then feel good in your presence. Loving and accepting yourself can only support others in feeling the same way about themselves—which then increases the amount of love that you are able to share with them.

On the other hand, the second kind of love—the co-dependent, needy kind—is fear-based. You are afraid that you might not get what you need and want from the other person. You radiate negative energy, based on your beliefs in lack and separation from love. You push the other person away, because subconsciously you don't believe that the relationship will work out. You are afraid that you will be left alone, which is what you ultimately create.

Of course, this process is unconscious. Consciously you want the other person to stay in your life. However, because of your deep negative beliefs, you tend to manifest the *opposite* of what you want—the person leaving you. Now you see why it is so important to do the necessary work, within yourself, to clear your subconscious of unwanted debris.

If you don't do this inner work, you will continue to attract people and circumstances that frustrate you to no end. You will feel confused as to why relationships don't work out for you the way you want. You won't understand why your partner treats you in ways that you abhor, without your being able to make him (or her) stop. Life will continue to be an unpleasant mystery for you, and worst of all, you will feel like a victim again and again.

However, once you understand the true nature of life and love, you will feel motivated to embark on this wondrous journey that will re-connect you to the source of love—within you. You now have a choice as to how you want your life to be. Such a choice empowers you to direct the course of your life, bringing back a sense of meaning and purpose to all that you do.

THE PATH TO TRUE LOVE

Trust this: The love that you want is within you. Learn to love yourself and treat yourself the way a best friend would. Cherish yourself. The life force that flows through you is a most precious gift, one that *you* can appreciate and treasure more than anyone else. And although you may not have learned to do this in childhood, you are learning to do so now.

You can change old learned habits of how you treat yourself—which are generally based on the way that your parents treated you or each other. It is time to step out of that mold, to re-think your life and how you deserve to be treated. Trust that you can have wonderful, loving relationships that support you in being who you are and feeling good about yourself.

Act in ways that honor yourself. Groveling for love certainly isn't one of those. Hold yourself in high regard and do things that feel good to you, from within. And ironically enough, the more you let go of needing love from others, the more love you will experience from everyone in your life.

Whenever you come from a needy place, your subconscious fears actually push the people around you away. When you let go of *needing* them for love, you unconsciously free them to shower you with love. It's funny how that works, but true.

When you are *attached* to having the love you want in a particular way, you hold on tightly to your expectations of how you think people should be and what they should do, in order to please you. Deep inside, you fear that you won't be okay if your expectations aren't met, so you try to control the people and circumstances in your life, in the hopes of getting the love you want.

You resist receiving love in any other fashion than the one you expect, and are not open to experiencing something different, that might even be better or more fulfilling for you. Because of the rigidity and fear underlying your feelings and actions, such attachments to having love in a particular way serve only to keep the love you want at a distance.

Love can flow only in present time—when you let go of how you think people *should* be and are willing to be with them as they are. Attachments to a particular outcome in relationships take you out of present time and make you focus on the future, preventing you from experiencing the love that is available to you here and now. Such attachments keep you stuck in a constant need to judge people, to see if they measure up to your expectations of them. And, the more you judge others, the less you are able to love them.

Let go of what you want another person to do for you or what you expect from him (or her). Be willing to accept the person as he (or she) is, and enjoy the time you share together. Only in giving other people the space to be who they are can you genuinely love them. And, in truth, it is only in giving yourself the space to be who *you* are, that you can comfortably support others in being who they are!

Do your best to work on clearing your subconscious programming, the "old baggage" you've been carrying for so long that your Higher Self is now guiding you to release. As you work on telling the truth about your negative patterns and use the techniques you've been given to help clear them, you will get more in touch with the loving being that you are at your essence.

It will be easier to love and accept yourself, and others as well. Love will flow more naturally and spontaneously for you, replacing the fears and doubts that once accompanied your old subconscious patterns. And although this process does not happen overnight, it is well worth the effort. You will be rewarded along the way with ever-increasing feelings of happiness, well-being, and the joy of being fully alive.

TAKE RESPONSIBILITY... FOCUS ON WHAT YOU WANT

Yes, you are in charge of your life, and you can have it the way you want. Hold a vision, within your mind and heart, of how you want life to be, how you want to feel, and how you want others to treat you. Imagine what your life would be like—how it would actually look and feel—if your vision were absolutely real.

By imagining your vision as real in your mind and heart, it will become real. Your thoughts and attitudes—both conscious and subconscious—do indeed create your experience of life. Your reality will continue to shift as you work to clear your negative programming from the past and envision what you want to manifest for yourself.

Be sure to focus on what you want, rather than on what you don't want. Many times, it's easier to complain about what happens to you and blame others for your fate. However, this only reinforces the idea that you are a victim and *not* in charge of your life and attracts more of the same kinds of unpleasant experiences to you. The energy you radiate, both consciously and subconsciously, always attracts matching energies in your life.

If you constantly dwell on negative thoughts in your mind, you will attract negativity from others and negative circumstances in general. Your inner negativity will always magnetize negativity to you from your environment. It is not your *fault*, of course, that you are being negative; there is no blame here. It is that you are now receiving a "wake-up call"—to work on yourself and bring your life to a higher level of truth, joy, and satisfaction.

Do your best to focus on the positive aspects of your life and keep a vision in your mind and heart of whatever you want to attract to you, knowing that you are powerfully creative with your thoughts, attitudes, and intentions for yourself. Do your best to be present and enjoy this process of waking up to who you really are. Love and accept yourself as best as you can, here and now, and continue to work on improving yourself, in order to achieve all that you want.

HAVE FAITH

Above all, trust in God/the Universe/that Infinite Life Force that flows through you and funds your needs and desires, according to your beliefs and attitudes. Know this: That unseen "Hand"/Energy can truly move mountains, according to your faith. It's all up to you, and there's really nothing to stop you.

Be willing to be open to the ideas presented in this book, even though they may stretch your current boundaries as to what you thought was real and possible. Trust that there is a Power, a dimension of Energy and Intelligence, greater than yourself which guides you and supports you in creating the life that you want. Your openness to such an energy allows you to make use of it, to expand who you are and what you are capable of achieving in life.

A genuine openness and receptivity to this Higher Power can flood your being with an incredible joy that you probably never imagined possible. Be willing for your skepticism to diminish, as you open yourself to the lofty possibilities that life holds in store for you on this wondrous, heart-opening journey of self-discovery.

RELAX AND TRUST THE PROCESS

Yes, the process takes time, but that is what being on Earth is all about. Life here simply takes time. That's how it is. There is generally quite a long interval between birth and death, so, for most of us, we have a great deal of time to spend on this journey. The key is to be patient and trust the process.

Wherever you are on your path is the perfect place for you to be. You could be in no other place than the one you are in. Accept that, and continue to move forward, for it is all good. You will get to where you want to be. Whatever time it takes, in the "Grand Scheme of Things," is okay. Make peace with where you are.

As Meher Baba, the great spiritual master of India, once taught his disciples, and as Bobby McFerrin vocalized merrily in accord, "Don't worry; be happy." Love flows in the absence of worry. And happiness is love's natural companion.

Make this the goal of your life: to open your heart to love and to trust the process of life. Then, everything that happens will ultimately support you in realizing your goal. This is how to create the life that you want for yourself. Life *can* work for you. Make the commitment, deep within your heart. And begin the process, now.

Afterword

The phone rang. A pleasant male voice spoke. "Is this Phyllis?" the caller politely inquired.

"Yes," I replied, curious about his identity.

The man introduced himself as "Richard" and proceeded to explain, "I was hired to do a review of your book, **Prince Charming Lives!** and after reading the book and all the information I received about it, I felt compelled to call you."

I smiled, intrigued by his words, and allowed the caller to continue.

"I write dozens of reviews, you know, and this is the first time I've ever felt like I really *needed* to contact the author."

"I see," I acknowledged. "So, what can I do for you?"

"Well, first, I was really taken by your book. You brought across your message of Truth so clearly, and you really help people to understand and resolve their relationship issues. But there is something that puzzles me...," he stopped suddenly.

"And what is that?" I asked.

"You know, the information you send out that goes along with your book, the sheet entitled, 'A Note From the Author' that talks about the healing power contained within the book...?"

"Yes."

"Well, I've never heard of that before, and I think it's phenomenal. A book that actually helps you heal while you read it—or even TOUCH it! It's wonderful," proclaimed Richard enthusiastically.

"I agree. It's been a real blessing to learn that the healing energies I work with in my private sessions are also available to help everyone who comes into contact with the book. In fact," I continued eagerly, "I'll tell you a little story."

"One time, I was selling my books at a book convention in Denver, and a man was standing at my booth who was clairvoyant. He quietly observed a lady who purchased a copy of my book, placed it in her bag, and walked away, quickly disappearing from view as she rounded the corner booth on the next aisle over. A minute or two later, she emerged on the other side of the booths on that aisle, and the man leaned over to me and made the most astonishing remark.

"That lady's aura totally changed from the time she touched your book until now." He shook his head in amazement. "The colors around her had been fairly dark, somber, with a lot of grays. Now she looks lighter, brighter, and her energy field has more of a glow, radiating more light. What an amazing transformation!"

"So, why didn't you write about this in your book?" Richard blurted out excitedly. "People need to know this!"

"Er, uh," I stammered. "I guess I didn't want to turn anyone off. I mean, the information in the book is so valuable in itself that I didn't want to push people too far past their comfort zones. I thought if I told them all that the book was designed to do, they might get stuck in their skepticism and never give the book any credence."

"I understand your reasoning," Richard replied thoughtfully, "but I still feel that people NEED to have this information."

"You mean it's time for me to come out of the closet?" I laughed aloud.

"Seems like it to me," he heartily agreed. "You mentioned that you were in the process of getting your second book published. Why don't you include 'A Note From the Author' in it, and let people know the real, behind-the-scenes story?"

"Well," I hesitated once again, "it's already done. I mean, the manuscript is complete. So, I'm not sure where I could add it at this point."

"Phyllis!" the tone of Richard's voice became stern. "You NEED to put this information into your second book. People need to know!"

"Well, it's interesting that you say this, because my guides have recently informed me that this second book will be "encoded," just like

Prince Charming Lives! is, and will have the same energetic healing benefits."

"Then, there it is. It is time. Let the people know...."

A "Divine Hand" must have been responsible for Richard's call that day, for it gave me the courage I needed—to be who I really am and to share my once secret truths with an apparently ready public. All that this book can do may indeed prove to be life-altering for you and for your loved ones, so it is obviously for your (and my) "Highest Good" that you should know more about it.

Since I am here to help humankind progress to higher levels of Love, Truth, and Understanding, I share the following information with you, which was given to me by my guides. I suggest that you once again willingly set aside any skepticism or disbelief that may surface, and be open to the incredible opportunity for healing and transformation that is available to you here.

A NOTE FROM THE AUTHOR

Dear Friends,

I want you to know the "behind-the-scenes" truth about my book, *Prince Charming Lives!* *Finding the Love of Your Life (*Princess Charming Does Too)*. This book has tremendous healing potential!

After thirty years of intensive self-healing and research, I have developed the ability to clear negative programming stored throughout the depths of the subconscious mind and repair the human energy field. I call this work, "Telepathic Healing," and I've been given the gift of help from Higher-dimensional Beings (healing guides) in this process.

Here's the magic: The healing guides are present, through my consciousness, to help people who read the book—just as they help my private clients. Not only does the book contain valuable information, it also provides actual subconscious clearing and healing for the reader! According to my guides, reading the book will help:

- Remove blocks to:

    a) intimacy

    b) being true to yourself in relationships

    c) being in touch with what you really want in relationships

    d) feeling that you deserve to have what you want in relationships

- Reawaken the thymus gland (the "love" gland, which is completely atrophied in most adults)

- Clear negative energy around the heart, caused by people thinking that they are not okay the way they are and the guilt that entails.

- Clear "Anti-Faith Units." These are small, sometimes numerous energy blockages that people attract and accumulate by the age of twelve, based on their attitude and beliefs. They reside in the area of the seventh or crown chakra and block the influx of spiritual energy, keeping people locked into a certain degree of skepticism and lack of faith in a "Higher Power."

Even *touching* the book will provide healing benefits. According to my guides:

1) Within each human being is an extremely large mass of negativity stored around the pelvic floor, which keeps people scared of change and makes them cling to their old ways. This mass must be released in order for humanity to move forward and evolve to a higher consciousness. All people who touch the book shall have this mass of negativity cleared from within them.

2) There is an energy blockage that all humans have, located along the front of the body—from just under the nose to just above the navel. This relates to the belief in suffering that exists in every single human being on the planet. This blockage of energy exists primarily in the spiritual and higher mental bodies, but also permeates the other subtle bodies as well. When people touch the book, this blockage will be released from within them.

3) There is a web of confused energy around the third eye of nearly everyone on the planet. It is the result of ancient negative energy in the collective unconscious about not being able to see or know that which is out of the realm of the five senses. Over the eons, this has stifled mankind greatly. When people touch the book, the detrimental effects of this negative energy will be cleared from within them.

Now, all of the above is true not only for **Prince Charming Lives!**, but also for **Love Now, Here's How**. Please, share this information with your friends and loved ones. Do whatever you feel inspired to do to share these blessings with others. My prayer is for maximum healing for our entire planet, and I appreciate all the support you can give toward helping my books reach as many people as possible.

Sincerely,

Index
of
Common Experiences in Relationships

The following list is intended as a guide to help you to determine which of the twenty-six "roadblocks to healthy relationships" or negative, subconscious patterns you have. It is not the final word, though. Just because you attract "strong-willed partners," for example, does not absolutely guarantee that you have a "Fear of Being Dominated." However, there is a strong correlation between the two, and a likelihood that you have that particular pattern. You must simply judge for yourself, as you read about the pattern, whether or not it applies to you. You may also have more patterns than the list below suggests.

Sometimes, certain experiences may be stated in several different ways and included under several different listings. For example, you will find the following listing: "Not true to yourself in relationships," and you will also see a listing, "Sacrificing yourself." Although they may be quite similar in terms of your relationships, you may see them listed with different patterns. Because of slight nuances, it was impossible to list every experience in the exact same manner. Again, the index is designed to be a helpful guide, rather than a set of ironclad rules as to which pattern you have. Be flexible as you work with it.

Remember, you can also use the "flash of light" visualization technique, on page 40, to help you determine which patterns you have. And, again, if you recognize any of the following as characterizing your relationships—whether in you or your partner—it is likely to be one of your patterns.

About the Author

Phyllis Light, Ph.D. in Psychology, has been working as a teacher, counselor, and researcher in the personal development field since 1973. Her specialized training has qualified her as a:

- Professional Rebirther
- Certified Practitioner of The Rubenfeld Synergy Method® and Gestalt Therapy Practitioner
- Neuro-Linguistic Programming (NLP) Facilitator
- Center Manager for Sondra Ray's Loving Relationships Training (LRT)
- Professional Meditation Teacher
- Jin Shin Jyutsu (Japanese Acupressure) Practitioner
- Certified Pulsor Therapy Consultant
- Certified Consultant/Instructor for Educational Kinesiology and Circles of Life (Technologies for Whole Brain Integration)

As a result of years of intensive personal research into the area of consciousness and spiritual development, Dr. Phyllis Light has developed highly intuitive and healing gifts. She has created "Telepathic Healing," an effective, almost mystical way in which she can help people, at any distance, to clear their subconscious minds of negative programming that causes problems, frustration, and unhappiness in their lives. Dr. Light helps people, in both private and workshop settings, to free themselves from the burdens of the past, and to move forward with greater ease, joy, and peace of mind.

Dr. Light is also the creator of Rejuvenizers® (unique devices that help protect the physical and subtle bodies from a number of environmental hazards—including electromagnetic fields from computers, TV, radio, cell phones, satellite and microwave frequencies, chemical toxicity, and high virus and bacteria levels—while energizing and strengthening the individual physically, mentally, emotionally, and spiritually). She owns and operates Light Unlimited/Stress Free Environments, an organization dedicated to teaching people how to alleviate internal stress, as well as reduce the negativity and stress absorbed from life in today's busy, high-tech world.

Dr. Light has also developed a series of unique and transformative seminars that she conducts nationwide. A dynamic public speaker, Phyllis Light has made numerous presentations of her work to help thousands of people throughout the United States, Canada, Great Britain, Europe, Australia, and the Middle East to find greater peace, happiness, and fulfillment in their lives and relationships.

To receive a complete listing of Phyllis Light's books, tapes, and healing products, or for further information about her seminars and private phone consultations, contact:

Dr. Phyllis Light
c/o Light Unlimited
P.O. Box 92316
Austin, Texas 78709-2316

1-800-935-0128

www.lighthealing.com